HOW TO

VOLUME 2

SELL MORE IN LESS TIME

WITH
NO REJECTION

Using Common Sense Telephone Techniques

Art Sobczak

Business By Phone Inc.
13254 Stevens St., Omaha, NE 68137   402-895-9399   Fax: 402-896-3353
www.businessbyphone.com

How to Sell More, In Less Time, With No Rejection, Using Common Sense Telephone Techniques- Volume II
By Art Sobczak

Published By:

Business By Phone Inc.
13254 Stevens St.
Omaha, NE 68137.
(402)895-9399
Fax:(402)896-3353
E-mail arts@businessbyphone.com
http://www.businessbyphone.com

Cover design by George Foster, Foster & Foster, Fairfield, IA

ISBN 1-881081-07-9

Dedication

To Rita and Art Sobczak Sr., my mom and dad, for your love and support, and giving me everything I needed to get where I am today, and where I will go in the future.

Special Thanks . . .

To Tricia Lewandowski, for not only your work on this book, but for helping everyone who calls our office feel like family. You are the definition and picture of outstanding customer service.

Contents

Contents
(continued)

Contents
(*continued*)

More Great Stuff

Teletips

About Art Sobczak

Art Sobczak specializes in one area only: working with business-to-business salespeople—both inside and outside—designing and delivering content-rich training programs, seminars, and products packed with ideas, tips, and strategies that users and participants show results from the very next time they get on the phone. Audiences and readers love his "down-to-earth," entertaining style, and low-pressure, easy-to-use, customer-oriented ideas and techniques.

Since 1984 Art has written and published the how-to tips newsletter, *TELEPHONE SELLING REPORT,* read by thousands worldwide.

Art is a prolific producer of learning resources on selling by phone. He authored the audio-tape training program, "Ringing Up Sales," published by Dartnell. His video program is "Getting Through to Buyers . . . While the Others are Screened Out." He wrote the books, "How to Sell More, In Less Time, With No Rejection, Using Common Sense Telephone Techniques—Volume 1," "Telephone Tips that SELL!" and has an entire catalog of other popular training tips tapes and books.

Art's how-to ideas and tips appear regularly in the print and electronic media. He has written a regular column for "Teleprofessional" magazine since the magazine's inception and is called its readers' "most popular columnist". He also writes for "SELL!NG" newsletter, and is frequently quoted in numerous sales and trade publications and on-line publications.

He holds the popular Telesales Rep College two-day public training seminars nationwide 8-10 yearly, and also customizes the program for on-site, in-house delivery. Art also delivers how-to programs on effective telesales ranging from one-hour to several days.

Clients include IBM, AT&T, Ameritech, Hewlett Packard, Norfolk Southern, Baxter Healthcare, and other companies and associations in virtually all business-to-business industries.

His speaking and training reputation has been built as someone who knows what works and what doesn't in telesales because he's done it (corporate telesales positions with AT&T Long Lines and American Express), and still does it. He also conducts extensive research to customize his programs, listening to tapes of actual sales calls of client reps in order to learn the language of the industry, company, and strengths and weaknesses of sales reps and strategies.

He built his reputation on providing ideas that work ... the same type of material you will benefit from in this book.

Introduction

Hi, again, and welcome back! (If you weren't with us for Volume 1, welcome for the first time. And DO get Volume 1—I guarantee your results.)

You're about to dive into the finest collection of telesales ideas I've ever assembled in one place. If you're one of the thousands who enjoyed, and more importantly, gained from Volume 1, you will absolutely love this book. The same type of how-to, no nonsense material, and more of it.

If you're familiar with me you know the stuff you're getting here is real. No theory ... no salesy old school manipulative garbage ... just real world conversational ideas and techniques that work. I know it, because I personally use this material, other reps have told me they've built new houses and bought new cars and boats because of it, and so can you.

What You're Getting

Let me give you a tiny preview.

We start with what sets you apart from those who sell primarily nose-to-nose, and that's with the section on **Persuasive Telephone Communication.** You'll get great tips on listening, speaking, and word usage so that you will "look" like the professional you are by phone.

I continue with the parts of the call in the order they occur. We have **Voice Mail, Screeners, and Pre-Buyer Conversations.**

Following that we look at the first crucial few seconds of your call, your **Interest-Creating Openings.** It is here where you either pull them into a conversation, or not.

The next logical step is **Selling With Questions.**

Once you've collected great information with your questions, you're ready for your **Persuasive Sales Recommendations.**

Some people might call it "closing" but I prefer the term **Getting Commitment.** We need to get commitment on every call, and you'll get plenty of ideas to help you do just that.

I believe that the best way to deal with **Objections** is to prevent them from occurring. We'll explore ideas in this section on how to do that, as well as ways to deal with them when we do hear them.

Many of us place multiple calls in our sales process in order to sell. The section on **Follow-Up Calls** shows us how to end calls to ensure successful follow-ups, as well as what to say on those calls.

Prospecting is perhaps one of the toughest tasks salespeople perform, and many are scared to death of it. We cover ideas to make it easier, and more successful.

One great feature of using the phone is that we can accomplish so much without leaving the comfort of our home or office. Our section on **Time Management** will help you accomplish even more.

I firmly believe that most of us don't even scratch the surface of what we are capable of, and that we truly control our own destiny in sales. To get closer to realizing our potential we must have the proper attitude. You'll get pumped up by the ideas in the **Self Motivation** section.

In my *"TELEPHONE SELLING REPORT"* monthly newsletter—in which most of this material originally appeared—I do a regular "Call Clinic" column where I analyze calls I receive, calls of reps that are submitted to me on tape or that I hear live, or questions regarding specific call problems or challenges. The section, **Case Study Examples,** is a collection of these real-life situations and is one of the most popular features in my newsletter.

As I compiled this book, I had a bunch of chapters that didn't necessarily fit cleanly into the other sections. No problem. You'll see them all in the section, **More Great Stuff.**

Finally, everyone loves brief, meaty, to-the-point, nugget-sized tips. You'll get over 30 pages of these in our **TeleTips** section.

Sounds good, doesn't it? I must warn you though: as good as this material is, there is no magic potion or phrase that is a cure-all that might ail someone, sales-wise. If there was, everyone would be using it. Judging by the calls I get every day, I know that's not the case.

The most successful salespeople I know are the ones who do lots of little things right, and consistently work to get better. And that's what you must do, fellow sales professional. I don't care if you've been in sales one day or 60 years, if you're not consistently working to get better you are losing ground. Period. The most successful (and wealthiest) sales pros I know are the ones who have that insatiable desire to get better. I think you fall into that category.

About the Style of this Book

For those of you reading me for the first time, let me alert you to the style you'll see. I'm heavy on how-to, word-for-word, real-life conversational examples. You'll see examples of what not to say:

"The bad examples look like this in italics."

You'll also spot the better alternatives:

"What you should say appears in bold face and is indented."

At the end of almost every section I have **"Action Boxes."** These are spots for you to take notes and personalize these ideas ... to jot down your own **Action Steps**. That's right, I encourage you to mark up this book. Mutilate it. Highlight ideas. Dog ear the pages. I'll even look the other way if you take a tip here or there, enlarge it to a ridiculously large size on the copy machine and post it there next to your phone. After all, unless you take action and put these ideas into practice they are worthless.

Final Thoughts

I reviewed my Introduction from Volume 1 and saw how long it was. Before I reach that length, I'm going to end here. After all, that's why you invested in this thing. (To reset it briefly, I justified the title, "How to Sell More, in Less Time, With No Rejection, Using Common Sense Telephone Techniques," and touched on a few other issues I won't cover here. Get out Volume 1, and reread it—you'll be glad you did. If you don't have it yet, get it. I'll buy it back from you if it doesn't help you increase your sales.)

So, let's get right into the meat of this book and helping you get better results on your calls.

Enjoy and prosper!

Art

Art Sobczak
November, 1998

Persuasive Telephone Communications

Chapter 1

Talk Less, Listen More, Sell More

The caller said, "We're looking for training, but what you do isn't right for us. I'm hoping you can refer us to someone." I paused, resisted making a defensive comment, then responded with a profound, **"Oh?"**

She proceeded in explaining what she wanted: a customized business-to-business telesales training program, covering each step of the call process. I asked a few more questions in response to her answers, helping her further explain, in detail, why she needed such a program (she explained her problem), and in what form she ideally wanted it, and the ultimate results (the solution).

My turn. I calmly stated that what she wanted was precisely what I did, and how I would deliver it for her. She agreed. Even though a few moments earlier she had a different belief (for whatever reason), she now had changed her mind. And *she* did most of the talking. There was no magic here. Just good listening, and logical questions. Here are a few listening tips you can use right now.

Listening Tips to Use Right Now

❑ **Separate the facts from the speaker.** There are people whose credibility is so questionable in your mind, that whatever they say is filtered through extreme skepticism. For example, consider the slow-pay customer who told you over and over "the check is in the mail," or a prospect who outright lied to you about what he was paying elsewhere. If they offered you criticism or a valid objection, the tendency might be to respond, *"Well, yeah, but consider the source."* Instead, listen to the facts of what they say, and ask yourself,

"In what circumstances could this be true?"

1

❏ **DO Consider the Source.** Words aren't always a good conveyor of meaning. They might say, "Your system isn't the right one for what we do here," but what does that really mean? If it's coming from a techno-type, it could mean something logistical or operational, compared to hearing it from a human resources person.

❏ **Question Key Words and Phrases.** Again, depending on a person's background and frame of reference, their interpretation of words could be far from yours—and that could cost you a sale. What does "a fair price" mean? Think about that from the perspective of someone who was just gouged by a scam artist. Compare that to the person who thinks you might have a higher price than the competition, and just wants you to be in the ballpark with yours. Always get clarification:

> **"Our customers tell us we have fair prices. What does that term mean to you?"**

❏ **Listen for Emotional and Favored Words and Phrases.** Here are a couple of simple, but hugely important communication principles: 1) people are more comfortable with those they feel a bond with, and, 2) we all have pet words and phrases. Therefore, to help others feel comfortable with you, listen for their favored sayings and sprinkle them back into the conversation. I was paired up with an auto mechanic for a round of golf the other day. He peppered his speech with words and phrases like, "that swing needs oiling," "the putt ran out of gas," and, "I'm going to wrench this drive up a few notches." Picking up on this, I drew on my limited vocabulary of mechanical terms and casually dropped them into the conversation (mainly adapting the ones he used):

> **"You really put it to the floor on that putt!"**

By the middle of the round you would have thought we'd known each other for years.

This Will Leave You Breathless

If you have a tendency to interrupt, hold your breath for two or three seconds before speaking. This ensures they are done, and gives you an opportunity to think of your next statement or question.

Ways to Improve Listening

To be the best listener possible, you need to be adept at focusing in on the speaker's words, while shutting out external distractions. Here are some exercises to help you do that.

1. At home, turn on the TV and the radio to an all-news or talk station, *and* an instructional audiocassette. Practice focusing on the cassette message while the other sounds compete for your attention.

2. Gather several colleagues together. Each of you take turns listening to one person speak while the others have a conversation within earshot.

3. Again play the TV or radio and practice counting by 15's. This will polish your ability to concentrate.

Get Agreement on What They Mean

A critical part of listening is ensuring you understand what the speaker said. If you are a bit cloudy, try saying,

> **"Let me see if I understand what you're saying ..."**
>
> **"So if I'm following you, you're saying that ..."**
>
> **"What I'm hearing is that you ..."**
>
> **"It appears that what you want is ..."**

When you're more certain, paraphrase with,

> **"As you see it ..."**
>
> **"It seems to you that ..."**
>
> **"What you feel, then, is ..."**

Listen for Names and Titles of Others

Listen carefully when a prospect mentions the name or title of others, as it relates to the purchase of what you sell. For example, "I'll ask Chuck what we've been experiencing in that area." Instead of wondering who this guy, Chuck, is, ask,

> **"I see. What does Chuck do there?"**

Then you can continue questioning to learn what role this person plays in the buying or influencing process.

Listen Carefully When They Lower Their Voice

Be particularly aware of what prospects and customers say when they lower their voice, or whisper so as to not be heard by others in their area. Typically this is sensitive and important information.

You Can't Talk With Your Mouth Full

Ingrid Gurzynski with Thomas Publishing keeps a water bottle at her desk. To force herself to listen and not ask multiple questions or answer her own question, she asks a question then takes a sip from the bottle.

Don't Listen Negatively

Negative listening sabotages effective communication, according to Joe Batten, in his book *"The Master Motivator: Secrets of Inspiring Leadership."* Negative listening doesn't really involve listening; it's simply waiting for the other person to finish speaking so you can make your point. Or worse, finishing someone's sentence, or giving an answer without knowing the question. Instead, be certain you're asking well-planned questions about their needs, and then listening intently to the answers, and absorbing them before replying.

Action Steps

Chapter *2*

Give Complete Attention To the Speaker

When it comes to dealing with people, sales representatives are no different than other professionals such as psychologists, ministers, and marriage counselors. To accomplish their respective objectives, each must believe one simple, common sense—but not always easy to apply—principle. And that is to give your whole-hearted attention to the other person.

The desire for attention is present in everyone. Think about your own situation for a moment, and recall when you were snubbed by an inefficient waiter, or stood waiting in a store check-out line, slowly simmering, while other clerks who could have helped you were standing around, pretending they were busy. You know the feeling. The concept of giving attention to your prospects and customers certainly isn't a new one. The trick is practicing it consistently. Here are some common-sense ideas.

Practical Tips
1. Be genuinely interested in your prospects and customers. Too many telesales reps start the day by saying, *"OK, I'm going to sell a lot of people today,"* instead of, **"I'm going to help people today by asking questions, determining specifically what their interests and concerns are, and then positioning the value of my products/services."** There is a major difference.

2. Always think in terms of what *they* want. We've all been subjected to salespeople who have pitched us what they wanted to sell— even going as far as arguing with us about their "benefits"— instead of what we wanted to buy, or had a need for. People buy for their reasons, not yours. Before every call, put yourself in their position, and ask your-

5

self, **"If I were this person, what would I want?"**

3. Listen with everything you've got. Without listening, the other points are meaningless.

4. Have a purpose for listening. All the listening tips ever written don't matter unless you have a desire to listen. Think about times when you were zoned in to a speaker's words, in a hypnotic-like trance, oblivious to everything else going on around you. You had a purpose. Contrast that with conversations where you spaced off a few seconds at a time ... even though you were staring at the other person, nodding your head. Obviously, no purpose for listening there.

5. Practice patience. For people who are in the habit of being concerned primarily with themselves, patience comes with some difficulty. But by practicing and intently focusing on the other person, patience grows.

6. Never take the prospect or customer for granted. Especially customers. Your customers are your competitor's prospects. Some will stay around regardless of any attention they do or do not receive. However, others are fickle, and will accept offers from anyone who courts them.

7. Be concerned. Treat everyone you speak with each day as the only call for the day.

Action Steps

Chapter 3

Developing a Selling Telephone Image

I read the story of the star baseball pitcher whining about how the press always misquoted him and took his words out of context. He claimed they never printed exactly what he said. The next time he pitched, here's how his remarks appeared in the paper:

"I, uh, ummm, had the curve, uh, ball really working, ya know? It, ah, was, like really, um jumpin, uh, if you know what I mean. It was, it was, uh, it was bafflin' them hitters, ya know? They, like, uh, ain't got no chance, when ... it, ahhhh, ummm, does dat."

Upon reading his remarks the next day—quoted *exactly as he said them*—he was livid. He felt like his words made him look like a fool. He was right.

The way you speak is like the artist's palette and brushes ... the carpenter's tools. Your speaking skills create an image in the listener's mind.

As a professional who spends a bulk of his/her time communicating non-visually, you must be a superb speaker to enjoy optimal success. You wouldn't dream of striding into a decision maker's office wearing the clothes you have earmarked for the rag bag, sporting your ultimate Saturday-morning-bad-hair look. Why, then, would you tolerate anything less than the most polished "appearance" to the ears?

Here are just a few ideas to keep your phone image sharp.

1. Tape your calls. It gives an added dimension to your self-evaluation. You never learn as much from an activity while you're engaged in it as you do afterward, especially when you have a chance to review it in a non-stressful environment. (We've sold thousands of our Recorder Links that plug into your phone handset or headset, and your standard tape recorder. Call us at 1-800-326-7721.)

7

2. Transcribe your calls. Have your taped conversations transcribed into the written word. Talk about a rude awakening! Just like the baseball player, *seeing* what sounds come out of your mouth can be humbling. But more importantly, educational. You'll see not only the annoying habits you'll want to rid yourself of, but also a visual version of how you react in various situations.

3. Target areas for improvement. After taping yourself, if you're typical, you'll likely pick out more than a few aspects of your speaking you'll want to work on. Be on the lookout for credibility destroyers like fillers (ahhs and umms).

4. Get more knowledge. Head to the "Self-Improvement" or "Communications" section at your local bookstore. Select a few titles on public speaking and voice enhancement.

5. Practice at every opportunity. I'm often appalled by the speaking skills displayed by some sales reps, both on the phone and in front of groups. Whenever you have a chance to speak, seize it! I'm not referring about coffeepot chitchat; I'm talking about small- and large-group presentations. Seek out and join a local chapter of a Toastmaster's group (an organization of people from all walks of life that helps you practice your speaking skills and receive feedback.

Roger Ailes, the communication and media consultant to several presidents and personalities, said, "You are the message." People can, indeed, see you—in their own mind, *every* time you open your mouth.

When you analyze it, selling by phone is primarily being skilled at collecting and presenting organized thoughts in a clear way. Continually work on the image you present *every* time you speak, and not only will you increase your sales, but you'll build and refine a skill you'll use the rest of your life ... in all areas of your life.

Be Careful With Grandiloquent Words (Like that One)

Be aware of your audience when speaking so as to not use extravagant words when a simple one will do. Joe Barlow, the Telesales Manager at *"Christianity Today"* tells his reps that when using words that are above the level of the general public's working vocabulary be sure to pause momentarily after saying them. Certain words might trip up the person's flow of thinking, causing them to get hung up on the word. **When In Doubt:** Don't use the words. Why risk it?

Other Word Ideas

• **Post Lists.** Be sure everyone, especially new hires, have a list of words and phrases to avoid ... those that are sure to create tension, or anger. Likewise, there are terms to avoid that reveal a rep isn't knowledgeable in the industry. (To this day, whenever I return from a hunting trip, my wife will say, "Did you 'catch' anything?" She knows better now, but says this simply to playfully irritate me.)

• **Use Proper Context.** When you do add new words to your vocabulary, be sure you use them in the proper context. When used improperly, listeners think all kinds of things—other than the effect you desire. One rep told me he was being "prosecuted" by some of the other, less-ambitious reps in his department because he always stayed late and made more calls than anyone. I admire his ambition, but perhaps he was watching too much Court TV in his spare time—I think he really meant "persecuted." And you'd be surprised how many people interchange even simple words like "objective" with "objection" in training programs.

• **Cliche Carefully.** Don't butcher cliches. A salesperson told me that *"It was water under the creek."* Must have been some deep water.

• **Speak Confidently.** When you do use fresh words for the first time, state them boldly. Don't mumble them under your breath. Practice saying them in context, with confidence. Although not recommended, mistakes committed with confidence can occasionally *sound* correct.

Be Careful of Threatening Language

Some language can be perceived as salesy or threatening. For example, instead of ,

"When will you send back the signed contract?", try,

> **"By when do you think we'll get back the OK'd agreement?"**

Instead of, *"Write us a check ... ,"* consider,

> **"Have the invoice submitted for payment ..."**

Shhhhh ... Whisper

To ensure that you're presenting a clear message over the phone, practice whispering your presentation (not to the prospect!) from time-to-time.

When we whisper, we must open our mouths WIDER and poke out our lips to be understood. When you return to your normal volume, use the same techniques as when whispering.

Say Nay to Hoarseness

To prevent and treat mild hoarseness,

- if you smoke, quit

- drink plenty of water

- be sure there's humidity in your house

- don't use your voice too long or loudly

- avoid speaking when your voice is hoarse (it's like walking on a sprained ankle)

- get professional voice training

(SOURCE: HOARSENESS PREVENTION & TIPS, American Academy of Otolaryngology—Head & Neck Surgery Inc., One Prince St., Alexandria, VA, 22314)

Project Energy With Your Voice

In his book, *"You've Got to Be Believed to Be Heard"* (St. Martins Press), Bert Decker tells the story of a CEO who gave the dedication speech for a new building before a thousand people. He began reading his speech, in a deadly monotone. Worse yet, someone inadvertently copied page 10 twice, and he *read it twice*. But no one noticed, including him, because no one was listening (many had already left). The importance for us on the phone is to be sure we're projecting energy with our voices. Decker suggests a few exercises:

✔ **Get on a Roller Coaster.** Visualize your voice on a roller coaster. Practice lifting it over the summit, then let it plummet. This helps you be aware of the dynamic range of your voice, and puts you in the habit of extending that range.

✔ **Move.** Get up! Walk around. Even if you're sitting, gesture a bit. It puts more excitement in your voice.

✔ **Be Aware of Your Nonwords and Replace Them With Some-**

thing More Powerful. Listen to yourself on tape and, although you might wince, count the number of "uhh" sounds you use. Awareness leads to action. Replace them with a pause. That's infinitely more powerful than nonwords.

Be Certain You're Understood

Leroy Gross, author of *"Phone Power: Telephone Selling and Prospecting," (New York Institute of Finance, Prentice-Hall, New York)* says that a lot of salespeople, especially in his industry of securities, feel the best way to sell is to impress prospects by flooding them with an overwhelming number of statistical facts. But in doing so they often build resentment on the part of the listener.

Not many people can comprehend a stream of numbers thrown at them very rapidly, particularly by an unknown caller. Gross suggests that people comprehend only about 25% of what is said to them over the phone. And they understand even less if the information is given rapidly, and *less yet* if the words are loaded with various sets of numbers.

To increase your impact, Gross suggests you,

❶ Speak slower.

❷ Use more inflection.

❸ Enunciate clearly.

❹ Use few numbers, and have them relate in an understandable way.

How to Build Rapport

After about two minutes into a call—or sooner—the prospect knows how he feels about you, and is well on his way to determining whether or not he'd be comfortable doing business with you.

Setting others at ease doesn't rely on technical skills—it's your people skills. And those skills aren't easy to learn if they're not present already. Dr. Kerry Johnson, author of *"Mastering the Game"* wrote in *"Registered Representative Magazine"* about four areas that can boost your rapport building ability (I'll add my own suggestions for taking action).

1. Project High Self Esteem and Confidence. Optimism and pessimism are both catchy. Do you know anyone negative that you truly enjoy being around? People respond to confidence more positively than nervousness and apologies. **Actions to take**: ensure your tone is a positive, confident one. Know what you'll say before you call to eliminate "umms" and "uhhs."

2. Communicate Creatively. *Actions to take:* Have a great opening and move to the open-ended questions quickly to get them talking. To paraphrase Dale Carnegie, you'll get people to like you much sooner by asking about them than by telling about yourself.

3. Project Empathy. Focus your **full** attention on them. *Action to take:* Listen reflectively:

> **"I see,"**
>
> **"Interesting,"**
>
> **"Tell me more."**

Paraphrase often. Layer questions on the topic they're on. Don't work from a list of unrelated questions without reacting to each of their answers.

4. Add Reassurance. Make them feel good about themselves and their choices. *Actions:* When they hint at an accomplishment they've attained, acknowledge it sincerely.

> **"That's a phenomenal growth in just two years. I bet you're proud."**

Other ideas from the same article:

Establish Common Ground. Say something that shows you understand their needs, industry, or problems.

> **"I just read where the President now is talking about taxing the income from annuities. Has that had an effect on your business yet?"**

Go With the Flow on Small Talk. This might seem contradictory to building rapport, but with some people the chit chat is annoying. Assess their receptiveness by their tone of voice, and if they start small talk, go along with their lead.

Practice Your Descriptions

People usually think in terms of pictures when they hear descriptions. What do you think of when you hear the word "sunset"? Naturally, you probably picture the colors of the sun as it falls below the horizon.

To evoke more emotion in your prospects and customers, improve your ability to create vivid mind images. Practice by describing objects or activities you see while driving in your car. Be as specific as possible, and use exciting, colorful action words.

Energize Your Language

The words "love" and "hate" evoke emotion that can aid in your sales effort. For example, **"Wouldn't you love** to go a month without having your copier fail?" And, "Don't you **hate** it when your order is late?"

Another language tip is to use active verbs. For example, "Our products are used by the Smith Company," is dull compared to **"The Smith Company uses our products."**

Commonly Confused Words

As the ever-present radio commercial implores, "People DO judge you by the words you use." And most of us will never know about the prospect we lost simply because we totally turned him off with an incorrect use of a word. Here are a few common blunders.

❏ **"Fewer" and "Less."** Fewer refers to numbers: "Fewer customers asked for refunds on this product." "Less" refers to volume: "There was more inventory in the warehouse, but it took up less space."

❏ **"Imply" and "Infer."** "Imply" means to hint at something: "He implied that he was having a delivery problem." "Infer" means drawing a conclusion: "I inferred that the prospect was ready to buy, based upon the statements of agreement I heard."

❏ **"Irregardless."** It's not a word. "Regardless" is what people really mean.

❏ **Avoid "Very."** Instead of,

• very smart, try "brilliant,"

• very good, try "excellent," or, "superb,"

• very strong, try "powerful," or, "mighty."

(SOURCE: "PHC Profit Report," 3150 E. River Rd., Suite 101, Des Plaines, IL, 60018-4218)

Action Steps

Voice Mail, Screeners, and Pre-Buyer Conversations

Chapter 4

Leave Messages That Have Impact

Here's a letter I received from Steve Beck of Omnicomp Software: "I make almost all of my sales calls by phone. It seems that I spend my whole day just leaving messages for my customers. Sure, once in a while I may get lucky and get to speak with them, but most of the time I end up leaving a message with the secretary or on their voice mail. My problem is that I never seem to have much luck getting calls returned to me. Is there something that you could suggest that would encourage my customers to call me back?"

My first response is "Why?" Not why do you want them to call you back, but why should they? That's the question we all need to answer before even considering leaving a message. Without a compelling reason for them to talk to you they'll either hit their "6" button (or whatever "delete" is), or instruct their screener to "get rid of this salesperson when he calls back."

Two Possible Objectives

When leaving a message, you likely have one of two objectives: either to stimulate a return call from them, or to have them be in a positive frame of mind when you call back (which inherently means they don't tell their screener to get rid of you when you call).

The way to accomplish both of these objectives is to have a valid item of interest; a hint of the desired result you might be able to provide them. And make it vague enough so that they want and need to talk to you to learn more. Actually, your message could look quite similar to your opening statement. For example,

> **"Ms. ____, the reason for the call is that we specialize in working with facility managers, helping them reduce the paperwork associated with maintenance**

jobs, while also providing an easy way to track the progress of each job. Depending on what you're doing now to manage your maintenance, this might be worth taking a look at, and I'd like to ask you a few questions to see if you'd like some information. I will call you back tomorrow ... "

Use Voice Mail to Presell Them

When placing a follow-up call and you reach voice mail, don't waste the opportunity. Seize the chance to set the agenda for your next call, to remind them of what they said they were going to do since your previous call, and to tease them a bit with a benefit you'll discuss on the next contact. Here's an example of an effective message.

"Hi Pat, it's Dale Wilson at Kenmark Services. Wanted to let you know that I collected the information you requested on compatible applications, and I'm confident you'll find this to be great news. I'll share it with you when I call back this afternoon. Also, I'll be interested to get your feedback on how the sample measured up to your expectations in the area of pliability ..."

If It'll Be Short, Let Them Know

On voice mail messages, if you will be brief, let them know that up front. **"Mary, I'll be brief here."** It helps them pay attention to the entire message, knowing they won't have to sit through a monologue.

Get Voice Mail Messages Returned
By Asking a Question

Here's an idea that might get calls returned when you're prospecting: begin your message with a question, then follow it with a potential benefit or result they might be able to get. For example,

"Ms. Prospect, this is Pat Dallas with Integrated Systems. My reason for calling is to ask you a question: What audience are you primarily targeting with your promotions? Depending on your answer, we might have a few ideas that would be of some value to you in reaching likely buyers."

17

Chapter 5

Know for Whom You Left Messages

One way to get calls returned is to leave just your name, maybe your company, and your regular direct-dial phone number. My feeling when I get messages like this is that it might be a potential customer, therefore I can't risk ignoring the message.

However, I don't recommend leaving messages on cold calls, as it can backfire quite easily. For example, take the case of a decision maker returning a call to someone he/she *hopes* is a prospect or customer for him, only to be disappointed–maybe even angered–by the fact that the caller was a salesperson. Double the pain when the sales rep is awful. Consider this example:

The pink message slip read, "Call ___ with Media Relations at (direct dial phone number)."

Hmmm, upon scanning my database, I knew it wasn't a customer or previous inquirer. Someone from the media perhaps? Maybe a salesperson hoping to sell me. I returned the call.

"This is ___."

"Hi, this is Art Sobczak returning your call."

After five seconds of nervous silence, he shuffled a few papers and asked, *"Uhh, yeah, Art, did I call you today or yesterday?"*

"I don't know."

"Let me see here. Hmmm. I call a lot of people, and I might have called you for a few different services I sell."

By now I figured out this was a sales rep prospecting haphazardly, leaving messages at every opportunity, hoping a few might call him back. I grew irritated as he diddled away my time.

"Look," I said, "If *you* don't know why you called me, I certainly don't know. I don't have time for this."

"Ok, Ok, I know now. I just called basically to tell you about my company."

Just as I suspected. A guy who was not able to articulate a benefit that would grab my attention and salvage something from the call. "Let me save you some time. I talked to someone from your company a year ago (I did recall it at that point), and I'm not a prospect for you. Thanks."

Analysis and Recommendation

If you must leave a message, be certain you're prepared to instantly recognize the person when they call back, and then take control of the call.

And that means having a valid, interesting reason for them to listen to you. Saying, "I want to tell you about my company," is a sure way to put someone in a resistant frame of mind. People don't care about your company. They care about *their company*, and what they could potentially gain by talking with you.

From what I recall about this business he could have said something like,

> **"My company specializes in helping experts in their field get free publicity in publications and on the radio, putting their message in front of hundreds of thousands of potential buyers. If that's something you'd have interest in, I'd like to ask a few questions to see if we'd have a good fit."**

If you leave messages, know who might call back, and be prepared to wow them quickly.

Action Steps

Chapter 6

Professionals Don't Need Trickery With Screeners

The exasperated sales rep called me looking for advice: "What tricks can you give me to get around or through the gatekeeper?"

I shake my head when I hear questions like that. It's a sign the person just doesn't get it. Anyone who relies on tricks to get "through" the screener likely experiences the following: the screener puts the caller on hold and says to the boss,

"Hey boss, there's another shady-sounding bozo on line 2 who's trying to schmooze me into letting him through. He's sellin' sumthin' but won't give me any information. Should I can him?"

"Yeah."

"Gladly."

Screeners are Your First Sale

At the precise moment an executive assistant or secretary picks up the phone in response to your call to the boss, that person (the screener) is the most important individual in your life for the next several seconds or minutes. Treat her/him that way.

Too many sales reps feel that they don't have to sell until they reach the targeted buyer. Wrong. You need to be prepared to sell whomever answers the phone. Let's examine why.

Understand Their Job

The role of the screener is protect the buyer's time. It's not to get rid of **all** salespeople (although for some dolts who treat screeners like dirt, that's what it seems like, and deservedly so). Therefore, you can reach the buyer a greater percentage of the time by being prepared to help the screener do his/her job. You do this by communicating that you are not there to merely waste the boss' time, and articulating very concisely and clearly that you have something worth talking about.

Therefore, whenever a screener asks, "What is this in reference to?", you need to have a persuasive reason ready. If you don't, you fail the first test, and have positioned yourself in the screener's mind as someone just "selling something." That prompts more questions—of you. Questions usually designed to disqualify you, followed by statements such as "Please send any information ...", or "He's/she's in a meeting right now." Therefore, your goal is to help the screener understand that you have ideas of value that can potentially help the buyer in several ways.

Tips to Use

Here are some points to keep in mind that will help screeners, and help you get through a greater percentage of the time.

☐ **Prepare a "screener strategy."** As part of your pre-call planning, know what you will say if you're questioned by a screener. It's just as important as your opening statement (and can be quite similar).

☐ **Be in an information-collecting frame of mind.** Upon reaching a screener, you don't want to speak with the decision maker—yet. You want information which will help you help the buyer. And in the process of questioning you position yourself as a person who really cares, as opposed to a salesperson with an attitude. Say to the screener,

> **"You probably work closely with Ms. Bigg. There's some information you could probably help me with so I'm better prepared when I speak with her."**

☐ **Use a confident, expectant tone of voice.** Some reps whimper their requests: *"Uh, I was wondering if Ms. Fremont is maybe available?"* This instantly brands the caller as insignificant. It doesn't matter if they are or not, since the **screener** thinks so, and that's all that matters.

☐ **Have a powerful justification reason ready to roll.** Who are screeners told to get rid of? Time wasting salespeople. And the only way you can avoid that label is if the screener feels you have something worthwhile. A piece of garbage I've heard spread by some so-called experts is that you shouldn't give any information to the screener. What nonsense! If they want to know why you're calling, be ready to eloquently explain:

> **"The reason I'm calling today is that my company specializes in helping trade show exhibitors gener-**

ate more prequalified booth traffic. I'd like to ask Ms. Bigg a few questions to determine if this would be of any value to her."

❏ **Make it interesting, but non-objectionable.** This means you don't want to present an idea they are qualified to say "no" to. For example, you wouldn't want to say, *"We sell office supplies and I'd like to introduce my company to him."* They'd likely respond, "We're happy with who we're buying from, thank you." There are about a zillion companies selling the same product, and the screener and decision maker need to know why you are special. Ideas, concepts, and methods are less objectionable than "products." Talk about the **results** of what you can provide, not the product or service itself.

Help screeners do their job, and you'll be able to do yours a greater percentage of the time.

Get My Video Program on Getting Through to Decision Makers

I've developed an entire 50-minute video program on getting to more buyers: "Getting Through to Buyers, While the Others are Screened Out." Complete with a workbook you will get plenty of how-to ideas to help you work with screeners, assistants, and voice mail to spend less time chasing decision makers, and more time selling to them. Go to our website at http://www.businessbyphone.com/GTTB.htm or call us at 800-326-7721, or 402-895-9399 for current pricing.

Action Steps

Chapter 7

Don't Make Screeners Skeptical, Or Insult Them

When prospecting or otherwise trying to reach someone who doesn't know you, and they're not available, you probably are quite often asked by screeners if you'd like to leave a message. If you do choose to leave one be certain you have something of interest and value for the prospect, and that you talk about results of what you have, not the product/service itself—the product/service can too easily create an objection.

If you tell the screener, "No, that's OK, I'll call back,"

be aware of the possible negative vibes you might be sending. For example, some screeners might be personally offended that you don't leave a message, wondering if you don't have faith that they could record and deliver it accurately. Or, they might get skeptical when you decline to leave a message, wondering who and what exactly you are. I'd bet the way you're labeled in their mind is not in a positive light. Of course, this could be a needless worry in some cases, where they're actually relieved you didn't leave a message.

Listen Carefully

To ease any possible skepticism, listen for the way the screener reacts if you say you'd prefer to simply call back. For example,

Screener: "Would you like to leave a message?"

Caller: "Oh, that's OK, I'll try again later."

Screener: (With a bit of hesitation, and an icy tone.) "I see."

Caller: (Time to backpedal and squelch any flicker of skepticism) **"Well, on second thought, maybe you can leave her a message ..."**

Remember, screeners are some of the most important people you'll ever run into They can take you by the hand and clear the way to the decision maker, or they explode the bridges in your path.

"She's Not at Her Desk Right Now"

When the screener answers your request with "He/she is not at his/her desk, don't simply leave a message. Continue questioning.

Often, screeners will ask the caller to leave a message, therefore leaving it up to the decision maker to decide whether or not a callback is in order. However, the caller should take control with questions. For example,

"Oh, is she in today?"

"What time is the meeting expected to conclude?"

"Will she stop at her desk before she leaves?"

These queries will help you obtain information which will give you an edge in reaching the decision maker.

It IS Important

I heard this while listening to a rep's prospecting call:

Screener: "Would you like to leave a message?"

Rep: *"No, it was nothing terribly urgent. Just tell him I called. I'm Joe Schmoe with Precision Specialties."*

Now THAT really positions the rep favorably for the next call, doesn't it? (sarcasm intended)

If you leave any type of message, keep in mind that the person you leave it with—a screener or anyone in the area—likely interacts with the buyer. Based on what you say and how you say it, they might communicate one of the following in response to the buyer's question, "Any calls for me?"

• "Nah, nothing important. Some sales guy called. I'll get rid of him next time if you want."

• "Yes, there was one that you might have interest in. Joe Schmoe with Precision Specialties called and mentioned something about the upgrade we're now planning, and how his company helped a few other fabricators keep down the transition costs of the whole project. He said he'd call you back to ask a few questions to see if you'd like more information."

Prepare for what you'll say to a screener—or to anyone you speak with other than your targeted buyer, including on voice mail—just as you would prepare your opening statement.

Work With the Screener

Nancy Yartz with Hemocue enlists the assistance of an office manager or screener when mailing information to the hard-to-reach doctors she targets. After building rapport with, and gathering information from this person, Nancy says,

> **"I'm sending information to the Doctor. So that he is sure to get it, may I put your name on it so that you can then give it to him?"**

Dealing with the "Informal Screener"

At a Telesales Rep College, Heide Ewell with the Sachs Group brought up the situation of dealing with "informal screeners," those people who technically aren't the real screener for the person you're looking for, but who nevertheless still perform the same function when they take your prospecting call and say, "I don't handle that, but send me the information and I'll give it to the person who does." What they're really doing is protecting the real decision maker from what they perceive to be a salesperson.

My suggestion here is treating this person like you would a real screener: helping the person understand that what you have could be of potential value for the buyer, and that you indeed need to speak with him or her to determine so for sure. For example,

> **"Carol, I understand that the person I'm looking for probably gets lots of calls, and that's one of the reasons why I'm reluctant to just send information. I don't want to waste his or her time, and yours or mine. You see, what we have could potentially be of value in helping the marketing department more accurately target the groups most likely to utilize the hospital's various services, therefore helping them create better advertising while saving money in the process. I'd really need to speak with the appropriate person in order to have any idea what I should send."**

Try The Fax Machine

Having difficulty getting through to your buyer? Consider the fax.

According to a survey by the National Association of Purchasers of 420 buyers in small businesses (fewer than 500 employees), the fax machine was listed as the most essential machine in their organization's operations. It was mentioned 93% of the time, compared to just 60% for voice mail. You might want to consider an enticing fax message you could send directly from your computer.

Talk to the Same Screener

Some organizations have more than one secretary or executive assistant handling the phones and screening calls. If you've called such a company in the past, says Elaine Walstad with NewsCurrents, ask for the same secretary you spoke with last time. Hopefully you will have already built rapport with this person and won't have to start from scratch.

Action Steps

Interest-Creating Opening Statements

Chapter 8

13 Ways to Create Resistance at the Beginning of Calls

What do you think when you see an apparently spaced-out person sauntering down the local shopping mall with a buzz-cropped haircut, but with a rainbow-colored 12-inch braided pony tail (protruding from the *side* of the head), shiny gold studs in each nostril, another in the lip, and one in the eyebrow for good measure, sporting ripped up four-sizes-too-large parachute pants and a shirt with "Hemp is OK."? (And this is the female of the couple!)

Call me unenlightened, but that first impression has so much of a negative impact that I would have a hard time ever looking beneath to the person if she applied for a job with me. Even if I tried, the continual reminder of the first (and the ongoing) impression would cloud whatever message this person could possibly present.

The first impressions you create are long-lasting, too. Within seconds on a phone call your listener forms multiple opinions of you. And if they're negative, your battle is uphill. Even if what you have to offer could be of some interest, you might not have an opportunity to get that far in the call. There are about a hundred things that can go wrong with a golf swing that cause the ball to react unfavorably, and about the same can be said about calls. In this chapter I'll cover what causes tension and resistance at the beginning of—and before—phone calls. In subsequent chapters (and really, in the remaining chapters of this book) we'll discuss what to do to ensure we're creating only positive impressions instead.

1. Uninspiring Letters or Faxes. Several times per week I get a bulging package of information irrelevant to anything I have use for. The form letters babble on about how great the writer thinks his company is, then says he will call me to talk about what he has. He probably doesn't know that the decision to not even talk to him has already been made.

2. Poor or Evasive Communications with Screeners. People who think they're too important to talk with screeners or explain why what they have is important typically find themselves in a losing battle each time they encounter one. Interestingly enough, these are the very people screeners are told to get rid of. Sales reps who commit any of these other errors with screeners are also sealing their own negative fate.

3. Unintelligible Accents. For reasons we won't discuss here, some individuals have deep-rooted prejudices against certain types of people because of where they're from in the country or the world, or their ethnicity or race. We can't control that. What can be controlled, however, is an accent. I'm not talking about totally eliminating an accent, just ensuring the words are understandable. Some—me included—love listening to English accents, or the friendly twang of the South. My late grandfather from Poland had a very distinctive sound, and I still enjoy similar dialects. What I am suggesting is that if a person has to strain to understand you, they probably won't work that hard. Let's face reality: speaking so that your prospects can understand you is as much of a requirement for successful selling by phone as being able to hit a 90 mile-per-hour fastball is for playing major league baseball.

4. Speaking Too Fast. Remember, their mind isn't totally immersed in two-way communication yet. If they're greeted by a speed-yapping salesperson, tension might set in.

5. Sounding Dumb. I'll be blunt here. How does someone who sounds like Elmer Fudd or Edith Bunker expect to build any credibility?

6. Speaking Too Slowly. See the previous point. I'm not saying speaking slowly is always a sign of low intelligence. But what matters is the impression the listener forms.

7. Sounding Salesy.

"If I could show you a way to save money, you would want that, wouldn't you?"

"Of course you'd be interested in how you could increase sales, right?"

8. Talking too Much Without Getting the Listener Involved. Enough said.

9. Lack of Confidence. It is magnified by phone

10. Annoying Habits.

"Uhhh, ahhh, like, I mean, ya know?"

11. Talking about Yourself and What You Want.

"I want to ask you some questions."

"I want to find out why you haven't bought from us in a while ..."

"I'm updating my accounts and I want to ..."

12. Talking about Products. People don't care about your products, only the results. Saying *"We sell office supplies"* is almost guaranteed to elicit, "We're happy with who we're using."

13. Asking for, or Alluding to, a Decision in the First Few Seconds.

"And I'd like to arrange a time for us getting together to ..."

"I want to talk with you about renewing your contract with us ..."

Action Steps

Chapter 9

How To Stimulate Interest at the Beginning of Calls

L ast chapter we discussed sure ways to create resistance at the beginning of calls. Let's go through what we can do to stimulate interest instead.

The Starting Point: The Potential Value You Offer

Creating interest begins long before you think about picking up the phone. It's a state of mind. An attitude. You must have a selfless, other-centered view of what you want to accomplish, as opposed to the "me"- and "gotta sell something"-attitudes of many reps. If one's primary focus is on pleasing himself, it's virtually impossible to genuinely create interest.

Remove all thoughts of what you personally want, and think instead about the people you call in your market. Ponder and understand their jobs and how they are evaluated ... what they try to accomplish ... pains and problems that hinder them. Then you're of the right mind to prepare for and execute call tactics.

Do Your Homework

The more someone knows about you, the more you're impressed about how much they cared to find out, right? Conversely, when a sales rep has to ask the most basic questions of the decision maker, he's perceived as a time-wasting buffoon. Ask questions of receptionists, screeners ... others in the buyer's department. Don't overlook users of the product or service. Always use the "H" word: "Help." You can then employ this information to personalize your opening and to ask more intelligent questions.

Effective Preliminary Non-Verbal Communication

Bulging file folders with form cover letters end up in the wastecan. Unless yours is a direct response mail package designed to elicit a reply on its own, save your materials. Prospects have no reason—nor the time—to plow through them. If you want to pave the way for an introductory call, write a short letter that touches on two or three potential results you could deliver, and mention you'll call soon. The more personalized the better. And I'm not talking about knowing how to work your word processing program's mail merge; I'm referring to information you might have gleaned from your sleuthing.

For example,

> **"I understand that you are now in the process of considering an addition to your manufacturing facility. Our firm specializes in the design of energy-efficient structures through some unique methods, helping companies in your industry reduce utility expenses by an average of 30% over typical buildings. I'll call you the week of the 20th to ask a few questions about your plans, and to determine if it would be of mutual benefit to discuss the situation further."**

Whether you mail information, fax it, courier it, e-mail it, or send it by pony express, be certain you discuss the potential results that can be gained by the prospect.

Professional Communications With Screeners

I made this point in the previous section on screeners, and I'll emphasize it again: Here's what you want the screener to announce to the boss: "There's a Mr./Ms. _____ on the line who really sounds like they have something you'll be interested in." Quite different from the message the screener would give about a slimy huckster employing shady, evasive tactics to con the screener. Introduce yourself, question the screener, answer with benefits when questioned, and always position yourself as the professional you are. Remember, the screener is sizing you up from the second you open your mouth.

A Phone Image That Exudes Confidence, And Competence

Sounding like a radio announcer doesn't guarantee you'll generate interest, but speaking like Dopey from the Seven Dwarfs will ensure resistance, regardless how good the ultimate message might be. Tape yourself, look for areas to improve. Go to your book superstore and pick out a few on speaking. Read the chapters on voice control in this book. Ensure you are proud of the way you "look" by phone.

Opening Statements

We're at the end of this chapter, and we're just now getting to what we actually say in the first 10 seconds of the call. That tells you something about the importance of the other areas, doesn't it? It's true that here you create curiosity and interest, and doing everything else well up to this point contributes greatly to your chances of success.

The remainder of this section specifically covers opening statements. Get your pen and paper out, and work on your own openings.

Action Steps

Chapter 10

A Fill-in-the-Blanks Opening Statement Template

Without an opening that seizes attention, sparks curiosity, and piques interest, it's like trying to climb a mountain with concrete building blocks strapped to your feet; you make the journey much more difficult than it needs to be, and as a result, you'll be stopped before you reach your destination.

Here's a fill-in-the-blanks formula and menu of word and phrase choices that I've used with sales reps for generic prospecting opening statements, which can be customized by most anyone for their own industry and types of calls. Use this as an idea-starter and template for your own perfect opening.

Fill in the Blanks to Create Your Own Opening

"Hello _____, I'm _____ with _____. I'm calling today because depending on what you're now doing/using/experiencing in the area of (fill in with your area of speciality) **there's a possibility we might be able to help you** (fill in with 1. Minimization Verbs) **your** (fill in with appropriate 2. Undesired Noun), **while at the same time** (fill in with 3. Maximization Verb") **your** (fill in with appropriate 4. Desired Noun). **If I've caught you at a good time, I'd like to** (fill in with 5. Action Verb) **your situation to see if this is something** (fill in with appropriate 6. Ending Phrase).**"**

Use these choices to fill in the blanks, or modify them and come up with your own.

---

1. Minimization Verbs

save	salvage	free up
consolidate	minimize	decrease
cut down on	eliminate get	rid of
reduce	lessen	cut
lower	soften	slash
shrink	slice	trim
combine	modify	

---

2. Undesired Noun

costs	trouble	difficulty
problems	restriction	obstacle
annoyance	inconvenience	time
expense	charges	taxes
waste	hassle	burden
work	drudgery	labor
effort	paperwork	bother
worry	anxiety	

---

3. Maximization Verb

strengthen	intensify
reinforce	boost
increase	xpand
add	grow
maximize	enhance
create	build
enjoy	ease
help	

---

4. Desired Noun

profits	sales	dollars
revenues	income	cash flow
savings	time	productivity
morale	motivation	output
attitude	image	victories
market share		

---

5. Action Verbs/Phrases

discuss
ask a few questions about
review
go through
analyze

---

6. Ending Phrases

you'd like more information on
you'd like to discuss
that would be of value to you
that would be of interest
that would be worth considering
that would work for you

Examples

This formula is intended to be tool for you to use when creating your own opening. Let's look at some examples using this template.

❑ **"Hello Ms. Dillon, I'm Dudley Denton with Able Supply. I'm calling today because depending on how you're now handling your receivables processing, there's a possibility we might be able to help you cut down on the time you spend preparing invoices, while also increasing your cash flow by getting bills paid to you more quickly. If I've caught you at a good time, I'd like to discuss your situation to see if this is something that you'd like more information on."**

❑ **"Mr. Grillo, this is Jill Nostrel with Slumlord Services. We specialize in working with multiple-unit property managers. Depending on how you're now tracking your accounting and owner reporting, there's a possibility we might be able to help you cut down on the hassle and paperwork involved in those tasks, while at the same time enhancing the amount of useful information you can put in a report, along with making them easier to read. If I've caught you at a good time, I'd like to ask you a few questions to see if this is something that you'd like to take a look at."**

❑ **"Hi Don, I'm Dale Fallon with Fishbreath Supply. My purpose for calling you is quite simple: depending on what items you're carrying now, there's a possibility we could help you lower your costs on many of the same supplies you're stocking, while at the same time free up more cash to carry other fast moving, high margin items. If I've caught you at a good time, I'd like to ask a few questions about your store to see if we should talk further."**

Apply this formula ... whip out your thesaurus and come up with other words more descriptive for what you sell, and what your customers want. Tinker with it, then test, edit, and retest your openings.

Chapter 11

One of the Worst Opening Statements Of the Year

H ere's one of the leading contenders for the worst opening statement I've heard so far this year:

"Hello, this is _____ with Action Pak Advertising. I was cleaning out some old files here from a sales rep who didn't do a very good job, and I see you had some interest at one time a couple of years ago in advertising with us, and I'd like to talk with you about that again."

I know there are skilled, professional sales reps out there selling advertising—but they're not the ones I get calls from. I hear from people who give that business a bad name.

Let's look at what is wrong with this opening:

1. *"I was cleaning out some old files here ..."* Wow! Doesn't that make one feel special! Consider the same approach, different situation: *"Hello, Myrtle, it's Tad Johnson. Hey, I was just cleaning out my glove compartment and I found one of my old black books with your phone number in it ..."*

2. *" ... from a sales rep who didn't do a very good job ..."* Nice way to build credibility in the first 10 seconds of a phone call, eh? So, before I hear a results-oriented reason why I should spend any time with this guy, he's hinting at the inefficiency of his personnel department and sales management.

3. *" ... and I see you had some interest at one time a couple of years ago in advertising with us ..."* This statement only serves to put someone on the defensive. Even if I had expressed interest at one time (which I had not; this company comes nowhere close to reaching my market), it was over two years ago! For example, think about all the telephone solicitations you've received during the past six months but didn't buy from. How many of those can you remember the precise details of? Now, can you even recall *any* of the calls you received over **two years** ago?

4. " *... and I'd like to talk with you about that again.*" Am I missing something here? Where's the benefit ... the results? This next point is true for everyone, but many advertising sales reps seem to be the worst culprits: prospects do not buy advertising (or any product or service itself). They might even have negative impressions of advertising in general. When they invest in advertising they do so with the hope of the end results: increased store traffic, more phone calls, more leads, or more sales.

Recommendation

OK, smart guy, you might be thinking, what approach should he have taken? Easy. Treat it like any other prospecting call:

❏ **In his preparation** he should realize that it's probably a good idea to not even mention any past conversations until he's well into the call with the prospect. After all, if the old sales rep was as bad as he says, what kind of impression did that leave on the prospects he contacted, even if they remember?

❏ **He should collect information** from others before speaking with the prospect. What my company does might have been a logical place to start. He could have quickly realized we weren't a prospect. (No, on second thought, it wouldn't have mattered to this guy. Even after I told him my buyers are not Data Processing Managers and Directors, he still tried to pitch me on the number of people I could reach, and the "low" investment per contact.)

❏ **The opening** has got to hint at results the person would be interested in, and then get him involved. Let's assume he did indeed target my market, and learned a little about me before speaking with me. A good opening would be,

> **"I'm ____ with Action Pak Advertising. We specialize in helping marketers get their message out to people who buy sales training materials for their companies. If that's an audience you promote to, we might have a few alternatives to help you acquire customers at a relatively low investment per account. What types of promotion do you use now?"**

Learn from these mistakes, and avoid them.

Chapter 12

Avoid Salesy, Manipulative Openings

What a coincidence! In my research I saw this old, tired, salesy technique in a book (which by the way had a sticker on it that read, *"Rated #1 best business book in America today—Success Today",* whoever they are), and the next day I heard it from a salesperson, almost verbatim.

Caller: *"Mr. Sobsi ... Sobee ...?"*

"Yes."

Caller: *"Would it be convenient for you to take a few moments to talk?"*

"I'm quite busy. It depends on what you have."

Caller: *"Uhhh, well, there might be a way to reduce your inventory, free up your cash, and get rid of problems that cash shortages generate. If that were true, you <u>would</u> want to talk about it, <u>wouldn't</u> you?"*

"No."

Caller: *"No? I don't understand."*

"I know you don't understand. Even if it were true, which it's not, I wouldn't spend time with someone who used a technique that tries to paint someone into a corner."

Analysis and Recommendation

First the guy calls me out of the blue and before introducing himself asks if I could take a few moments to speak with him. The only reason I was as nice as I was, was because I thought it just might be a customer. I wish someone could explain to me how asking someone for a few moments of their time on prospecting calls, *before* you've told them what you can do for them, supposedly succeeds more than it fails. My experience clearly shows it doesn't, and I don't like those odds. What we're trying to do immediately is put the listener in a positive, receptive frame of mind, and this question shrieks, "I want to sell you something!" If you insist on asking for time, I'll give my favorite idea in a moment.

Next, if he would have asked the person answering my phone what we do and sell here, he would have realized we aren't the type of company that ties up tons of cash in inventory, so the entire call was really a non-issue.

Finally, he used that dreadful question, *"If I could show you ..., you would want to hear more, wouldn't you?"* People who use and promote this phrase—including the author of that "best selling" book—ought to get a clue: It puts listeners in a resistant position. Sure they might respond the way the sales rep wants, but they're trapped into it, and then are left bracing themselves wondering what's going to come next.

If I was a prospect for what he was selling—which I didn't stay on the line long enough to find out exactly what that was—a simple rewording of the opening would have caught my interest:

> **"Mr. Prospect, depending on how your current inventory level compares to what you'd like it to be, and what type of cash position you're in, there might be a way to reduce that inventory and free up more cash. We've worked with other (manufacturers/wholesalers/suppliers) to help them do just that, and if I caught you at a good time, I'd like to ask you a few questions to see if this would be something worth looking into."**

Notice this is non-threatening, doesn't come on strong, and leads nicely into the questioning with someone who is open-minded, not resistant.

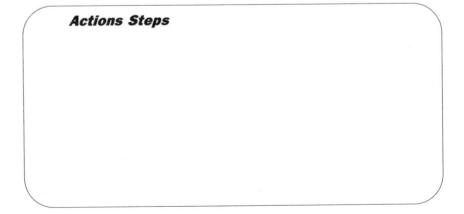

Actions Steps

Chapter 13

Creating Great Openings After Inquiries

Fairfield Processing Corporation in Danbury, Connecticut, sells fluff.

No, really. They do. The fluffy stuff that goes in pillows, quilts, even teddy bears (scientifically called Poly-fil-R®).

Gina Kuchta, one of the sales reps, wrote to me looking for help and explained her existing sales process and tactics.

Most of Fairfield's new prospects are phone inquiries resulting from people who've either heard about, seen, or used the product. (Fairfield also sells through distributors, and their phone number is on the packages.) Typical prospects and customers are ma & pop crafters working out of their homes looking to save a buck wherever they can. However, they also have many larger customers who mass produce. (My own mother is a crafter, and as it turns out a retail customer of Fairfield products. She confirmed that they are the Lexus of the fiber fill business.)

The Incoming Call

On the incoming call, reps ask questions to learn about the business (Gina did mention they could expand on the questioning and subsequent sales opportunities. I agree and will address it later). A package of fluff then goes out (I couldn't resist that). Actually it includes pricing, product and company info. They place a follow-up call about two weeks later, and that's where the difficulty comes. Gina asked for help with her opening, which she characterized as "weak."

"Hi, _____, this is Gina Kuchta calling from Fairfield Processing in Connecticut. About two weeks ago you had phoned/written to us requesting some information regarding our Poly-Fil products. I'm just calling to make sure that you received it."

Since she wasn't lighting anyone's fire with that, she was desperate for something stronger. After discussing the matter by phone, we came up with a few ideas.

Analysis and Recommendation

The main problem isn't with an uninspiring follow-up call opening. The problem is with what happens—or doesn't happen—on initial calls, leaving sales reps nothing of substance to work with when trying to come up with a good opener on follow-ups. We need to squeeze all the potential we can from that initial call, and I suggest several tactics to do so.

Sell on the Incoming Call

Granted, you might not close a sale with everyone on this call, but why not start there as a primary objective? After all, if they're calling about fluff, and they've used your exact same stuff(ing) before, why do they need to see something else? I've seen too many reps create unnecessary work by feeling (wrongly) they needed to stretch out the sales process over several calls, because they should always just send out material on a first contact. Hey, go for the gusto. These people called for a reason. If the need is there, don't prolong the process. That would be like a cashier at a retail store telling customers in line, "Go home with the price list and a few brochures, and then, in a week-to-ten-days, let's get back in touch."

Tightly Qualify Them

Question with CIA-like depth. Bottom line, will they buy or not (at some point), find out when, in what quantity, and how often.

> **"How much do you use now?"**
>
> **"How much are you planning on using within the next year?"**
>
> **"How are you selling your stuffed rhinoceroses now?"**
>
> **"So if the Wal-Mart deal goes through, how many do you think you'll sell per year?"**

Learn the Decision Criteria

If they do need to see your material first, ensure they're a serious player. Learn their decision-making criteria, and what they'll do and when.

> **"What will you look for in the sample?"**
>
> **"How will you decide between us and Foam-R-Us?"**
>
> **"Who else will evaluate it?"**
>
> **"By when will you have a chance to look at it?"**
>
> **"When do you need the material?"**

Get a Commitment

> **"If the sample meets the requirements you men-**

tioned, will you buy from us?"

"Can we be your supplier?"

"Will you be ready to set up an account the next time we talk?"

If everything's sailing smoothly, build the anticipation by preselling them on what you'll send, so they have an idea of what to expect, and of what to do when it arrives.

"Mary, I'll send you a sample of our pillow insert in the two sizes you need. You mentioned you want inserts that retain their shape under pressure. Well, these are the best you'll find. I'd actually like you to test these by putting them under a concrete building block for a couple of hours. Do you have one available? Great. Then notice how well it snaps back and retains its cushiness."

Assuming everything discussed thus far was executed flawlessly on the initial contact, it would be a breeze to assemble a smooth introduction on the follow-up.

"Hi Mary, it's Gina Kuchta with Fairfield Processing, calling to continue our conversation from last week, where we discussed our inserts for your new line of Barney pillows. If I caught you at a good time, I'd like to discuss your evaluation, plus I have some additional information I came across on marketing through consignment stores that I thought you might find interesting."

Notice that there's something new at the end of the opening. I suggest that on *every* call you bring some additional value to the table.

The quality, ease of development, and subsequent success of any follow-up opening—and call— is directly dependent on how well the previous call set it up. Focus more on the initial call, and the follow up is a breeze.

Action Steps

Chapter 14

Ideas For Follow-Up Call Openings

Your follow-up call opening should serve to smoothly bring the customer's state-of-mind back to the point where it was when you ended the previous conversation. The opening should not,

• ask for a decision: " ... *calling to see if you're ready to buy now ...*"

• be simply reactive: " ... *and I was just checking to see if you had any questions ...*"

• be a quality test of the postal service or their internal mail handling: " ... *wanted to see if you received the material I sent ...*"

First, your follow-up call needs to be based upon an objective for this call. When you think about it logically, there must have been some reason why you've agreed to follow up, right? (If not, this might be a sign you're getting the brush-off from lots of folks, causing you to waste time chasing shadows. For example, "Well, just call me back in about six weeks.")

Good reasons for following up include either,

• they were to do something between the last call and the scheduled follow-up that would make this call worthwhile, or,

• a future event would take place that would make the follow-up more appropriate, such as a new budget year beginning.

The opening needs to bring them into a conversation that readdresses the hot points fueling their interest last call, and also serves to move the process closer to the ultimate action you're seeking (the sale).

Follow-Up Opening Format

Here's a simple format for the opening.

1. Identification. The less the familiarity, the more formality. If you've only spoken once, first and last names and your company should be included. If you're well acquainted, you be the judge as to what sounds appropriate.

2. Bridge. Again, you want to bring them back to a point they were emotionally when you ended. You often need to remind them of their interest and the previous call. Use words like,

> " ... **calling to continue our conversation from two weeks ago ...**"
>
> "... **I'd like to pick up where we left off ...**"
>
> " ... **calling to resume our discussion of ...**"

Mention what their main interest was.

> " ... **where we went through the savings you'd show with internal management of your ...**"

3. The Agenda for This Call. This part needs to be proactive:

> "**I'd like to go through the material I sent you to point out the specific cost-cutting features that apply specifically ...**"

Other proactive words and phrases include,

> "**discuss**"
>
> "**analyze**"
>
> "**cover**"
>
> "**review**"
>
> "**walk through**"

Remember, you're not calling to just check in, or slap them with a goofy question like, *"Well, what'd you think? Are you ready now?"*

You also should bring something new to the table ... some value-added reason for this call, beyond what was covered last time. This way, if their interest has waned since the last contact, and/or they didn't follow through with what they said they'd do (which happens quite often) you still have a basis for continuing this contact. For example,

> "**And I also did some research and came up with a few other examples of something you showed interest in the last time we spoke: how other engineering firms have used this process.**"

The opening is a small, but integral part of the follow-up contact. When well prepared and executed, it takes them to the next phase of the call, which is your questioning.

Chapter 15

Opening Statement Tips

What to Do When They Say, "Make it Quick"

It can be a pain when prospects and customers say, "OK, you've got two minutes, make it quick." This triggers some reps into a panic, shifting to frenetic speed-talking data-dump mode, racing the clock, spraying words like a firehose.

So what should you do? Unless you detect they do indeed need to hurry off the phone (when they say they need to actually go somewhere, or they have someone in their office), keep these ideas in mind.

❑ **Understand why people say this.** They often make these statements as a natural, resistant, defense mechanism. It gets rid of salespeople who self-destruct under the pressure.

❑ **Go for it!** Since you have them on the phone and it might require several more attempts before you get the opportunity again, jump in. Compose yourself, and resist turning on a verbal waterfall. You might even consider saying,

> **"That's fine, unless of course after a few minutes you'd like me to continue."**

❑ **Present your brilliant opening statement.** Just like any call, you want to grab their attention. Time flies when you're talking about something interesting, it's here that you help take their mind off their previously-stated time constraint.

❑ **Don't rush.** You know you can't effectively cram a call into a tiny box of time, so don't try. It will only tense you up like a tightly-wound spring.

❑ **Check on the time.** After a few minutes, and you've involved them, ask,

> **"I know you're pressed for time. Shall we continue now, or arrange to talk again?**

❑ **If they're not a prospect, you've saved your own time.** By seizing the opportunity, you've realized you don't need to call them back, therefore saving time you can use more wisely.

Show the Benefit First

In your openings, always be sure you're explaining what you can do before you ask for something. For example, consider your reaction if you heard,

"Ms. Prospect, I'd like to ask you a few questions and find out about your manufacturing process to determine if our new flange-resistor system might be able to shave time off of repetitive quality control checks."

> Compare that to, **"Ms. Prospect, we've been able to help other manufacturers shave time off of repetitive quality control checks in their manufacturing process through an innovative new flange-resistor system. To see if you would have interest in getting information on this, and if it would fit with what you do, I'd like to briefly discuss your manufacturing process ..."**

The premise here is that if you blindside someone with an immediate demand (asking them questions) before they see any reason to comply, skepticism—or even resistance—immediately sets. in. Conversely, by first explaining how they'll potentially gain, they move into a positive, receptive state of mind.

Get Them to React

Try a variation of this opening statement:

> **"Ms. Prospect, I have an idea that might be able to help you** (fill in here with something they really want, i.e. more store traffic, higher average sale, etc.) **and I need your input on it."**

Wait for their response, ask a couple of qualifying questions, and tease them with a vague hint on what the idea is about,

> **"It's regarding how we've worked with other stores**

to sell more to their existing customers through some
innovative point-of-purchase techniques."

Then ask more questions.

How to Handle Rushed Prospects Who Say
"Just Tell Me What You Have"

A question I received via e-mail asked,

"How do you build a relationship with prospects who insist on positioning you as a 'vendor,' by saying very quickly at the beginning of a call,
'tell us what you have to offer,' or, 'We won't answer your questions until
you tell us what you have to offer.'"

My feeling is that people who say things like this either aren't serious
about listening, or haven't been convinced that the sales rep has anything
of potential value, or both. I've responded in several ways to this situation:

**"Trying to tell you what I could do for you, without
knowing anything about you would probably waste
your time and mine. By learning a little about your
situation regarding _____, I'll be in a better position
to discuss what the mutual value might be ..."**

**"Giving you a presentation without having any in-
formation about you would be like buying a birthday present for someone I don't know—it likely
wouldn't be appropriate. By asking you a few questions ..."**

**"I likely do have something to offer you, but until I
know specifically about your situation in the area
of _____, I won't know how you'd benefit. Let's discuss how ..."**

My feeling is that people most often say things like this to test sales
reps, and to separate the pros from the "pitchers," the reps who rattle off
the same spiel to everyone. Maintain your composure and dazzle them
with the value you can deliver.

A Dead-End Question on an Outbound Call is a Good One on an Inquiry

I've always suggested avoiding go-nowhere questions at the beginning of prospecting calls, especially *"Are you familiar with us?"* As in, *"Mr. Prospect, I'm Jan Mackerel with Zygon Industries, are you familiar with us?"* My reasoning is that if they aren't familiar with you, you'll have to explain your company anyway, so why do it after they've given you a negative answer? Plus, you haven't given them a reason to answer your questions, or to care about your company. If they answer that, yes, they are familiar with you, but they're not a customer, it leads to the beginning of a potentially uncomfortable situation, almost putting the person on the defensive.

You do, indeed, want to find out what they know about you—just do not make that the focus of your opening statement. After you've generated some interest and curiosity with a brilliant opener, you can say,

> **"By the way, so I'm not being redundant with my questioning, does our company name sound familiar at all to you?"**

Incoming calls are an entirely different matter. If they inquire to you for information, you should definitely find out—early—what they already know about you. This pinpoints where you need to start with them. For example,

Prospect: (who called in to the sales rep) "Yes, I'd like to get some information on the Performacal Trioxin you had advertised in Chemical Journal."

> **Sales Rep: "I'll be happy to help you with that.** (after getting name, company, etc.) **So I can give you the best information for your application, let me ask a few questions. First of all, how familiar are you with our company, and the Performacal product?"**

Listen carefully and take notes, as this simple open-ended question could provide you with the basis for some great information. It's quite likely they'll mention some positives which you naturally can build upon, and if they by chance bring up any negative perceptions, you can question further and hopefully dispel them.

Don't Say What You "Just Wanted to Do"

In openings avoid using the phrase, *"I just wanted to give you a call today and ..."* Don't talk about what you "just wanted to do." Instead,

TELL them why you're calling, including your reason why they should be interested.

> **"I'm calling because we've worked with other people in a similar situation as yours, and helped them to ..."**

Have Something of Value Every Time You Call

Here's another go-nowhere opening that, to me, sounds like long fingernails dragging slowly across the blackboard: *"I was recently assigned to your account as the new rep handling your territory, and I was just wondering if everything is OK, and if we could be of service in any way."* I feel sorry for the unsuspecting greenhorn sales reps who are thrown into situations like these, often with very little training, and are told, "Call these people up and see if there's anything we can do." It's as if the prospect was waiting for the call, list in hand of all the items he would like to buy from the caller. Yeah, right. Usually, the customer isn't really a customer—maybe someone who purchased something minor at one time or another—and hasn't a clue about the calling company, and couldn't care less that there is now someone assigned to his account. Actually, he's probably thinking that now he has some sales rep who will be bothering him. If you're handed a pile of old "accounts," keep in mind these people may not know your company from one plucked randomly from the Yellow Pages, let alone care that you're now the person assigned to him. Therefore, treat these like prospecting calls and be certain to have something of value when you call ... a reason for them to listen and share information with you.

You're Not a "Talking Mail Piece"

Keep in mind you are not a "talking direct mail piece." That's a caller who spews the same information, call after call, with little regard for questioning and the needs of the listener. For example, the caller might repeatedly say, *"The reason for the call is to let you know about our special on muffler belts this month. They come in six colors and are only $5.95 each. Would you like some?"* A tape recording could give that same message, for gosh sakes! Ensure you're calling with prepared questions, and only present after you've learned of their needs.

By the way, you *can* take a specific offer, and make that the premise of your call—you just don't give the entire spiel at the beginning. Instead, you might start with,

> **"Pat, when I saw this month's special, I thought of**

you, and how it would be perfect for you because of what you told me last time about how muffler-related items move well in your store. (pause) **Tell me, what brand of muffler belts are you carrying now?"**

Then, after layering questions further—questions designed to uncover needs-related information—then the listener would be in a much more receptive frame of mind to hear about the belts, plus the rep could tailor his presentation to fit snugly with the prospect's situation.

"Could I Have 43 Seconds of Your Time"

In an issue of the *"Guerrilla Marketing Newsletter"*), I read where financial planner Michael Marteloni cold calls prospects and asks for 43 seconds of their time. The article didn't say how many agreed to give him the time (other than saying he talks to a lot of people), but out of those who do, 10% agree to a 50-minute face-to-face meeting, and 10% of those become clients.

The key here seems to be the gadget technique of asking for "43 seconds." I wouldn't recommend this for most people, but in the financial planning business (and probably life insurance) where most prospects would rather have their toe nails removed by needle-nosed pliers than talk to a salesperson, it could be a way to at least buy a few seconds to deliver a value-laden opening statement.

Read Your Opening Into a Tape Recorder to Test It

After cobbling out an opening statement you feel is ready for field testing, put it through a few more trials. Speak it into a tape recorder—this ensures it sounds conversational. Role play it with a partner. Have them throw resistance at you. You'll be better prepared when you get on the phones.

Action Steps

Action Steps

Selling
With
Questions

Chapter 16

Questions: The Key to Professional Sales

H ere's the secret of sales that can double your income: Get information before you give it. It's that simple.

Selling isn't *convincing* anyone of anything. It's helping them get what they value.

A cab driver ask what I did for a living. After hearing the answer, he said that he couldn't sell because in a job interview he had taken a test requiring him to sell a pen to a person who already had a similar pen. He failed miserably, and asked me what kind of pitch I would have suggested.

I responded that there's no possible way I would *even consider* trying to put together a "pitch" under those circumstances because you're predestined for failure. I told him that you'd first need to find out why and how the person uses pens, what he likes and doesn't like about them, ideally what he desires most and least when it comes to pens, and what value he places on that. Only **then** could you effectively tell him about your pen and have a snowball's chance of getting him to consider yours.

The Same is True With Your Calls

And that's no different than your sales calls. To enjoy gargantuan success in sales, you need to be a master questioner, able to open up your prospect and customer, unlock their needs, concerns and desires, and move them into a state of mind where they begin wanting a product or service like yours even before you begin presenting it. Think about it: offer someone a drink of water when they're not thirsty, and they decline. When they're parched, they seek out the water. Your job is to help them recognize the thirst.

Here is a very effective exercise I recommend you engage in to help your questioning be as effective as possible.

Generate Need-Development Questions

People only take action when they are dissatisfied with their present situation, or want to avoid such dissatisfaction. What dissatisfaction do you ease?

Benefits are only benefits if the person hearing them perceives them to be benefits. Therefore, I suggest you work backwards from benefits to create questions. Take a "benefit," then think of what dissatisfaction it soothes, the need it fills, or problem it solves. Then, write out the appropriate question you'd ask.

For example, an order-entry software program offers instant notification of out-of-stock merchandise, allowing you to suggest alternative items. But it's only a benefit if a listener runs into backorder situations and feels it's a hindrance because they lose sales, or have paperwork headaches, etc. Therefore an initial question would be,

"How often do you run into backorder situations?"

Followed by, **"When do you realize it?"**

"Have you ever lost sales because you had to notify the customer later their item was going to be late, and they just told you to cancel it?"

Notice that technique isn't simply, "Are you having any backorder problems?" That forces them to think too much. You want to help them recall and feel the dissatisfaction.

Begin each call thinking of the dissatisfaction you can fill, and what questions you'll need to ask to determine if it exists, and to what extent, or how you'll help them recognize any latent dissatisfaction.

After you've accomplished this on a call, then and only then are you in a favorable position to begin presenting what you offer.

More Tips

Here are additional questioning tips.

❏ **Prepare your questioning plan.** You are not adequately prepared if you prepare only for the questions you'll ask. The real pros know what they'll do with the answers—all possible answers. That's how you become smooooth. You can't script out an entire call; there are too many possible ways the conversation could branch. But you can be totally prepared for whichever artery it travels. As part of your preparation, take just one path at a time and brainstorm every possibility. Just as a road is more familiar the second time you take it, so too will be your responses to questions, since you've already traveled that path in your mind.

❏ **Embellish needs.** Again, people only take action when the dissatisfaction is strong enough. You probably have some need right now, but they are not major, so you let them slide ... you know, those "I'll get around to it," kind of things. With prospects and customers, you need to compound their perception of these needs. If they tell you they waste time now, ask how much. If they think sales are lower than they could be, ask how much lower. If they're losing money, find out how much. This gets them thinking about and feeling the pain.

❏ **Clarify the "Fuzzy Phrases."** Don't get put off by an abstract phrase like, "We might do something next quarter. We'll take a look at it. Let's stay in touch." What does THAT mean?

> **"When you say 'do something', does that mean you'll go with it?"**

> **"What exactly will you be looking at?"**

> **"Does 'stay in touch' mean I should call at a certain time?"**

Help Them Shop Around

When your prospect or customer is shopping, ask,

- who else they'll talk to,
- what they'll look for, and,
- how they'll make their final decision.

With this information in hand you can also help them judge the competitors. Give them additional questions to ask. If you know the other contender is weak in quality, and that's your strong suit, tell the prospect to be sure they collect the quality control facts and figures. And if they're fuzzy on how they'll make their final decision, help them set the criteria. This way, they'll know specifically how to evaluate the other players as they're shopping.

Sell More to Existing Customers

Would you say that you have customers who buy some of the same things you sell, from your competitors? This is true for most sales reps. Especially those who have large customers representing significant revenue, but yet buy only one or two products in large quantities to generate that revenue. Some reps have told me they don't want to jeopardize the existing business by going after more.

NONSENSE! *Not* building on the relationship is doing a disservice to the customers. Approach them by saying,

> **"We really appreciate the opportunity to work with you, and given the fact you've been satisfied with the _____ you've been getting from us, we might have several others ways we could work with you and provide the same quality, service, and competitive pricing you're getting now. I'd like to find out more about what you do/use/buy to determine how else we might be of service."**

Questions to Use

Here are questions you can adapt or use as-is on your calls.

> **"What are some of your responsibilities in this position?"** (Helps you understand how they are evaluated in their job, and how you can help them)

> **"What process did you go through in selecting your present vendor?"** (Gives you an idea of how difficult it might be to win the business?)

> **"How are you handling _____ now?"** (Fill in with a problem they likely are experiencing, or one you think they might encounter.)

> **"What are you doing about it?"** (If they say, "Nothing," ask the next questions.)

> **"What effect is that having on your business, and other departments?"**

> **"What is it costing you?"**

> **"What will happen if you do nothing?"**

> **"What is keeping you from solving the problem?"** (These are all designed to help embellish and magnify the problem so they see it as being severe enough to do something about.)

> **"What do you see as possible solutions?"** (To get their idea of what they'd like to do.)

> **"What do you think is the best solution?"** (Narrows it down.)

"Why is that one most important to you?" (Gives their emotional reason. Helps them sell themselves.)

"If you decided to go that route, what is the overall decision making process?" (Gives you an idea of what channels you might have to go through.)

"Who else might be involved?" (Gives you the names of other players.)

"Will they go along with your decision or recommendation?"

"What will you need to do to win their support?" (Uncovers the degree of difficulty of getting the decision passed.)

WHY are They Interested?

In dissecting every potential sale I've lost over the past couple of years, I can always point my finger at one reason: I either didn't learn enough about the need/problem/interest, or I didn't develop it enough. Quite often we think that just because someone has voiced an interest, we should shift into presentation mode.

Don't. Dig deeper, like an archaeologist mining for fossils. Most importantly, discover what's behind their interest. Ask,

"What prompted your decision to expand?"

"What were some of the considerations that led you to search for a new machine?"

"Is this decision part of a new direction for the company?"

"How did you arrive at this decision?"

The more you know about the core reasons behind a need or problem the better able you are to deliver results that satisfy them precisely.

How to Be a Problem-Solver

You'll sell more if you're a problem solver than if you're a sales person. And you'll build stronger customer relationships.

"Telemanaging," a publication for newspaper classified advertising sales managers, listed the following problem-solving model, adapted from a workshop given by Anne Antony.

Help Identify the Problem
"What is happening?"

"What is not happening?"

"What happens as a result of the problem?"

"Where does it happen?"

"Where does it not happen?"

"When does it happen?"

"When does it not happen?"

Investigating the Causes

"What are the possible causes?"

"What are the most probable causes?"

"What cause is most likely the real one?"

Envisioning the Desired Result

"What do you want things to be like?"

"What do you want to fix?"

"Are you after short- or long-term effects?"

Choosing a Course of Action

"What possible actions could be taken?"

"Which actions are most likely to lead to your vision of the solution?"

"Which course of action is the best?"

Take this model, and adapt the questions to your own selling situation. Apply them to the very real problems your prospects and customers experience, the ones you help solve.

(SOURCE: "Telemanaging," The MacDonald Classified Service, 14 N. Second St., Lafayette, IN, 47901)

If I Could Share Just One Idea With You ...

A middle-aged man approached me at a presentation and said, "I'm moving into a sales position, and I'm a bit fearful of it because I'm not sure I can be a typical salesperson. What one piece of advice could you give me that would help me be successful?"

I first asked him what he considered a typical salesperson to be, and he described a slick-talking pitchman who has all the answers and often pushes people into decisions.

My answer didn't require a lot of thought:

"Don't be a 'typical' salesperson. Instead, be certain you get a lot of information before you make any type of recommendation. That will ensure success."

It really *is* that simple. Brain strain isn't required to understand that you couldn't fit a person with the right pair of shoes unless you knew his size. A doctor couldn't write the appropriate prescription until he knew the patient's symptoms. Why "typical" salespeople "pitch" product and service data before knowing anything about the listener is beyond me. Yet, it happens more often than not.

Pitching (I hate that word used in a sales, rather than a baseball context) product details without understanding the listener's needs, problems, concerns, desires, and interests is like throwing a handful of pebbles from 50 yards through a wedding ring. The pebbles scatter haphazardly, and just maybe one finds its way through the target.

When a salesperson launches into a data-dump monologue,

❏ people view the product pitch skeptically, actually looking for faults in what the speaker presents. We do that instinctively because of a natural resistance to being sold or pushed, and,

❏ they are passive, not really into two-way communication.

On the other hand, questioning not only serves to provide us with great information,

❏ prospects become participants in the interaction,

❏ initial resistance is diffused because they are talking about themselves, and what they want and need, and,

❏ they become mentally and emotionally moved into a state of mind where they are now thinking about their pains, problems or desires, and are more open-minded to hearing the recommendation. As the saying goes, "No one likes unsolicited advice," which is exactly what a pitch is without prior questioning. Conversely, again using the doctor example, think of how receptive you were of the prescription your doctor gave you for that nagging ailment.

Here are a couple of simple ideas which I know will help you to be more effective.

1. Instead of making a statement, or giving an instruction, try to think of a question which would help the listener reach the

same conclusion. Use it with prospects and customers, and make it a life long habit. Do it with friends, co-workers, spouses, and children. For example, in place of, *"You should enter the data first, then you wouldn't have the extra work,"* consider,

> **"How would first entering the data affect your workload?"**

2. Never, *ever*, present until you've asked questions first. Make it a policy. Before presenting, simply ask yourself, "Do I know if they're interested in what I'm about to say?"

Do you think these ideas would work for you? I do.

More Dumb Questions And Vague Statements

As I've said before, there are dumb questions in sales; those questions that give you virtually worthless information and require another question to clarify the answer.

Dumb question: *"Will you be using the program for a long time?"*

> **Better: "How long will you use the program?"**

Dumb question: *"Does that happen often?"*

> **Better: "How often per day, approximately, does that happen?"**

Dumb question: *"Do you anticipate getting approval soon?"*

> **Better: "When do you anticipate getting approval?"**

Dumb question: *"Do you use quite a bit of that chemical?"*

> **Better: "How much of that chemical do you use per week?"**

Dumb question: *"Should I check back with you later?"*

> **Better: "When do you anticipate finishing the evaluation so I can check back with you?"**

Vague Statements

Likewise, there are statements that also communicate vague information to your prospects and customers.

Vague: *"I'll be back in the office later."*

> **Better: "I'll be at my desk and available after 2:30."**

Vague: *"We'll get the proposal out as soon as we can."*

> **Better: "You'll have the proposal no later than Friday's Federal Express delivery."**

Asking About Money Makes You Money

Asking money-related questions can clear the fog in the sales process. You can quickly qualify your prospect, plus get a feel for what you will recommend during the presentation stage of the call, plus you can get a feel for where you are competitively.

Sadly, though, many sales reps neglect this all-important question. And it usually hurts them later by causing them to waste time with people who ultimately turn out to be nonbuyers, are unqualified, or don't have the amount of cash it takes to buy from you.

Keep one thing in mind: real, serious prospects don't mind hearing money questions. Pretenders, however, are wounded by money questions because it exposes them.

When you do ask money questions be sure you position them in terms of how they'll help the buyer. For example,

> **"I want to make sure we're in the same ballpark here ..."**

> **"I'm asking the next question because it will help me determine exactly what I'll recommend ..."**

> **"Just to be sure we don't invest a lot of time up front needlessly, I want to be sure that our price ranges are compatible with what you're looking for ..."**

Then ask the question,

> **"Approximately what were you looking to spend?"**

> **"About how much has been set aside for this project?"**

> **"What budget range were you thinking about?"**

Notice that these don't ask for a specific amount ... just a range or approximation. That way you leave room for negotiating them up by positioning your value—if you're close.

Don't Sell; Be a Problem Solver

Reviewing the newsletter my son's school sends home, I saw a wise piece of advice, that, although basic, again should be a staple for what we do by phone. It was about solving problems. I'll adapt it for phone use.

1. Gather Data. Collect information about events and feelings:

"What do you do when ...?"

"What happened?"

"How did you feel?"

"What did you do next?"

"What are the implications of that?"

Restate the situation clearly. It's easier to solve a problem when the other person has a clear understanding of it. For example,

"What you want to do is_____. Is that right?"

2. Generate Ideas. Encourage them to state a solution.

"What ideally would you like to see?"

3. Evaluate Ideas. Examine the consequences of their ideas (but don't criticize bad ones). Help them tell the difference between good and bad ones.

"What might happen if ___?"

4. Ask for a Decision. Ask them to take action. Help them make the choice.

"Is this what you'd like to do?"

Finish With This Question

As you conclude your fact-finding phase of your call, conclude with a question which may provide information you might have overlooked. For example,

"Karen, before I make my recommendations, what else should I be asking you about how you're now handling this situation?"

Let Them Tell You Their Problems

When a prospect says, "This is what we're doing now ...," a salesperson's instinctive tendency might be to attack their present system or vendor, and fire off the "benefits"of what they sell. Instead, let the prospect tell you his problems. Consider asking,

> **"Have you thought of any disadvantages to doing it that way?"**
>
> **"What's the downside of that?"**
>
> **"In what ways does that not meet your expectations?"**
>
> **"What would you change about that if you could?"**

Use Trial and Direct Commitment Questions To Move the Sales Process Forward

During the presentation/recommendation phase of your call you want to get feedback to learn how they're reacting to your statements. Since you can't see their expressions, we must ask for them with trial commitment questions. For example,

> **"Is there anything I've covered so far that I can explain more fully?"**
>
> **"How would that work for you?"**
>
> **"How does it sound so far?"**

After you've made your recommendation, and you've heard statements of agreement from them, it's time to move the process forward. Here are ideas for direct commitment questions to move them towards action.

> **"I'm ready to talk terms if you are."**
>
> **"I'm reading the feeling that you're ready to schedule delivery. Is that accurate?"**
>
> **"Shall we iron out the details right now?"**

Sales Training Lesson From The O.J. Trial

I observed a great lesson from the O.J. criminal trial. One of defense attorneys was questioning the curbside baggage check-in guy from L.A. International airport. The lawyer confidently stated, *"And of course you didn't see Mr. Simpson anywhere near that trash can, did you?"*

"Uh, as a matter of fact, I did," responded the witness.

OOOPPS! The lawyer violated a cardinal rule of cross-examination, according to one of the TV network attorney/analysts: asking a question when you don't already know the answer.

Applies to Sales Also

The rule for salespeople is similar: Don't ask a question unless you know how you'll respond to the answer. *Any* possible answer.

When a rep says to a prospect, *"Tell me about the service you're getting with your present vendor,"* I guess they're hoping the prospect will say, "Service! It's non-existent. They couldn't even spell it, let alone deliver it!" In actuality, though, when they hear the more likely answer, "Service is fine," they're stumped, not sure what to say next other than, *"OK, keep us in mind."*

The well-prepared rep confidently responds with a question designed to get the prospect visualizing an occurrence of inadequate service he likely has experienced:

> **"I see. What do you do when you need to get technical questions answered quickly, and you reach a recording asking you to leave your name and number so they can call you back?"**

Or, let's say their answer truly leads this branch of questioning down a dead end. No problem. The prepared caller smoothly shifts the questioning in another direction:

> **"What do you do when you need an item that is either discontinued or back-ordered?"**

More Tips

Here are a collection of tips and ideas to use.

❏ **Have a strong belief system regarding questioning.** I've seen timid reps carrying a preconceived notion that people are offended by qualifying questions. Nonsense. This is business! They're actually more offended when salespeople don't get to the point. Project a self-assured image and tone ... one that says questioning is a necessary part of your process (it is!) in order to determine how you can help them. Let your demeanor indicate you expect an answer.

❏ **If you must ask for what really is touchy or private information, don't apologize.** *"I hope you're not thinking I'm getting too* *personal here, I know this is normally confidential."* Instead, preface your remarks with your justification for asking, which puts the answerer more at ease:

> **"The reason for the next question is that it will help me identify the best recommendation for your company's size range."**

☐ **Use "Assumptive Problem" open-ended questions.** Instead of saying, *"Do you have any problems with defects now?"*, say,

> **"How are you handling defects in the manufacturing process."**

If you know your industry well enough, you're aware of problems everyone has. You're asking them to quantify and explain the implications of the problems.

☐ **Use "Parrot" questions.** Repeating back what the person just said. For example, when they say, "We haven't had much luck finding the right system to track our process," you could parrot back,

> **"You haven't had much luck?"**

Their comment is just the tip of the iceberg. By repeating a part of their comment, you encourage them to continue.

☐ **Use "Instructional Statements."** Don't ask for information. *Tell them* to give it to you. Use phrases like,

> **"Tell me a little about ...,"**
>
> **"Share with me ...,"**
>
> **"Fill me in on ...,"**
>
> **"Give me some idea of ...,"**
>
> **"Detail the ways that ...,"**
>
> **"Let's go over the reasons for ..."**

☐ **Remember that some of your "benefits" are actually liabilities to others.** Your benefits are not universal. Some people could actually say, "We don't need that, and we don't want to pay extra for it!" Therefore, for each benefit you have, make sure you ask a question to determine if it's really perceived as one by your prospect. For example, if the laser printer you sell races through at 20 pages per minute, you might ask,

"For what types of jobs do you use your printer?"

And depending on their response,

"How much of an issue is speed?"

☐ **Ask yourself questions before calls in order to develop the best prospect/customer questions.** Ask, "What do I want them to do as a result of this call?" This gives you your primary call objective. Then ask, "What information do I need from them?" This provides whatever qualifying or data-gathering questions you must ask. Finally, ask, "What do I need them to think and believe in order to take the action I desire?" The answer to this question provides the points you'd ideally like to get across ... without actually making the points yourself. They are ideas you want them to discover through your questions. The reasoning is that people always believe more of what they say and think than of what you say. For example, let's say you need them to believe that they are missing sales opportunities because their incoming business reply card leads age too long before their sales people unenthusiastically call on them, and, that their salespeople would be much better off calling on hot leads that had already been qualified. You could develop questions such as,

> **"How long do your leads normally set before your reps get to them?"**
>
> **"Have they ever had situations where the prospect already purchased before the rep got around to calling?"**
>
> **"How often do your reps complain about the quality of the leads?"**
>
> **"Do you think they might even avoid calling them sometimes because they perceive them as bad?"**
>
> **"If so, do you think they might miss a few of the good ones that undoubtedly are still in there?"**

After these questions the prospect would be much more favorably conditioned to hear a presentation on your lead-qualification service.

Get Examples of the Problem

When you uncover a need or problem, ask the prospect to give you examples of the situation. This way they relive the pain of the problem, plus it gives you something concrete to deal with.

Prospect: "We have noticed a tardiness problem here lately."

Sales Rep: "I see. What specifically have you noticed?"

Prospect: "There have been a few times when their service hasn't met our expectations."

Sales Rep: "Oh? What are some examples?"

Prospect: "We used their service before, and the result wasn't what we were looking for."

Sales Rep: "What did you get, and what specifically did you want?"

It's Just Like Shopping for a Gift

Let's pretend for a moment that upon arriving at work tomorrow you read a note telling you that your task for the day is to go out and buy the boss' daughter a birthday gift with the $100 enclosed in the envelope. You'd likely have all kinds of questions, wouldn't you? How old is she? What does she like? What does she want? What doesn't she want? What does she have already?

Logical questions, to be sure. We'd all ask them. But why, then, do some salespeople not even flinch when it comes to pitching their product/ service without knowing diddly about the other person? Without this information we have the same chance of satisfying them as we would buying a present for someone we didn't know. Be certain that you always question before you present.

Listen for the Word, "Problem"

Whenever a prospect uses the word "problem" to describe their experiences with their situation or another vendor, read that as an opportunity to further explore their comments, and even more so, the emotions and reasons behind them.

What you're hearing is just the surface level. They might have much more bugging them. Do not jump in with a presentation, thinking that you have just what they need to solve their problem. You need details so you can present your solution in the best light.

Layer your questions and dig deeper. Since they might not yet fully realize the magnitude of the situation, embellish and enhance it.

For example,

Prospect: "We've had a problem with the quality of the workers provided by the other agencies."

Premature Response: *"Well let me tell you how we train our workers here ..."*

> **Better Response: "Tell me about the workers they provided you ..."**

Another:

Prospect: "My main problem is trying to figure out these complex reports the service provides us."

Premature Response: *"Our reporting is very detailed and it ..."*

> **Better Response: "What information do you use from reports, and in what form do you need it?"**

Listen With Your Mind, Not Just With Your Actions

Some sales reps feign listening by pausing to let the other person talk for awhile. To truly listen, you need get emotionally involved, and react to what the speaker says, understanding why they say what they do.

Get Agreement on What They Mean

A critical part of listening is ensuring you understand what the speaker said. If you are a bit cloudy, try saying,

> **"Let me see if I understand what you're saying ..."**
>
> **"So if I'm following you, you're saying that ..."**
>
> **"What I'm hearing is that you ..."**
>
> **"It appears that what you want is ..."**

When you're more certain, paraphrase with,

> **"As you see it ..."**
>
> **"It seems to you that ..."**
>
> **"What you feel, then, is ..."**

Give Choices of the Problems They're Experiencing

Don't say, *"So, what are your needs?"* early in a call. That asks them to do your job, which is to uncover those needs. One way to get them to tell you about their real problems, is to help them.

For example, you might say,

> **"Pat, quite often I hear the same things from people in your business: that they can't find good people, the ones they do hire don't stay; it's difficult to keep them motivated, or they don't feel they get maximum production from them. Which of those hit home with you?"**

The key here, of course, is to provide choices that most likely are experienced by everyone you'll speak with, concerns and problems you're able to address and solve. If, however, they respond negatively, perhaps you don't have a qualified person on the phone. At that point you have nothing to lose by saying,

> **"What are your biggest challenges?"**

Questioning Tips

Here are effective questioning tips you can use.

Weak: *"Is your present vendor doing a good job for you?"*

> **Stronger: "What do you like about your present vendor, and what would you like to get if you could?"**

Confrontational: *"Why did you choose them?"*

> **Non-Adversarial: "What was the process used to make that choice?"**

Invasive: *"So, what's your budget?"*

> **Justified: "The reason for the next question is that my recommendation will be based on what's best for the amount of money you have to work with. Can you give me an idea of what your budget is for this project?"**

Keep in mind also that every answer your hear is perceived as correct in the mind of the person giving it. Respect them, even if you don't agree.

What Do They Really Want?

Needs are the bare minimums we must have. Wants and values unlatch emotions, bringing more creative—even impulsive—thinking to the forefront of their minds. After all, needs for the most part are pretty mundane ... the wants and values get us dreaming, thinking more creatively.

And when we want something passionately enough we typically connive a way to get it. Your prospects and customers will do the same. Ask questions to free up their emotional thinking:

> **"What's on your wish list for what you'd ideally like for your department this year?"**
>
> **"If you had no internal restraints, what would you get?"**
>
> **"OK, you've told me what you need, now let's talk about what you really want."**

Learn Their Buying Criteria

When you're working with commodity-type products in bidding situations, such as with governments, the contract doesn't always go to the lowest bidder. Marceline Rogers, with ASAP Software Express likes to ask this question:

> **"How will you award the contract if pricing is tight?"**

By learning the selection criteria, you can maintain margins, and get the business.

More Questions to Use

Gene Foster sells electronic components to manufacturers who use the parts in their final product. Here are a few of Gene's ideas.

Instead of *"Do you have any other projects that I could look at?"*, ask instead,

> **"What other projects are you working on that could use the cost saving, space saving features of the new Bourns switch?"**
>
> **"If all restrictions of cost and time were removed, what would you like to add to the design?"**
>
> **"Who else at ABC Co. would you suggest I work with? What is his position? What project is he working on?"**

"To Buy, You Need to ..."

I saw a rerun of a Saturday Night Live routine where David Spade plays the annoying reception person, and communicates primarily through fill-in-the-blank questions.

"And your name is ...?"

"And your purpose for being here is ...?"

When used at the right time, in moderatic n, this is an effective technique. For example, you might say,

"So, your main goal for this project would be ...?"

Use Statements to Question

You can use statements to probe. For example,

"Steve, your thoughts on what you'd like to see in a landscape plan will help me provide you with the best information."

DO Ask a Question They Can Answer "No" To

One of those old-school sales myths passed through the generations is, *"Never ask a question the person can answer 'no' to."* What a joke! This assumes that if we don't give the prospect an opportunity to verbally express resistance, that means it doesn't exist.

The opposite is true: if you don't give the person a chance to vent a problem or disagreement, it will grow and ultimately appear at the end of a conversation—as an objection. And by this time it's tougher to deal with.

Use what some people call "trial closing" questions. I prefer to term them "temperature checking" questions. Use them strategically between your presentation points.

"How would that work for you?"

"Would that option be of value?"

"Do you feel this would solve your problem?"

"Sound good so far?"

A Question To Wrap Up With

As you finish your questioning, ask a final general one to uncover any important points not yet discussed:

"Is there anything of importance to you regarding this issue that I haven't asked you yet?"

Persuasive Sales Recommendations

Chapter 17

Present With Power

Here is the not-so-secret secret to a powerful sales presentation: present only what people are interested in, based upon what they told you in your questioning.

Too many sales training courses spend inordinate amounts of time on sales presentations. Not mine. I tell people I want them to talk *less* about their products or services. It's called "objection prevention." Here's how:

1. Transition From Your Questioning. Let them know you're done questioning, and spark interest—again—in having them listen to you:

> **"Luke, based on what you told me about the existing insurance coverage on your business, and the added liability exposure you have, I believe I have something here that will cover you completely, at about the same premium you're paying now."**

2. Paraphrase Your Understanding. Right out of Sales 101, rephrase in your eloquently persuasive—and slightly embellished—way, the needs, concerns, desires, and values they just related to you:

> **"Let's just review what we've discussed so far to make sure I understand it completely. Bottom line, you feel you've been neglected by your present agent, except when it came time to renew your policy. And, you feel he's charging you an outrageous premium for the amount of coverage you now need since you're manufacturing toxic chemicals. Is that right?"**

3. Present the results of what you can deliver. Only talk about what they told you they're interested in. Period.

> **"Luke, by switching to my agency you would get the attention you deserve, and pay a reasonable premium for more than enough coverage. First, we would** (present proof of each claim) **..."**

4. Get Commitment. You're involved in a conversation at this point, either answering questions, or listening to buying signals. If the questions are buying or possession signals such as "That sounds good," or, "Do we pay the premium to your agency or to the corporate headquarters?", ask for commitment.

> **"Should we get started?"**

> **"You can pay it directly to us. Should we prepare the paperwork?"**

Make your recommendations conclusive. Leave no doubt as to what they should do. You're the expert here. Don't just *wish* they'll come to the conclusion you'd like, and *hope* they volunteer to take action on their own. I've heard reps leave things up in the air with a weak phrase like, *"So keep us in mind when you feel you'd like to make a switch."* Most people avoid tough decisions. State your suggestion explicitly so all they have to do is react to it—even if that means resisting it.

> **"Pat, based on everything we've discussed, you'd show a savings from day one on the program. I recommend I overnight the paperwork to you so you can OK it and have it back by Monday. Would you like to do that?"**

It's quite simple. Make a presentation before you know what someone wants, and you're selling. Make it after, and you help them buy. What would you rather do?

Presentation Tips

❑ **People buy results.** I like the word "results" in place of benefits. It's much more descriptive of what people really want. They don't care diddly about the product or service itself, they get excited about the end result—the picture or feeling—they enjoy from owning or using it. Forget about your product or service, and concentrate on the results you deliver.

❑ **Prepare sensory descriptions of your results.** Think about how your results are seen, felt physically and emotionally, tasted, and heard. Remember, you want to help them experience, in advance, the results they can enjoy. **"And just think how much easier it will be for you to prepare training. Instead of spending hours after work doing the research you said you hate, you can simply flip to the appropriate topic in your Leader's Guide for that month, circle the questions you'd like to use, and listen and moderate while your reps learn through their own discussion."**

❑ **Preface results with a reminder.** When presenting several results as part of your overall sales message, precede each with a reminder of the pain they want to avoid or eliminate, or the pleasure they desire. For example, **"And here's what will help you avoid those lawsuits you were worried about ..."** Or, **"And here's where you'll save big money ..."**

❑ **Use specific numbers.** If you present round numbers like 50%, or $100, they tend to be questioned more, or negotiated against more enthusiastically than specific numbers, such as 52%, or $104. People believe more thought and research went into arriving at precise numbers, whereas rounded numbers seem to be pulled out of the air.

Use Third-Party References To Build Credibility

A fundamental principle of persuasion and influence is that third party references and testimonials tend to add more believability to a story. For example, look at, *"I feel this is the best value on the market."*

Now compare,

> **"Four out of the top five engineering firms are now specifying this valve in their projects."**

Naturally the one that references others is more believable. There are several ways you can use this technique.

Testimonials

If you have names or companies which are recognizable and likely meaningful to the listener, use them (if you have permission).

> **"... and Steve Phillips, the President of the Association of National Widget Buyers is one of our customers and swears by this product."**

> "Some of our customers include IBM, General Electric, Ford Motor, and Union Pacific."

> "Judy Liston at Chemical Manufacturing here in town switched to our service over a year ago. She has cut her maintenance expenses by over $10,000 since then."

But be cautious. Prepare your testimonial statements before using them. Ensure they carry positive impact. Some names might result in a big "So what? Who is that?" from the prospect.

General References

This is simply referring to a third party. You don't need to mention names:

> "Customers who use this machine now find that it's much easier than ..."

> "I had someone just the other day who was in a similar situation and ..."

> "People who have been with us for some time say that they enjoy the fact that ..."

How to Help Them Assume Ownership

Visit a car dealer searching for a new vehicle and the salesperson puts you behind the wheel to "take 'er for a test drive."

Roam around a furniture store while shopping for a sofa, and you're encouraged to lay down on it, just like you would when relaxing in front of the tube.

Both are examples of assuming ownership. It's an extremely effective sales technique. That's because once we experience ourselves owning something, and we like it, it becomes difficult for us to give it up.

Helping prospects assume ownership is much easier for face-to-face salespeople since they can physically let the buyer assume ownership.

However, on the phone we can help prospects assume ownership through the pictures we create with words. For example, you can begin descriptions with,

> "Pretend you had this machine in your office..."

> "Put yourself in this position for a moment..."

> "Imagine yourself having this service already..."

> "If you did use it, how would that..."

Help them experience ownership in their own mind, and they might sell you on why they should buy!

Be the Last to Present

If you are working on a prospect where multiple calls are necessary, and you are bidding against a few other competitors, ask to be the last seller to speak with them. Ask them when they will have had a chance to speak with everyone else, and then arrange a time to visit with them. You will learn what went on between the buyer and sellers who preceded you. They might have a clearer picture of what they want at this point. Armed with this knowledge, you will be prepared to put together the information that has the greatest chance of meeting their needs.

Get Larger Sales By Making Bigger Suggestions

When in doubt, suggest to a prospect or customer the larger quantity, the bigger model, the higher rate, the longer term, and so on. This is effective for several reasons.

1. It can be insulting and embarrassing for the prospect if you suggest something too small. For example, if a real estate agent said to a couple, *"Well, we have several homes listed in the $200,000 range,"* when they had the intention, and the resources to buy a $350,000 residence, the couple may take the statement as an insult, implying that he/she didn't feel they could qualify for such a home.

2. By starting low, you might be "leaving money on the table." For example, assume a securities broker said, *"Would you like to put around, say, $5000 into this fund?"*, when the prospect had a figure of $7500 in mind. It's likely that the prospect would go along with the $5000 based upon the suggestion, whereas if the amount stated was $10,000, they either would have accepted that, or backed down to $7500.

3. Similarly, throwing out a low figure in price negotiations can cost profits. By starting higher, you have more room to come down, while still being able to stay within a comfort zone.

Explain Your Experience

"Experience" is another one of those words that may mean nothing to your listeners. If you feel they are interested in your track record, give examples of **results**. Instead of, *"We have experience in that area,"* tell them,

> **"We have worked with four companies in that industry and helped every one beat production quotas."**

> **"I have a list of satisfied customers who have used it."**

> **"For six years companies have been coming back to us, and referring us to others."**

Speak From Another Perspective

Phrasing your benefits as if they're coming from a third party is a great way to be more believable:

> **"Customers who use this system now tell me they've noticed increases in productivity of as much as ..."**

The reasoning is that someone else has experienced the results. A psychological-cousin to this strategy was shared by Linda Dugan Stennett of BNA Communications. She suggested speaking to the prospect from the perspective of the actual *user* of the product or service. For example, she sells video-based training. When talking to a training buyer, she'll occasionally say,

> **"Let me tell you what I experienced as I watched this film myself as a student."**

It wasn't Linda the salesperson trumpeting the virtues of the program, it was Linda the student sharing her experience. And of course the training managers are interested in what their trainees will think about the program, which ultimately is a reflection on them as training managers. Think about how you can do something similar. For example,

> **"I use this system myself, and here's my experience as a user ..."**

> **"Now I'm nowhere near as technically-astute as the engineers who actually use this material daily, but let me tell you I had the opportunity to spend a day working with it and here's what I found ..."**

> **"I've experienced this as a user, and here's my perspective ..."**

Present Just a Few Benefits

Instead of presenting all of your "benefits," present only a few, but in several different ways. After identifying their hot button, use various terms to describe the feelings they'll have by buying from you. The psychology here is that you are more likely to believe something if it agrees with thoughts already existing in your subconscious. And it's not always necessary that you've totally accepted the idea ... just that you haven't *disagreed* with it. It's like saying, "Yeah, I've heard that before. It must have merit." Then the more it's repeated, the more firmly embedded it becomes.

How to Communicate a Lower Price

When positioning a better price, use words like,

- **"smaller investment,"** or,
- **"best value."**

The words "cheaper" and "deal" can undermine the customer's perception of your value.

Action Steps

Chapter 18

How to Position What You Say as More Credible

While coaching my son's little league baseball game a few years ago, I noticed the opposing pitcher had an odd windup that technically was illegal. Since we're only talking about 11-year olds here, I didn't make a fuss, instead mentioning it to the other coach so he could correct his player and modify the motion before the bad habit became too ingrained The coach reacted somewhat indignantly and stated, "Look, I've coached at every level from grade school through junior college, and I tell you that move is legal."

Since my own personal experience wasn't a match—only studying pitchers as they were striking me out at every level consistently through high school, I felt at a disadvantage. In my mind, his opinion had credibility. Maybe he was right.

The next day, I analyzed why his opinion carried weight, at that moment anyway. It was primarily because of the way he established his credibility. (Although, as it turned out, I read the rule, and talked to a few people with even *more* credibility. I was right, and this poor kid will get called for balks and not know why.)

What the experience really did was prompt me to think about how we can get total strangers to believe what we say by phone. Let's look at ways you can position what you say as credible.

❑ **"It ain't braggin' if you've done it."** Excuse the grammar, but if you've earned your stripes in your business or industry, don't hide that fact under a rock. Trumpet it to add to your credibility! Drop in statements such as,

> **"In my seven years in this business, I've learned that ...,"** or,

> **"I've worked with over 550 retailers, and I've always found that ..."**

81

❏ **If you're not on commission, it doesn't hurt if they know that fact.** Hey, I know most of us are paid directly based on what we sell, and there's nothing wrong with that ... except that when a customer knows a salesperson has absolutely no monetary stake in his purchase he might tend to relax a bit earlier in the relationship. Therefore, you might casually say,

> **"We've been so busy around here, I wish I was paid on commission."**

❏ **Use precise numbers.** If you told me you've worked with "lots of other businesses in my industry," that wouldn't even be close to the credibility wielded by,

> **"... and I've personally installed this system in 23 sales training firms."**

❏ **Use the praises of others to build your credibility.** If you say how good you are, well, they can naturally view that with skepticism. But they can't argue with the words of others—even if you're the one repeating them. For example,

> **"I was talking to Pat Jones at Indy Industries just this morning, and she told me how she has increased her production by 45 cases per day after just one month on the program."**

And just the fact that other people are doing something tends to lend credibility and influence behavior. The motivational speaker, Cavett Robert said, "Since 95% of the people are imitators and only 5% initiators, people are persuaded more by the actions of others than by any proof we can offer." The psychology behind this is quite fascinating, and the dynamics are at work around us every day. When you're out-of-town, driving around scoping for a good restaurant, would you pull into an empty parking lot, or a jammed-packed one? Direct mail and advertising copywriters use this theory quite frequently. Take notice of how many ad headlines are in quotation marks, as if they're the words of someone else. Quite often, it's *just a headline in quotes,* but it appears that someone else said it, therefore adding credibility.

❏ **Be a name-dropper.** Following a similar philosophy, sprinkle in the names of some instantly-recognizable customers, normally the larger ones, or the prominent ones in your industry.

Think of ways you can add credibility to what you say, make a conscious effort to use those ideas, and you'll be more persuasive.

Chapter 19

Here's a Secret Tip That Everyone Doesn't Know

D id that chapter title get your attention? If so, you've just experienced a principle that you, too, can apply on your calls: appealing to humans' innate desire to be in on exclusive information, censored information, and secrets.

Most people tend to place more value on information, and a product/service, that's not available to everyone. This is a powerful method of influence and persuasion you can use in your sales strategies and tactics.

In his book, *"Influence: Science and Practice,"* (Harper & Collins), Dr. Robert Cialdini cites a study by one of his grad students who used this principle. The student, a successful beef-importing company owner, had his sales reps call their retail food market customers as usual, and use one of three different approaches in asking for the order. One was a standard presentation and request for the order. The second was the standard presentation, plus notification that the supply of beef was likely to become more scarce in the upcoming months. The third was the same as the second, but also informed the customer that this information was not generally available, and it had come from certain exclusive contacts the company had. (All of this was true. There was an impending shortage, and the news did come from an exclusive source.)

The customers who heard the second appeal (about the upcoming shortage) bought twice as much as the first group presented with the standard approach. The third group (the ones let in on the upcoming scarcity via the "exclusive" information) bought **six times** as much. Not only was scarcity built into the supply, the *information itself* appeared scarce.

How You Can Use It

There are a variety of ways you can use this principle.

"Here is information everyone doesn't have ..."

"I'll let you in on an announcement that won't be made public until next week ..."

"These sale prices won't be announced until our flyer comes out, but here they are ..."

"Here's something very few people know ..."

Judges face this phenomenon regularly. Attorneys knowingly slip in inadmissible information that judges subsequently rule the jury can't consider in their decisions. Give me a break! That's like saying, "Don't think of the color red."

Roger Dawson, in his book, *"Secrets of Power Persuasion,"* (Prentice-Hall) cited a study of juries at the University of Chicago Law School. Juries were empowered to decide the amount of awards in injury lawsuits. When it was disclosed the defendant was insured against the loss, awards went up 13%. When they were instructed to disregard the information, average awards went up 40%!

I Really Shouldn't Do This ...

A related strategy is when you stretch the rules a bit (*sales reps would never do that, would they?*), and/or letting your prospect know they've gotten something that *everyone* else didn't. For example,

"I'm not supposed to do this but here's what I can offer you ..."

"This is something that we're not typically allowed to give, but here's what I can do ..."

"We're normally not able to offer this, but I might be able to make an exception ..."

"I'd have to get approval on this one, but here's what I might be able to do ..."

Cynics out there might be reading with a raised eyebrow, thinking this has the possibility of resembling the cheesy techniques of a plaid-cladded used car sales rep who "has to run it by the manager" to get approval. I agree. I can think of numerous examples where the ethically-bankrupt employ these ideas. My personal feeling is that these people should be strung up by their phone cords, and be publicly flogged with a handset.

The Scarcity Principle

Everything I've talked about here is related to the "scarcity" principle of persuasion, which, when boiled down, essentially means our desire for something intensifies inversely to its availability—or our *perception* of its availability. We want what we can't have, we desire to be things we're not (see basketball and football player/millionaires cutting their own rap albums), and we'll go to extreme measures to pursue things that might be just a bit elusive.

A Scarce Joe Montana Cap

I experienced this a few years ago on a family trek to Missouri for the weekend to catch a Nebraska Cornhusker road football game, and a K.C. Chiefs home contest. A cool sports apparel store advertised the "Joe Montana Cap," the one *HE* wore on the sidelines. And, oh, by the way, only 500 were to be shipped from the manufacturer, and nobody else in Kansas City (and *certainly* not Omaha) had them, or could get them. Instantly the scarcity principle kicked in, wreaking havoc with my new desire for that hat. I feebly tried to justify my lust with the logic that I needed a Chiefs cap, ignoring the fact that I have only about 50 other sports lids on my shelf. But, hey, I didn't have a Chiefs cap (there I go with the logical justification again). The clerk told me—and everyone in line ahead of and behind me—that the caps weren't yet in (further fanning the scarcity flames). They were sold-out of that initial allotment anyway ... but they were taking advance orders for the additional supply they managed to wrangle from the supplier (imagine their timely stroke of luck!). Naturally I ordered one. With shipping I paid a mere 40% more than I normally would have for a cap ... one that I never had seen prior to that day, and in all objectivity, isn't even as attractive as some of the other more plentifully available caps.

Do you have information or products/services which are genuinely scarce, exclusive, forbidden, or censored? Do you ever live on the edge, testing the rule-limits in order to help your customers? If "yes" in any of these cases, my gosh, let the person know, and your persuasive impact can be far more powerful than ever imagined.

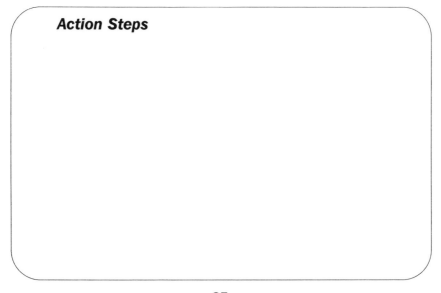

Action Steps

Chapter 20

How to Use Stories to Sell

People are interested in other people ... their lives, experiences, successes, and misfortunes. Just glance at the daily line up of TV talk shows exploring the outrageous tales of dysfunctional social misfits. Obviously *someone* is watching.

People enjoy entertainment, on the job as well as off. And the more interesting you make your sales message, the more impactful and memorable it will be. That's a fact of communication. And, by the way, facts are mostly boring. Facts can't come close to evoking the feelings and emotions you need to tweak in order to help people take action. That's why stories are effective in helping people understand and accept your ideas, and why you'll sell more by using these powerful tools.

An Ancient Idea

This isn't a new phenomenon. Jesus used stories extensively (parables). Politicians use stories to simplify complex issues ... and sway public opinion. Ronald Reagan was a master. Before he finally saw the light, Bill Clinton demonized the balancing of the budget by telling stories of tossing grandmothers out of nursing homes into the streets, able to afford to eat nothing but cat food. Whether or not you agree with the politics, the stories create vivid images.

Stories, metaphors, analogies, and examples all help listeners gain a better understanding and retention of a message. Sometimes at seminars, sales reps who had been at a presentation of mine up to three years prior have actually asked me to repeat stories that I've since forgotten. But obviously the stories worked with the listeners. I'd wager that if you described your favorite teachers in school you'd likely remember some of their stories ... although, in many cases, few of the facts of their lessons.

Listeners tend to apply stories to their own lives, which helps them gain a firmer grasp of the message. You can make a suggestion in a story (or have a person in the story make the implication) that you wouldn't dare attempt yourself.

Stories also tend to relax people. They don't feel like they're being pressured or pitched when you employ a story or anecdote.

As salespeople, we can present the boring features and benefits. Or, we can arouse, electrify, and sometimes poke at tender emotions with stories, metaphors, and analogies.

When to Use Them

Everything we discuss regarding stories happens after your questioning. Your examples are most powerful when they're on target. Spinning a tale that's irrelevant to a listener's situation is like surfing the cable channels in search of ESPN, only to have your remote control batteries die on the Nature Channel's discussion of rock fungus. It's pretty likely you would tune out. Again, rule one: understand their needs and interests before presenting.

How to Do It

When we weave stories into our calls—whether they be one sentence or a few paragraphs—we're bridging the visual gap inherent to the telephone. Customers place themselves in the picture or mind movie you create. They experience, in advance, the emotions they'll get when they own and use your product or service. And that's why they buy. Here are specifics you can use in making your presentations more visual, emotional, and memorable, and your offers more desirable.

❏ **Put them in the story.** Help them visualize owning or using your product or service, or experiencing the problem you can solve.

> **"Let's assume you did get the other system. It's two years from now, the warranty is up, the motor goes out, you likely have to open your checkbook again. Now, with our system, you wouldn't pull out your wallet, you'd just pick up your phone ..."**

❏ **Using similar-situation examples.** This is the premise of the old "feel-felt-found" technique. Compare their situation to someone else.

> **"I had another shop owner tell me he wasn't sure he could afford it. But he did it anyway. He didn't regret the decision during his busy season, since he was able to handle more jobs and double his profits with the extra capacity."**

❏ **Represent your results with word pictures.** Just one picture can unleash a flood of memories. Think about the last time you thumbed through a picture album of your childhood. A single image caused you to recall emotions, dates, people, and facts.

> **"Mr. Manager, just visualize every check-out counter in your store with customers lined up four-deep ..."**

❑ **Use Third-Party Similar-Situation Examples.** Think about the effect this has on you, personally, "I saw someone who looked and sounded just like you, and they ..." You were probably curious and interested. You can do the same with your products/services and prospects/customers.

> **"I was talking to another dentist last week who told me he was experiencing exactly the same thing with his practice. Let me tell you what he did ..."**

❑ **Animate and Humanize Your Products and Services.** TV commercials give us everything from talking toads to walking remote controls. PSSSST, guess what? This inane stuff works! By humanizing otherwise boring objects we sell, you can make your points more memorable. Dr. Donald Moine and Kenneth Lloyd, in their book, *"Unlimited Selling Power"* (Prentice-Hall) give an example:

> **"This computer system will hold your hand when you're learning how to use it."**

❑ **Horror Stories With Others.** Your goal, after all, is to get them to take action. And fear is a powerful motivator. Some sales reps prefer to use subtle fear as opposed to bashing them over the head with it. One way is to tell stories where *someone else* experiences the danger. Customers will put themselves in the story so you won't have to.

> **"I know of one shop that was sued for a million dollars by a guy who was trespassing after-hours and fell in a hole, in a fenced off area! And they didn't have coverage. They thought it couldn't happen to them because they were so small."**

❑ **Exaggerate Competitive Comparisons.** Compare and contrast with the competition. The boring example is "apples to oranges." Think of your own.

> **"Using a lesser machine for the major project you have planned will be like getting on your hands and knees and cutting all the grass on a golf course with nail clippers."**

❑ **Complex-to-Simple Comparisons.** Often we lose sales because the buyer thinks it will be too much of a hassle to change what he's doing now. Or, he feels that it would be mind-numbing to learn a new system, or the technology is over his head. Use an example of something familiar and simple that he can relate to.

> **"Using the system is a lot easier than most people think. It's like when you set your alarm clock for the first time. It took a minute to learn what buttons to push, then you had it mastered."**

❑ **Your Personal Experiences.** I was catalog shopping for Christmas presents and asked the phone rep about an oversized fleece sweatshirt. She bubbled,

> **"Oh, your wife will absolutely love that! I have one myself, and it is the most comfortable thing I own. I slip it on when I just want to vege out, nestle in my favorite chair by the fire and get lost in a good book."**

Of course I bought it—and one more for myself. If you own it, use it, or wear it, tell them how it makes your life better, and how theirs will be as well.

❑ **Self-Deprecating Remarks and Humor.** People enjoy those who can poke fun at themselves and admit their shortcomings and mistakes. Plus it helps to drive home memorable points. I often mention the fact that I'm "mechanically challenged" when describing my handyman aptitude. Consider this illustration:

> **"I'm so inept when it comes to tools that I don't know which end of the hammer is supposed to be plugged in, but even *I* was able to open up my computer and slip the modem card in the slot. It's that easy."**

❑ **Personalize It.** The more you know about them, the more tailored you should make your stories. If you know your listener is a huge golf nut, weave in a golf term or two.

> **"This will be as simple as tapping in a gimme putt."**

If they talk about their kids, use familiar examples:

> **"It's amazing! My son says that his basic math is too hard, but he can figure out the codes to get to the 10th level of difficulty on Nintendo. That's similar to what we're talking about here with ..."**

❏ **Have Them Tell You Stories.** The beauty of stories is that you know you have them visualizing when they offer you a story. If they don't volunteer one, ask for one:

> **"Sam, I bet you've had situations where someone at a retail counter simply ignored you while they were back there pretending to be busy. What comes to mind?"**

These are even more powerful than the ones you tell.

❏ **Look for "Material" Every Day.** You don't have to be a born storyteller. You do need to have the desire to work at it. It's like people who say, "I can never remember jokes." What they're really saying is, "I never work hard enough to store in my memory the jokes I'd like to repeat." When you happen across an example, a testimonial, a situation you observe, or anything ... write it down, quickly. Don't trust it to memory. As soon as possible, sit down and apply more thought to it, stretching, kneading, beating, molding and shaping it into a story that will work for you.

The Ten Most Powerful Types of Sales Stories

1. Introductory Stories. Tells about who you are, how you've helped others.

2. Attention-Grabbing Stories. Gets people interested in listening.

3. Product Information Stories. Instead of laundry-listing the features and benefits of your products or services, you use this information in a fascinating story.

4. Stories to Overcome Fear. Illustrates how others experienced the same fears the listener has and how they later learned they didn't need to worry after all.

5. Money Stories. Gives examples of how they can afford your product/service. Shows how they will make or save money.

6. Improved Productivity Stories. Shows how your product/service helped others increase their efficiency, output, sales, and decreased errors, trouble, hassles, and flaws.

7. Ego Enhancement Stories. Shows how owning and using your product/service has increased other customers' self-confidence, pride, self-esteem.

8. Family Togetherness Stories. Shows how your product/service has brought families closer together.

9. Security Stories. Reveals how doing business with you has given people peace of mind, and emotional and financial security.

10. Closing Stories. Wraps up the commitment and gets the sale!

(SOURCE: UNLIMITED SELLING SKILLS—HOW TO MASTER HYPNOTIC SELLING SKILLS, by Donald Moine and Kenneth Lloyd, Prentice Hall. Get this book! Check your bookstore. If they don't have it, they can order it. ISBN 0-13-689126-8)

Action Steps

Chapter 21

Don't Sell On Price. Focus on Value Instead

If you at all feel that your sales strategy has been reduced to a commodity price war, I strongly recommend an article in the February 1996 issue of *"INC. Magazine"* detailing a printing company's dilemma: their sales reps had fallen into the trap of selling on price.

The study of Booklet Binding company is similar to what I often see with telesales staffs. Reps call customers and prospects and ask, *"Do you have anything I can quote on?"* This might result in a few price quotes. Reps then follow up with the question, *"Well, how does our quote look?"* The buyer says, *"You have to do better."* The rep responds, *"How much better?"* The rep then goes to the manager or owner and pleads for a better price, whining *"Boss, we're gettin' killed out there on price."*

If this resembles your sales process, your margins are eroding like a river bank during a flood. And it's like Russian Roulette. Mark Ladniak, a consultant who turned around Booklet Binding's sales strategy, said, "If your salesforce is down to asking 'What's it going to take to get your business?' then they've basically said they don't have any worth. It's not the customer's job to care about your margins. And they won't."

Discuss the Use of the Product/Service

To shift the focus away from price, follow the advice of Jim Morrissey of Market Catalysts, quoted in the *INC.* article: "With any commodity, you've got to move the discussion toward how the customer is going to use it, and therefore what the important attributes will be. The value-added isn't in the product anymore; it's in the relationship between the salesperson and customer."

In a nutshell, Booklet Binding trained its sales reps to *help* their customers increase revenues, decrease costs, and retain and grow their customer base. Although the reps were still selling the same product—booklets—they were now focusing on the *use* of the booklets, not just on the cheapest printing of them. And you can and should do the same thing if you've ever lost a sale because of price.

Ideas for Selling Value

Tom Winninger's book, *"Price Wars"* (The Winninger Institute, 800-899-8971) details many ideas and strategies for selling on value, not price. Here are just a few.

❑ **Sell Cost Over Time, Not Price.** Discuss all the costs that will be involved in the long-term with a lower-priced alternative. Compare that to your price, not just a competitor's one-time lowball price.

❑ **Be a Specialist.** Most sales reps don't take the time to do this. And it makes the ones who do stand that much further apart from the crowd. When you provide information on how customers can grow their business, they feel like they're getting a great deal, even with your higher price. You've moved them out of playing in the price arena.

❑ **Fight for the Best Customers, Not All the Customers.** Many people don't like to buy their cereal and cleaning supplies in 50-gallon barrels just to get a lower price, therefore they don't shop at Sam's. They are willing to pay a premium for the value and convenience they receive elsewhere. Likewise, understand that only certain customers will pay a premium for the value you deliver. Be sure you know why. Those are your targeted prospects. Get a grip on the fact that you won't sell everyone, nor should you need or want to.

How to Define the Value You Deliver

Selling value involves much more than a pep rally/sales meeting proclamation. It's a culture ... a mindset, a strategy. To do it well, you first need to be able to define it. The book *"Competing on Value"* (Hanan and Karp, Amacom Publishing) lists questions you should answer to help define your value.

❑ **Do you help customers** reduce or avoid variable costs so that their prices can be lowered and margins improved? How?

> Or do you help customers improve margins by adding new features and benefits to their products, services, and systems? How?

> Or do you help expand market share by adding to productivity? How?

❑ **To truly add value** and set yourself apart from the competition you need to know how to help your customers control one or more of their critical costs or exploit one or more of their critical revenue sources.

Ask yourself two key questions about what you sell, and your opportunities to add value to your customers:

1. Where is it possible to impact overall and long-term cost savings and productivity improvements with customers?

2. Where is it possible to help customers increase their sales and profit margins?

❑ **Know what value means** to all the levels you sell to. At the user level, value could mean making their life hassle-free. A middle manager derives value when you provide a profitable solution to a cost problem, or a revenue-generating opportunity. At the top level, the solution is less interesting than the potential added profits or improved productivity of corporate assets.

Action Steps

Getting
Commitment

Chapter 22

Closing for Commitment

The "close" need not—no—*should not* be the major point in your sales or prospecting call. Just like the long bomb is not a high percentage or highly used play in football, "closing" someone early doesn't carry good odds either.

And just like the football team, by moving methodically downfield, getting nearer your target, you improve your chances of scoring. The closer you get, the better your odds of running a scoring play.

Therefore, after you've progressed through your questioning, and while presenting the benefits ideally suited for the listener's situation, ask questions to help move the prospect down the field. Over time these have been called many things, including "trial closes." I like to term them "check questions," or "first down" questions.

"Is that something that would work for you?"

"How does that sound?"

"Would that solve your problem?"

"How does that compare to what you were thinking of?"

"What are your thoughts?"

Those questions all ask for an opinion. As you gain more agreement, you should ask more action-oriented questions.

"What are your plans at this point?"

"Which way are you leaning?"

But wait a minute, you might be thinking. Don't these questions open you up to possible negative answers?

Yep. And if you're going to hear a problem, better to get it here while it's still small, instead of letting the obstacle brew into a major roadblock, while later going for the all-or-nothing "close" and then hearing about the major objection.

Assuming you're doing everything well and still hearing positive responses, then ask more action-oriented questions. Questions asking them to do something.

"Would you like to do this?"

"Shall we move forward?"

"May we set a date?"

"Would you like one?"

A "close" shouldn't be an all-or-nothing maneuver intended to ensnare a person into buying. Instead, look at using check questions, commitment questions, and action questions to help move the prospect/customer closer to the end destination.

More Closing Ideas

Brian Jeffrey, president of SalesForce Training & Consulting in Ontario, Canada, has some interesting ideas and suggestions about closing.

■ You have nothing to lose by attempting to close the sale. You don't have the business before the attempt, and sure, you might not have it after, but at least you will have had a shot at it.

■ To improve your closing rate keep in mind that the person who gets the most yes's also gets the most no's.

■ Many sales people can rattle off the names of closing techniques, such as the "Alternate Choice" or the "Minor Point," but are at a loss to recite the actual words to use in order to gain commitment. They know what to do ... they just aren't sure *how* to do it. Jeffrey suggests writing down actual commitment questions on 3x5 cards, and in-between calls, glancing at them and repeating the words until they're committed to memory. And remind yourself that you owe it to your company, your customer, and yourself to attempt a close at the appropriate times.

■ You need to prepare the customer for your closes. Use opinion-seeking questions such as,

"How does that sound?"

"If you were to get it, when would you want delivery?"

"How do you see yourself benefiting from ...?"

"How do you feel about this?"

Positive responses here indicate you should ask for the order. Commit these trial closes to memory. Practice by writing them on cards also.

■ There's no magic formula to closing. It's 70% attitude, 20% technique, and 10% skill. Prepare yourself, prepare the customer, and do the deed.

(SOURCE: Brian Jeffrey's SALESTALK, SalesForce Training & Consulting Inc., 1451 Donald B. Munro Dr., Carp, Ontario, Canada, K0A 1L0. 613-839-7355.)

Have Alternative Recommendations Available

When you present your sales message, and in turn close, be sure you have a fall-back position in case your recommendation isn't accepted.

For example,

Sales Rep: " ... and for all of these reasons Tom, you'll show an increased margin on your sales of widgets. So, shall we start you out with a supply of 10 cases?"

Prospect: "No, I just don't feel we could carry that much of a new product."

Sales Rep: "OK, that's understandable. Here's what I'll do. We'll ship you five cases now, and give you price-protection on the other five, meaning that if the price goes up for any reason during the next three months, you'll have the current price guaranteed, OK?"

Your alternate position should be a solution that helps alleviate the buyer's concerns, while still resulting in a sale. Without getting extreme, aim a little higher with your initial suggestion, therefore allowing you to back off with your fallback position.

Be Like a Waiter and Ask for the Order

Ever notice how busy waiters manage their customers? They always ask for the order.

"What would you like?"

"What can I get you?"

"What do you prefer today?"

In contrast, think about the results if they were wishy-washy, explaining every menu item in detail, but never asking for action. It would unnecessarily lengthen the experience for everyone involved.

Just like a sales call.

Ask yourself, "Do I just *finish* my presentations, or do I ask for and invite action at the end?"

Sadly, many sales reps invest plenty of time working up to the action phase of the call, then stop short of asking for commitment. They volley control back to the prospect/customer, when, in fact, like a restaurant customer, your prospects want to be led with requests and suggestions.

When it comes time, close. Ask. Get commitment. Without movement, nothing happens.

You Could be Richer, And You Will Be

Think back on all the sales, revenue, and perhaps commissions you might have enjoyed if you only asked for the sale more often. Even the best askers let a few slip through, and, for those who are shy about asking, they could probably be driving that nicer car or living in the larger house they're craving. On the other hand, have you ever regretted asking someone for a sale? It's rare. Even when you don't get a "yes," at minimum you can chalk it up in the "At least I tried" category. So if you haven't been asking enough, change today, and begin enjoying the things you've missed!

Ask Large, Ask Often

If telesales reps enter a call thinking what can't be done, or have only a small sale as an objective, the results will naturally be negative or the order will be small. However, by aiming at a larger target, the outcome is also likely to be greater. This point is illustrated in the book, *"Dealmaker."* Richard Grassgreen, president of Kindercare day care centers, says that newer, naive employees can sometimes get a better deal when they are sent out to negotiate the rental of new locations. The reasoning is that they don't know what they can't do, and they aren't afraid to ask for very favorable deals. He says, "Asking is easy, and it's cheap. Too many people forget to ask."

How true. We should approach every call expecting to achieve not just an acceptable outcome, but a very favorable one.

(SOURCE: *Dealmaker: All the Negotiating Skills & Secrets You Need, by Robert Kuhn. Wiley & Sons.)*

Try These Trial Closes

After you've presented a few benefits, and nothing but silence greets you at the other end, resist the tendency to continue with the presentation. What you are saying may not be of interest to the listener. Find out what they think and feel about what you've said:

"Am I going in the right direction?", or,

"Am I talking about what you're interested in?"

Practice Your Closing and Commitment Lines

As part of your call preparation you should state your primary objective, which I define as,

"What do I want them to do as a result of this call?"

Based on that objective you should also create and practice the closing phrases you'll potentially use to gain that commitment. For example, your objective might be,

"To get commitment that she will take my proposal to her purchasing agent and obtain a purchase order."

Therefore, the closing questions could be,

"Are you ready to request a purchase order?"

"Will you request a purchase order so you can get started?"

It's always easier to perform an activity after you've prepared for it.

Get the Order Form Out

Some old outside sales wisdom(?) suggests that sales reps have out the order form right from the beginning of the call. Kind of like the car salesman who fills out the order form during the in-office conversation, and says, "I'm just filling this out so we have all the information at the end should you decide to move forward."

This, of course, is annoying. But by massaging this idea a bit, it can have a positive effect for those of us on the phone. For example, consider having the order form out while talking with your prospects and customers by phone. It affects our attitudes positively, knowing we have that order form or appointment book in front of us, reminding us of the ultimate call goal.

Commitment Questions You Can Use

Here are more ideas for commitment questions you can use or adapt to move the relationship forward.

"What will happen between now and our next contact?"

"If you like what you see in the sample, will you buy?"

"Are you comfortable taking this to the boss with your recommendation that you go with it?"

"So you will have those inventory figures prepared by the next time we speak, is that right?"

"You're going to survey your staff and get their input on what features they'd like to see, and you'll have the information by our next call, correct?"

"By when will you have had a chance to go through the material so we can speak again?"

"Is this the program that you'd personally like to invest in?"

"If you do decide to change vendors before my next call, will you call me?"

"The next time you need supplies, would you buy them from me?"

"When you send out your Request for Proposals, may I be included?"

"Shall we get started?"

"Would you like to buy it?"

"Why don't I ship you one?"

"May I sign you up?"

"If the proposal contains all of these items, will you approve it and go with our plan?"

"Can we finalize the paperwork?"

"Do you think you would be happy with this model?"

"If we included _____, would you want to place the order today?"

"Are you thinking about getting two?"(or whatever appropriate amount is higher than what they likely will get)

"Is this better than what you had in mind?"

"Is there anything that's keeping us from moving forward?"

"Any reason why we shouldn't get started?"

"Seems like we should finalize this. What do you think?"

"Looks like it's what you need. Agree?"

"Do you think you would be happy with this model?"

Check Questions to Use

Here are more "check questions" you can use (also referred to as "tie downs" or "trial closes").

"Aren't you?

"Isn't it?

"Won't they?

"Doesn't it?

"Couldn't you?

Action Steps

Objections

Chapter 23

A Painless Way to Address Objections

When's the last time someone thanked you for telling them they were flat out wrong? It doesn't happen.

Even though *everyone* resents being told they're wrong—often getting defensive—most sales training suggests sales reps do exactly that: counter objections and resistance with slick, canned phrases, with insidious names like the "Boomerang Technique," which inherently tells people they're wrong and makes them feel just slightly lower than topsoil.

You'll never change anyone's mind by preaching at them. For example, think about beliefs you feel strongly about: something political, moral, or even a favorite sports team. If someone refuted everything you believed in, you would likely strengthen your stance and think of why the other person is wrong. You can, however, help someone to first *doubt* their beliefs, which is the initial hurdle in opening them up to your ideas. Get them to question their position regarding your offer or ideas. People believe their ideas more than they do yours. You can't tell them they're wrong and expect success, but you can help them doubt their perceptions, which causes them to lower their guard and at least be open to what you have to say. You do this with doubt-creating questions. Here's how.

How to Create Doubt and Address Objections

1. Understand the objections you commonly hear. Write them out. Then list **reasons** people voice them. For example, when they say "Your price is too high," does that mean they can get it cheaper down the street? Or, did they have a predetermined price figure in mind? Or, do they not have enough money in the budget? You'll need to know their rationale (their problem) before you can address the symptom: the objection.

2. For each of the objection reasons, write out questions that uncover their rationale, and plants seeds of doubt. For example, for the "price is too high," questions could be,

> **"Are we talking about just the price itself, or the long-term value?"**

> **"What are we being compared to?"**

> **"What price figure did you feel would be appropriate for what you're looking to receive?"**

> **"Take price out of the picture for a moment; do you like this unit better than any other you've seen?"**

Or, take the situation of a wholesale supplier trying to persuade a retailer to carry his product. The retailer says, "We don't need to stock any more lines." The wholesaler could use a canned "objection rebuttal," trotting out market share facts and figures that would prove the retailer wrong—but not change his mind. A doubt-creating approach would use questions:

> **"How often in the past month have people called and asked for this type of product and you're not able to provide it?"**, or,

> **"Have you ever had a situation where someone called and asked about a product like this, but they didn't come in because they found out you didn't have it?"**

Approach objections in a non-adversarial way, and ask questions to root out the reasons. Go through this process, and you'll be better prepared to ask the right questions to plant the seeds of doubt in their mind, opening them up to considering your ideas, therefore softening their resistance.

The Objection Autopsy

When dealing with objections, what we're really doing is backing up and revisiting the questioning part of the call. Because, if the person is resisting your recommendation, it's typically because you either didn't collect enough information to make the best prescription for what they want, or, they misunderstood what you presented.

Here's the best way I know of to prepare to address objections. It's called the Objection Autopsy, and it helps you think of all possible reasons for the objections you hear, the questions you'll ask upon hearing them, the possible responses ... and it continues until you have enough information to again make a recommendation that helps the prospect/customer understand why what you have will help them.

1. Select a common, real objection. For example, "Your minimum order is too high for me."

2. Brainstorm all the possible reasons why the objection could be stated. For any objection you might have multiple reasons.

3. Develop opening questions to address the objection (after isolating it). Isolation question:

> **"If it weren't for the minimum, would you buy from us?"**
>
> If so, **"Let's talk about the minimum then. How much would you say all your orders over a month total, even with your other vendors?"**

4. Think of their possible answers, and your next responses.

5. Continue the process. It looks like a computer programmer's flow chart. Ultimately you can reach an understanding and agreement together, or you'll determine there's not a fit. And a very important point about objections is that you will not, and can not, answer every one.

Action Steps

Chapter 24

Dealing With Price Objections

L et's look at various aspects of dealing with the price issue in selling, mostly as it relates to when your price is higher than the competition's.

People Buy Value, Not Price

In your customer's mind, your price is simply the monetary number at which they can acquire your value. If the value is perceived as higher than the price, they buy. If value is lower, they don't buy, or you get "the price is too high" objection.

No one buys on price alone. We've all been stung by taking the cheapest route on a purchase, personifying the "you get what you pay for" adage.

The first step in dealing with price is ensuring you personally are convinced that you deliver value far exceeding your price. If you now have customers, you do give such value.

Never Apologize for Your Price

I've heard sales reps—who were blind to the value they delivered— say things like, *"Yeah, it is pretty expensive."* Of course, that reinforces any feeling of low value by the prospect or customer.

Present Price with Conviction

Hem and haw while presenting price, and listeners either question the value, or feel they can beat the price down. I had some large pine trees planted, and asked the installer how much extra for staking the tree. "Thirty-five dollars," he stated resolutely. "Oh, how much better can you do than that for all of these trees?", I asked. He gave me a "whaddya crazy or somethin?" look, and responded, "The price is thirty-five dollars per tree."

I paid it.

Preface Price with Value

When you do present your price in your presentation, build the value first. People will view the price through the filter of value. Therefore, say things like,

> **"If you bought this elsewhere, you'd expect to pay well over ..."**
>
> **"If you performed all of these steps manually ..."**
>
> **"Purchased alone, all of these components would total over ..."**

Use the Theory of Contrast

This means contrasting your price with one that is much higher. While channel surfing late one night after ESPN SportsCenter, I saw an infomercial for an odd looking tool called a "skewdriver," which allows one to fasten screws around corners (if, for reasons beyond me, you had a need for that type of function). The pitchman was a master at contrast. He said,

> **"It would cost you over $400 dollars at the hardware store to buy all the tools this one device will replace."**

Ok, cancel the trip to Ace. Then he said,

> **"And the wholesale price on this thing is normally $125."**

Of course, most people associate wholesale with getting a good deal.

After some staged haggling, the host got the pitchman to concede,

> **"OK, I'm almost losing money on this, but I'll give you a price of two payments of $29.98."**

(Probably would have ordered it, but I'm still paying off my non-stick cookware.)

Reinforce the Price

After you've gotten a sale, validate their decision in order to fortify the value:

> **"You're getting a great deal."**

After haggling with a guy selling me landscape pavers, he said,

> **"I sold thousands of these at 50 cents. You're stealing these at 39 cents."**

Dealing With Price Shoppers

Most sellers hate it when someone calls them and says, "What's your price." Or getting the same question early in an outbound call. Especially when their price is higher than the competition. How you handle this tender situation can make the difference between getting the sale, or scaring away the jittery price shopper. Your best bet is to get their mind off the price by asking questions.

For example, when someone says "What is your price?" before you've asked any questions, respond with,

> **"Well, it could be as high as $6,000. Depending on what you want, yours could be much lower. Let's take a look at your situation."** Or,

> **"It depends on several variables. Let me ask you a few questions so I can quote you the best price for your situation."** Or,

> **"I imagine you're looking for the best price possible, so let me find out a little bit more about what you want so I can give it to you."**

The Price Objection

Stewart Issacson of Fidelity Investments made a good point during a seminar. In his business of selling 401K programs, his customers need to be able to justify the price not only to themselves, but to others. So when you hear the price objection, interpret it as the person saying, "Help me justify this price in my own mind."

Just like with any objection, you need to find out why they feel the price is too high. Begin by asking questions:

> **"What are you comparing the price to?"**

> **"How did you arrive at your price figure?"**

> **"Are you looking at just the one-time purchase price, or the total cost and value over time?"**

Giving Price Concessions

If you ever need to give in and lower your price, try to get a concession of your own in return. This way you don't compromise your value. For example,

> **"I could lower the price by a nickel per unit, if you**

can live with non-priority shipping."

And if you just flat-out have to lower price to get the business, do it grudgingly, kicking and screaming. Maybe even waiting until the next call. Giving one too soon indicates there could be more to be had. People feel smug when they feel they've gotten the best deal possible.

So, is your price higher than the competition? No problem; your value is as well. Communicate that effectively, and you'll sell more than you ever have.

Who's *Really* Objecting to the Price, You or Them?

Letting your own biases affect your conversations with customers can be fatal to your sales. I was listening to a call, and in response to a prospect's question about an item, the sales rep said, *"I have to warn you; that's the most expensive model we have."*

After that disclosure what do you think was going through the listener's mind? Probably not the value of the machine, but how expensive it was.

As I've often said, YOU need to be totally sold on the results of your product or service before you can sell it to anyone else. Quite often when I hear sales reps encountering price objections it's due to the tentative way the price was presented; no value was created in the listener's mind, therefore the rep hesitantly rushed through the price issue, darn near apologizing for it. Quite often it's really the sales rep who objects to the price, and it shows during the call.

Be unwaveringly confident in what you provide, and it will shine through in your voice and words, and that's contagious.

Help Them Understand the Value

Let's say you've reached the point where you've pointed out the savings you could show for the customer, yet they don't see the amount as significant enough to take action over. Your tendency is likely to beat your head against the desk and say, "Dummy, open your eyes." Don't. Instead, analyze the real problem: he simply isn't associating the dollar amount he's overpaying now as a big enough problem, or viewing the savings as a large enough solution to a problem. Therefore, your job is to present it in a way that helps him think differently.

As with any objection the first action is to determine if that truly is the only factor keeping him from buying. Ask,

> **"Is it that your feelings about the savings not being significant enough the only thing keeping you from moving forward?"**

After getting confirmation, then move to the next step. Consider,

❑ Putting the savings in terms of profits.

> **"That's money that drops directly to your bottom line."**

❑ Discussing profits, in terms of additional sales they would need to get.

> **"Let's look at this in terms of what you'd need to sell to realize this much profit. Based on your 10% margin, you'd have to sell another $10,000 worth of your products just to show the $1000 profit I'm basically giving you."**

❑ Relating it to common expenses.

> **"With this savings you could make the monthly payments on three of your delivery vans. It would be like we're actually buying your trucks!"**

Know the Payback to Win the Business

You don't need to be a mathematician to be successful in sales, but it's a tremendous advantage to be able to quickly calculate, and point out, how your product/service can pay for itself over time. This is especially true when your price is higher than the competition's. For example,

> **"You're right, our price is higher—on the front end. Over time, if you use ours just half as long as you've kept the existing unit, you'll make up the price difference, and show over $5,000 in labor savings."**

Action Steps

Chapter 25

Objections and Problems

The conventional wisdom on objections says that you should always call the objection a "question," and not a problem. For example,

Prospect: "Your price is too high."

> **Caller: "Hmm, that's an interesting question Ms. Flounder, let's see if we can answer it."**

While giving this some super-heavy thought the other day, I decided that there are situations where it's better to call the objection a *problem*, if they feel it is one. Then you can help them solve it.

Assume the prospect says, "We'd love to get your system. What's stopping us is the incompatibility with our existing unit."

The prospect apparently wants the system, but views a problem blocking a purchase. Treat it as such.

> **Caller: "Hmmm, let's see if we can work out that problem."**

Dealing with objections this way is a professional, conversational, customer-oriented approach to helping them, and getting what you want in the process.

The "No Money" Problem

Using the "problem" technique mentioned above, let's look at a situation we've likely all run into. When the prospect or customer says, "We just don't have any money available," keep in mind that what they're really saying is, "We only have money available right now for items or services deemed to be of strong enough value."

After all, they are spending money—it's just that their perception of the value you're offering isn't strong enough to warrant the slim funds that might be allocated. I suggest the first step in addressing this question is getting agreement that they are sold on what you present.

> **"Ok, well, let's see if we can solve that. First, I'm assuming that this is what you want, right?**

Then ask another question to judge how threadbare the money-cupboard really is,

> **"How are you addressing that problem ... I mean when you run across something like this that you want. Under what circumstances would you be able to justify getting the money?"**

Action Steps

Chapter 26

How to Handle "I Want to Think About It"

Thinking back to my early days as a naive, peach-fuzzed-face high schooler/part-time phone salesperson, I recall one of my grizzled managers giving a piece of seasoned advice that I've never forgotten and always believed: "Nothing will kill a deal like time."

How true. With prospects and customers, today's interest and perception of a pressing problem or need often becomes tomorrow's bottom-of-the-pile "to-do," until it ultimately vaporizes into the air, replaced by a new set of concerns. Like a fire on a winter night, left untended, it will extinguish itself with time. To be successful, then, it is your job to keep prospects' flames of interest roaring.

To avoid letting that thief, time, steal your sale, consider the way it disguises itself with these phrases:

"Let me think about it."

"I need some time."

"Maybe later."

Why They Delay

A couple of things to keep in mind here:

1) They might, indeed, be sincere and truly need time before making a decision. Fine. If so, find out what specifically is going to happen, and why the time is required.

2) If they have no intention of ever buying from you, or worse, never making a decision of any type, find that out, too.

3) If the matter is simply one of procrastination, and you both agree a decision would be in their best interest, it's best that you help them take action now, since their perception of urgency will likely diminish as quickly as interest in a losing lottery ticket the instant the drawing is over.

What you **don't** want to do upon hearing their stall is confront them with a slickly-coined phrase designed to push them into a quick decision. That only serves to annoy them, and perhaps even cause them to come up with more rational reasons for delaying. The professional approach uses well-placed questions to get them talking ... to help them turn their interest into action.

First we need to uncover the cause of the delay. If your reading of the situation tells you they are sincere, and there is something that truly needs to happen before they buy, fine. Just be sure they're on your side and help them be specific about the next action:

> **"So what you're saying is that my proposal is what you want to go with. All you need at this point is to write up the justification so you can present it to the acquisitions manager and get the funds, right?"**

Let's deal with the other situations, the ones that cause you grief and waste your time and money. The ones where they're either flat-out procrastinating, or just yanking your chain. Here are questions to help them open up and give you concrete issues you can deal with, or cause them to fess up and admit they're not going to buy from you—which I call a success in this situation.

> **"What concerns do you still have?"**
>
> **"What's causing you to hesitate?"**
>
> **"What questions are still unanswered for you?"**
>
> **"What are you still unsure of?"**
>
> **"What is it that you're planning to consider?"**

Or, you could provide choices that might help them give you a real reason for the delay.

> **"Is it the ____ that's holding you back?"**

Some might argue that this just offers them an easy excuse to select, one that isn't true. Could be. But like most attempts at deception, it's stripped bare by further questioning.

If you finally conclude that this person doesn't warrant further short-term effort on your part, politely let them know you'll be happy to work with them when (or, if) they make that decision. Then move on.

For the ones who are simple procrastinators, keep stoking the fire until it reaches the point where they act. Continue questioning to make them even more uncomfortable about their need or problem. Through questions, help them feel and verbalize how much better their life would be with your product or service.

Don't let "Let me think about it," or other similar delays take money out of your pocket. Move them forward, or move them out.

Chapter 27

What to Do and Say When They're Wrong

People will rarely change their mind if you tell them they're wrong, which is what most instruction on "overcoming" objections suggests you do. The natural tendency is the opposite of the desired effect: they tend to resist even more. The best way to deal with objections is to soften them (**"Let's talk about that."**) and then go back to questions to help them doubt their beliefs.

In situations where someone is flat-out wrong about facts that hinder your position, you need a tactful way to help them change their belief, while saving face. For example, consider a situation where they say, "The XZY Company has a product that can slice bread, and chew gum at the same time, plus it's cheaper than yours." You know this is not true.

❑ You can approach it from the source of the information:

> **"Hmmm, that's interesting. Where did that information come from?"**

This could reveal that it actually was heard from a friend's uncle's neighbor.

❑ You could add something about your credibility and expertise:

> **"We pride ourselves here on staying on top of all developments in this industry. Do you have some inside information?"**

❑ You might find a flaw in their stance by asking them to be specific:

> **"What specifications have you seen on that product?"**

Continuing down this vein could help them realize that, OK, maybe it wasn't cheaper, or that it couldn't actually slice the bread.

❑ You also want to make sure you're both talking "apples-to-apples":

> **"When you say it chews gum too, do you mean the entire chewing process, or that it just stores the gum?"**

> Or, **"When you say it's cheaper, in what quantities are we talking about, and what about the installation, delivery, and maintenance of the chewing and slicing mechanism? Quite often, those services are left off the quoted prices, while we quote the complete price."**

❑ **Consider agreeing** with one part of their stance before questioning on the flawed part:

> **"I know that they have something in a lower price range that chews gum, but the slicing bread would be revolutionary in the industry. Tell me more about what you know about it."**

❑ Or, let them know you had heard that before, but actually found out the facts.

> **"You know, I had heard that same thing a month ago. Then I actually did some research, and found out some interesting facts. When they say 'slicing,' what they actually mean is just making the perforations. And there is a cheaper model, but the deluxe is actually almost 50% more than ours."**

Action Step

Chapter 28

How to Ensure You Never Hear "We Don't Need It"

A participant at a seminar asked, "How do you suggest handling the 'We don't need it' objection?"

Easy. Never hear it again. Prevent it from occurring.

When a prospect or customer tells you they don't need what you have, it's a sign that something has failed in the sales process. And it's usually the salesperson's fault.

For example, if that's a real objection, it means that there is not a fit in the prospect's mind for what you're offering. And that means they heard your off-target product/service presentation before needs and problems had been fully identified, indicating the questioning was inadequate. Here's a closer look at the reasons people say they don't need it.

- **there really isn't a fit.** They *don't* need it. A business that rents its office space and has all maintenance performed by the building manager obviously doesn't need the replacement light bulbs and cleaning chemicals hawked by the phone salesperson who is simply smilin' and dialin' and pitching his specials. This business should have never heard the "pitch" (I hate that word when used in a sales context instead of its baseball one) in the first place. Instead, simple, obvious qualifying questions would have been,

    "Do you own or rent your office space? How much of the maintenance are you responsible for?"

- **there might be a fit, but the prospect doesn't realize it, or the potential perceived gain or avoided loss isn't valuable enough.** People will only take action if they see their need being severe enough, or the potential gain being worthwhile enough. For example, dentists suggest that you get a checkup every six months. Some who don't see the need, might only visit the dentist when the pain from a toothache becomes so excruciating they finally relent and go in—for a root canal. From a sales perspective, your goal would be to get the person to realize, on their own (you can't talk them into it), that the potential pain from a possible toothache and root canal far outweighs the minor inconvenience of the regular checkups.

Sales reps often toss up their arms in exasperated frustration with prospects who they feel are ignorant (dictionary definition: lack of knowledge or awareness of a particular thing). Instead of placing the blame externally, on the prospect, they need to look internally, and understand it's their failure to execute the sales process effectively.

What You Should Do

Here are specific action items to help you avoid hearing the "We don't need it" objection.

❑ **Never begin a call, or the planning of a call, from a product/ service *presentation* perspective**. Such as "I'm going to call today to present our new product line to customers." Instead, adopt the mindset of,

> **"What needs, problems, and desires must my customers be aware of in order for our new product line to be of value?"**

Take your product/service benefits and results and define what needs or problems must exist before the benefits truly would be of value. Then create questions you'll ask. For example, a sorter/collator attachment for the prospect's copy machine would only be of value if, 1) they don't have one already; 2) they have—or anticipate— copy jobs that require sorting and collating; and, 3) they're doing it manually and it's taking the time of a person who could be doing something else, or they want to prevent that from occurring.

❑ **Embellish their needs and problems.** The hungrier someone is, the better that scrumptious dish sounds, and the more desirous they become. You enhance their hunger with your questions so that when they hear your presentation, they're listening from an open, receptive, salivating state of mind. This is the key to helping them *want to buy* instead of selling them. Using the sorting and collating attachment example mentioned above, taking point 3, where the company had a person performing the tasks manually, embellishment questions would include,

> **"How much time are they spending?"**

"How often?"

"What does that cost in terms of labor?"

"What other things could they be doing?"

☐ **Only present after you've identified their needs, problems, and potential gains they desire.** Make this an unbendable rule! It's here that you ensure you won't hear the "Don't need it" objection. Get information before you give it. I define a "pushy" salesperson as one who presents something a person doesn't want or need. Asking the questions first eliminates that possibility.

☐ **Know when to punt.** In some cases you'll come up empty in the needs department. In that case, don't hesitate letting go without a time-wasting presentation that would only create objections. You might, however, want to ask one more catch-all question to drag your net through the sea to catch anything you might have missed:

"**Joe I'm not sure if what I have would be of any value to you. Could you see any possible circumstances changing where you would be expanding your assembly line?**"

Action Steps

Chapter 29

Objection Tips

In this chapter we'll look at a variety of brief tips on dealing with objections.

Don't Ask What They Like About Their Vendor

I've developed a new opinion on a sales technique that I'm sure I've suggested at some point over the past 16 years.

It deals with asking the questions, "What do you like about your present vendor?", and, "What would you change about your present vendor if you could?"

After much deliberation, I suggest canning the first question, and just using the second (or a variation of it). My decision resulted from a call that went like this:

Prospect: "We're pretty happy with the company we're using now."

Rep: *"I see. Tell me, what is it that you like best about them?"*

Prospect: "They're great. I really like the fact that they've built up my trust in them over the years. When they say they'll do something, they get it done. They deliver long-term value far beyond what we pay them." (The customer's voice cracked. Sounded like he was getting a bit weepy-eyed as he spoke with unwavering fondness of his vendor.)

At that point I realized, why should we present—*and encourage*—the opportunity for prospects to sell themselves on how great their vendor is? Oh, sure, you can rebut this reasoning with the logic that if they tell you what they like, you can respond with how you can deliver the same thing—and more of it. Yeah, right. *Telling* someone you can be trusted carries about the same perceived value as a politician's promise.

I do, however, recommend the second question ... about what they'd ideally like. Use variations such as,

> **"What would you like to get that you don't have now?"**

121

"What is on your wish list?"

"What would you change about your present situation?"

This way you get them thinking about their pains and their unfilled wants, which if you can fill them, will help accomplish your objective.

The Objections "Bridge"

When your prospect expresses an objection, they likely feel it's important. Be sensitive to that feeling. That's what the bridge is designed to do.

Just like psychologists put people at ease in order to get them to open up, your bridge has the same effect. Here are other bridge examples.

"That's a very logical concern for people in your business."

"I can certainly understand why you would say that, given what's going on in your industry."

"That's a question we hear quite often from Human Resource Managers running departments about the same size as yours."

"That's a valid question in light of the regulatory issues you're faced with right now."

Asking "Why" Can Create Tension

When my son misbehaves in some way that is just so strange I can't fathom what he was thinking when he did the deed, in moments of exasperation I often ask, *"Eric, WHY did you do that?"*

Usually the answer is, "I dunno."

I should know by now. With some people, "Why" is a threatening word. It implies they are wrong, and attempts to force them to justify their reasoning. (In my case, my son knows he's wrong by the time we're having this discussion, therefore I'm better off to not try to have him rationally explain an irrational action. He might come up with a good reason and do it again!)

What we should do in the sales process when we're looking for the reasons behind a prospect's/customer's opinions and actions is to coax out their beliefs in a nonthreatening, conversational manner, avoiding the word "why."

For example,

Prospect: "I don't think your system would work for us?"

Instead of *"Why not?"*, consider,

"I see. What were some of the factors considered in reaching that conclusion?"

Here's another,

Prospect: "We can't do anything about new machines until next year."

Instead of,

"Why?", try,

"What is it about next year that will make that a better time for you?"

Think of excuses and resistance you commonly encounter, and brainstorm for non-threatening questions that will help unlock the real reasons behind the words. Try to focus on the decision and the activity, not the person.

Become an Alternate Source

Some prospects are so entrenched in the habit of buying from one particular company that they tune out any suggestion of switching suppliers—unfortunately even if that means getting a better deal.

Instead of butting heads and trying to get them to reconsider, approach the problem from another angle. Get them to consider you as an alternate source. For example,

"Steve, I'm not asking you to quit buying from Dufus Supply. I'm just asking you to consider us as another source for some of the items we can save you money on. You'll have the best of both worlds. How about giving us a try?"

Clarify the "Fuzzy Phrases"

Don't get put off by an abstract phrase like, "We might do something next quarter. We'll take a look at it. Let's stay in touch." What does THAT mean? Clarify through further questions.

"When you say 'something,' does that mean you'll go with it?"

"What exactly will you be looking at?"

"Does 'stay in touch' mean I should call at a certain time?"

Dealing With Resistance And Objections

❏ **To get them talking** after they state an objection, say,

"Tell me more about that."

❏ **The old myth says** that "The selling doesn't start until an objection has been expressed." That's garbage. If the sales process had been perfectly executed, an objection wouldn't even occur.

❏ **Resistance early in a call** is easier to deal with than a major objection later on. Plus it helps you change course when necessary. So, ask for the resistance if it's there.

"What are your thoughts so far?"

❏ **Use the "Just suppose"** technique.

"Just suppose the money was in the budget. Would you go with it then?"

❏ **Never tell someone** they're wrong (even if they are!). Instead, take the responsibility.

"I don't think I explained myself clearly. Here is what I meant ..."

Give Them Choices in Response to Resistance

The only way to professionally answer objections is to get the other person talking about the reasons behind the resistance. One effective way is to offer them choices. For example,

Prospect: "We're happy with our present supplier."

"I see. Is it that you're locked in to a contract, or that you've not found a better value yet?" Or,

"Is it the quality you're getting there, or the service that you like best?"

Prospect: "We're not ready to do anything yet?"

"Is it because there's something that needs to happen before you buy, or that you don't see enough value in acting right away?"

Prospect: "We can get it cheaper elsewhere."

"Hmm. Is price your main concern, or are you looking at service factors also?"

You can't answer resistance until you get them talking. Giving them choices allows them an easy way to voice their concerns. Even if they don't pick one of your alternatives, you have something of substance to deal with.

Listen for the "Too's"

Listen for the word "too" when prospects and customers serve up resistance. Typically "too" is used in conjunction with part of their decision-making criteria, which is quantifiable. If they view something as too expensive, too small, etc., we need to find out what is acceptable. For example,

"It looks good, but I think it's too expensive for us."

"I see. What price figure did you have in mind?"

"The system is too small for us."

"Hmm. What size do you feel you need?"

Once you get them talking, you can then address the reasons behind their "too" response.

Look at Objections From Their Viewpoint

Think for a moment about why disagreements escalate into full-scale battles. Typically it's when both sides entrench their own positions more strongly with each verbal salvo, only considering why the other person is wrong and they're right. I believe that's why handling objections is such an uncomfortable situation for most people ... we just naturally prefer to avoid conflict. Therefore, upon hearing resistance, instead of trying to counter it, ask yourself, "Under what circumstances would their view be true?" And, "What would cause someone to say that?" Then you are in a much better frame of mind to discuss their resistance and deal with their concern conversationally, instead of trying to beat it down with a verbal baseball bat.

What to Say When They're Happy With Their Supplier

Scott Hodges sells material handling products to manufacturers. His are the highest priced in the market, so he naturally faces resistance like,

"We're happy with who we're using, and have no problems whatsoever." Scott's best response is to simply ask,

"When you replace the existing product, why is it replaced?"

What a great question! Notice the psychology here: the question doesn't address the reflex resistance response "we're happy." That's smart, since a lot of rational thought hasn't been devoted to that response. It's instinctive as blinking your eyes. Questioning the response would only frustrate them, and perhaps help them come up with good reasons why they are using their present vendor.

Instead, this question focuses on what Scott is really doing: solving problems. In doing so, he's positioning the real value of his product. Because when the prospect answers by explaining that he replaces his pallet jacks when the cost of repairs become higher than the cost of a new unit, he can layer questions deeper to get the prospect thinking about those costs. Ideally the prospects begins realizing how even though the equipment had a cheaper price tag initially, the real costs pile up in terms of replacement parts, labor, out-of-service time, and ultimately a shorter life span. Then the prospect is in a very receptive frame of mind to hear about Scott's products ... and, most importantly, how his problems could be solved.

How to Root Out the Real Objection

Get to the heart of the reason for an objection:

"It seems the real decision here is this: is (the ultimate benefit they'll receive) **more important than** (the objection)**?"**

For example,

"It seems the real decision here is this: is giving your salespeople a proven system for generating additional add-on sales more important than the time they'd be investing in the half-day training program, time off of the phone?"

Turn Objections Into Questions

Paraphrase objections and resistance as questions to ensure you understand the situation, and to position them as something to be answered—not overcome. For example:

"What you're asking is, will you get a return on the

extra $200 you'd pay with our system. Is that the question?"

Use Questions to Cause Them to Rethink Their Position

When prospects make unreasonable requests or objections, use questions to get them to reexamine their position.

Prospect: "I'll need that special order by tomorrow."

Rep: "Were you aware that special orders need two extra days for imprinting?"

Prospect: "We must have all of these stipulations accepted if we're to use you."

Rep: "We can meet most of these. How important is the one on restocking fees?"

Review the Progress You've Made So Far

Regardless of how pitiful a round of golf might be going for me, I always manage to crush a couple of monster drives splitting the middle of the fairway. And the poorer the game is that day, the more inclined I am, after walking up to my ball, to turn back towards the tee and admire the vast amount of ground that extraordinary shot had just traveled. It's a reminder that regardless of how difficult things might be, I've still accomplished something remarkably positive.

You should do the same on calls where you've screeched to a standstill with your prospect. For example, let's say you've been negotiating for awhile, but he wants a concession you're not able to make. Call a time-out to look "at your shot," to review the positives you've covered so far.

"Dan, let's back away from this issue for a minute. I think we're getting hung up on an issue that's really only a small part of the grand picture. Let's review all the positives we've agreed that will come from this relationship, once we get it finalized ..."

Ask Them to Explain Their Objection

Some prospects may not be clear in their expression of objections, or they might throw out some objections as stalling techniques. To clarify the situation, ask them to repeat, or explain their objection again. For example,

"Mr. Davis, I'm not sure I fully understood what you

just said. Will you please repeat that for me?"

Or, **"Pat, I heard what you said, but I'm not follow-ing the reasoning. Would you mind explaining it for me?"**

If their objection is truly a legitimate one, their explanation will pro-vide you with information which will help you answer it. If, on the other hand, they are just stalling, your question will help to smoke out the real objection.

Action Steps

Follow-Up Calls

Chapter 30

The Way You End a Call Makes or Breaks The Follow-Up

D o you ever have problems with follow-up calls, even after you felt the previous call went OK?

Or, how about that gut-knotting feeling of staring at your prospect notes from a previous call as you prepare for the next one, searching for—but not finding—what you'll say on this call that's more inspiring than, *"Well, ahh, I'm just calling you back to see if you got my brochure, and what you think about it?"*

If you've ever been there—and most of us have—chances are that your previous call didn't end strongly: with a clear summarization of that call, and of what was to happen next, both before and during the next call.

Ending a call with, *"OK, I'll just send you out some literature, and give you a call back in a couple of weeks,"* virtually ensures your demise on the next contact. And rightfully so; there's nothing specific here. No connection between this call and the next, no summarization of the problem, need or interest (if there was any at all), and no confirmation of who's to do what next.

Here's what you should do at the end of your calls to ensure a fluid transition from this contact to the next. (By the way, all of this presumes you didn't get a sale—we're all pretty good at wrapping up those calls.)

How to Wrap Up a Call and Plan the Next

Before ending the call you need to do an overview with your prospect/ customer. Summarize,

- **The Need/Problem, and Their Interest.** Revisit what they are interested in, and why.

- **What They Will Do.** At the very minimum you should get commitment they will read your material and prepare questions, test out your sample and evaluate it according to criteria you've both discussed, take

130

your proposal to the committee with their recommendation, and so on. THIS IS CRITICAL! If you don't get a commitment for action, this person might not ever become a customer. Asking for, and getting some type of action commitment is my way of tightly qualifying people. If they're not taking action, why are you calling back?

- **What You'll Do.** Review what you'll do, what you'll send, who you'll speak with, or whatever you promised.

- **When You'll Talk Next.** Don't say, *"How 'bout I call you in a couple of weeks?"* Let them give you a date, and tie it to their commitment:

> **"Carol, by when do you think you will have collected all of the inventory figures we'll need for our next conversation?"**

Not only do you have a date and time, but you have their commitment, again, they'll perform their duties.

- **The Next-Call Agenda.** Before you end a contact where you know you'll place a follow-up call, ask yourself, "What is the reason for the next call?" It should be that they are taking some action as a result of this call. Summarize what they're going to do, what you'll do, and the purpose for the next contact. It eliminates the tendency to begin follow-up calls with the loony phrase, *"I was just following up and wondered what you decided to do."* For example, a good ending would be,

> **"OK, so you'll survey your department to determine how many would participate in the program, I'll prepare the price quotes at the various levels of participation, and when we speak again next Friday we'll talk about dates for implementing the program."**

Go over what's to happen next. It plants a seed as to what they should expect on the following call.

> **"Let me go through what we've covered today. You feel that Advantage Inc. will provide you with better availability, and you like our customer service policies, and you do want to get going with that new inventory program we offer, but you need to wait to get funding in the next budget, which you're going to suggest, and we'll plan on talking around the first of next month when I call you again."**

How to Do a Post-Call Review
That Will Make You a Better Sales Rep

It's said that we don't learn nearly as much performing an activity as we do after it, by reviewing and analyzing our experience. You can take a quantum leap in your development by simply assessing your calls, committing to take action where improvement is needed, and then beginning preparation for the next contact to the same person. Here's how.

Analyze the Call

Ask, **"What did I like about this call?"** Reinforce a deed well done. What gets rewarded, gets repeated.

Ask, **"What would I have done differently?"** Keep it positive. Don't ask the destructive question, *"What didn't I like?"* And don't darken your attitude with negative self-talk like, *"I really blew that call."* Instead, be positive and action-oriented. By pondering what you could have done differently, you're replaying the call, doing a mental role play, searching for phrases you'll use next time. And that's how you improve.

Prepare Notes, and Plan The Next Call

Review and record what they're doing and what you'll do as a result of this call. Also put in your notes:

Info You Need on the Next Call. Remind yourself what to ask next time.

Possible Next-Call Objectives. Plan your next contact while this one is still fresh in mind.

Opening Statement Ideas. Ditto the previous reason.

What's that you say? Can't take the time after a call to do all this stuff? Think again. These steps actually save you time in preparing your next call, and ensures your calls are as solid as possible.

What to Do When You Win, or Lose, the Sale

When you lose a major bid or proposal, don't stew, burn bridges, or beat yourself up with negative self-talk. Instead, call the customer and thank him again for the opportunity to be considered, then,

• tell him you'd like to ask a few questions about the sales process.

• let him know that you're not trying to steal the business, but to understand how you can be more competitive and do a better job next time.

Let him know you are interested in his business in the long term, and the best way to keep him informed of whatever you might have is to understand what you could have done better or differently.

When You Win

Likewise, when you get that deal, ask your new customers,

- what they liked about you.
- what they didn't like about the competition
- what you did right and the competition did wrong
- what you could have done better
- what the competition offered that they wished you offered
- how they see you as being unique
- how the messages from the competitors differed

The answers to these questions can not only help you help your new customers, but also provide you with great information to help you win more new customers.

(SOURCE: "SELLING AT THE TOP," by Jim Pancero, published by Dartnell, 1-800-621-5463)

Help Them Sell For You

When your prospect or customer must discuss and/or get approval on your offer in order for a sale to take place, there are steps you can take to improve your chances of success.

➡ **Get agreement they are sold.** As I've mentioned so often, if someone else is doing the selling, they need to be sold first. Ask them,

"Is this what you want to do?"

"Are you personally sold on this?"

"Will you recommend this program?"

➡ **Arm them with tools.** Ask who will be in the meeting, and what they will likely want to know. Then provide whatever information, samples, brochures you both feel will help the process.

➡ **Stay familiar.** David Landy with International Automated suggests faxing a note a day or so before the meeting, letting your contact know you're available to answer any last minute questions. Kathleen Ashbey also with International Automated likes to let her prospects know her schedule. For example, she informs them that she will be available all day—especially during their meeting—just in case questions arise that they need immediate answers to. Calling them the day of their meeting with additional information is a good idea because it might give them something they can use to sell the offer, plus it positions you in the forefront of their mind if they also must present the offers of a few other vendors.

Another Benefit Of Taping

If you don't tape record and review your calls, you're missing out on one of the most useful self-development tools available. I also use taping for another sales-related purpose. On what I know will be very important follow-up calls, I'll tape the conversation and then review the content before the next call or action. Just last week I reviewed a taped dialogue very slowly and jotted down notes—especially the words and terms used by the prospect. I then made a point of using this person's exact terminology in the proposal, which naturally made an impact.

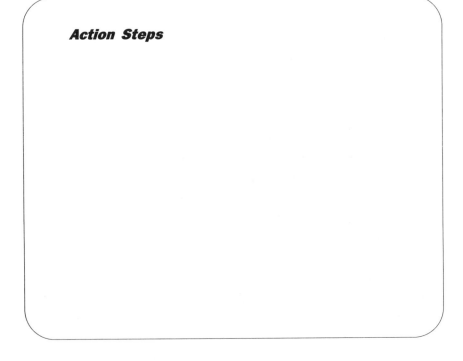

Action Steps

Chapter 31

Phone Appointments Show You're Serious

At a Telesales Rep College in Irvine, California, Nina Vultaggio with FINOVA made this statement regarding telephone appointments: "If you take yourself seriously, so will they."

If you suggest a specific time for a telephone appointment, and treat it just as you would a face-to-face appointment, you send a clear message that your time is valuable (as is theirs) and what you both will discuss is significant. Conversely, meekly suggesting that you speak again *"next Thursday afternoon"* is vague and easy to disregard by the prospect. They're really thinking, "Sure, you can call then. I don't know if I'll be here or not, and it's really not that important anyway."

I'm still surprised when people admit they're not using the powerful tool of phone appointments. Granted, you might not be able to logistically set an appointment for *every* call you place—nor would you want to—but everyone has those important follow-up contacts worthy of an appointment.

The Process

Here's how I suggest setting the appointment: At the call's wrap-up phase, after you've determined what you'll both do before the next contact, say,

> **"Great. Let's schedule our next conversation. You mentioned you will have tested the sample by next Thursday, so does Friday look good for us to speak again?"**

Assuming they affirm, continue with,

> **"Good, do you have your calendar handy? Is there any time better than another? Morning, maybe?"**

Wait for their answer, check your schedule, then narrow the choices:

> **"Ok, please write me down for 11:15, your time,**

and I'll call you. Does that work?"

Place emphasis on "their time," and "I'll call you," so you're clear on the responsibilities.

End with,

"I've got you in my book, and unless I hear from you otherwise, I'll call you next Friday at 11:15. And if you have the sample and your notes ready then, we can go over them."

This again reviews the details, and also reminds them of what they're going to do before the call, and sets an agenda for the next contact.

Set phone appointments. It's an efficient use of your time, and it sends a clear message of professionalism.

Action Steps

Chapter 32

Don't Invite More Delays On Long-Term Follow-Up Calls

ere's the scenario: On the previous call, two months ago, I told the caller, a sales rep for multi-media presentation equipment, "I'm not ready now," and agreed to accept a call back "in a couple of months" from the rep. He called back at the appropriate time, and opened the call with,

"I'm following up on our last call, where you had said you weren't ready yet for our system, but to check back with you to see if things had changed."

I was in my typical harried mode of trying to keep five plates spinning atop of sticks when he phoned, and responded with the first thing that came to my mind, "Still not ready yet. Nothing has changed. Check back later."

So what's wrong here? Put yourself in my position, that of the prospect: I hadn't given this salesperson or his offer any thought since the last contact. He then called and immediately reminded me of the stall/objection I used the last time to get him off the phone. I didn't hear any benefits from the rep, any reasons to speak with him (even though I am a real prospect for what he's selling, and will likely buy, sometime, from someone) therefore the easiest thing for me to say is exactly what he just reminded me of: the way I got him off of the phone the last time. It's like an actor being whispered lines he's forgotten while on stage—he simply repeats the first thing he hears.

Recommendations

What we all should do as sales reps in these follow-up call situations is instead open up the call on a positive, reminding the prospect of the benefits he had interest in last time, and mention why now would be a better time, as opposed to why the past wasn't.

Here's what I would have listened to:

"Mr. Sobczak, this is Pete Visual with MultiMediates.

137

We talked in April about your interest in making your presentations come alive with computer graphics, and felt that now would be a great time to talk since you're planning your Fall schedule. I've also got some new information about some systems that have been very popular with other trainers."

That would have kept me on the phone.

Notice the difference. It doesn't put me on the spot to try and recall my interest; it *reminds* me instead. It also doesn't leave the fate of the call in the vague hands of "things changing." It's specific about an impending event that was on my mind at that time. The suggested opening also offered up something new, information that a system that has been popular with others similar to me, appealing to the innate "keeping up with the Joneses" desire that many people have.

How to Ensure a Great Follow-Up

The real key, though, to ensuring you have a good follow-up call is laying the groundwork on your initial calls (which this guy didn't do). Before ending the initial call, ensure they are worth calling back. Calling back just for the sake of reactively "checking in" is a waste, and normally results in another stall. If they say something like, "Check back with me in a couple of months," ask them,

"I'll be happy to follow up. Do you feel at that time you'll be ready to move forward?"

If they waffle, you know they might be stalling. If they sound sincerely interested, you can probe further:

"What will make that a better time for you?"

On the other hand, if there's not a fit today for what you have and they don't suggest you call back, but you nevertheless feel they would be worth pursuing (for example, when they're a huge potential customer) find out if there *ever* would be a chance of doing business in the future. Ask,

"Would you ever see yourself using a service like ours?"

If so, ask,

"Under what circumstances?"

Most people you talk to won't buy today. It just makes sense, then, to increase your chances of success with your follow up calls.

Here are additional ideas to help you on your follow-up calls.

☐ Keep your name in front of them in the time between your initial call, and the longer-term follow up. You can fax or mail notes, articles of interest, information on new products they would be interested in, based on your last conversation, notifications of sales ... anything which would have some value for them. This strategy keeps you and your company's name at the front of their mind, just in case their situation changes. Then, you'd likely be the first they'd call.

☐ In the opening, use their specific hot buttons which you uncovered on the last conversation. Remember, they are not sitting at their desk, staring forlornly at the phone, hoping it rings, like a teenager wishing for a call from a potential prom date. They are doing something and your opening needs to instantly snap their memory and emotions back to the conversation where their interest was high. Therefore, use their terminology. For example,

> **" ... and I'm calling to pick up our conversation on the Manage Right software that you felt would help you to eliminate most of the paperwork you generate in your order processing."**

☐ A good follow-up opening example:

> **"Ms. Davis, I'm Duane Davis with Accurate Technology. I'm following up on our last conversation ... about two months ago where you had shown interest in our Hydro Gromolutzers to help you reduce your labor costs in your manufacturing process. You had mentioned that now would be a good time to re-open the conversation because of the new products you'll be retooling for. I also have some additional new information I think you'll be interested in hearing about."**

Action Steps

139

Chapter 33

How to Ensure What You Mail Helps—Not Hinders—Your Sales

The sales rep did a commendable job of piquing my interest, discovering my innermost desires through questioning, making a recommendation, and then offering to send information I needed to examine in order to move the process forward.

Then he negated all that goodwill by mailing a cover letter—with a bulging bag of brochures which didn't specifically address the detailed issue we discussed—that read,

"Dear Mr. Sobczak,

Thank you for your interest in Acme Company. Enclosed please find additional information. We are the recognized leader in the widget field. We have (blah, blah ...).

Our products (yadda, yadda ...).

We look forward to speaking with you in the future.

Sincerely ..."

The signature had a printed "D.G." underneath, signifying that it was actually signed by someone other than the rep. So what kind of personalization was this?!

My impression of what happened here—which is all that really matters since I'm the prospect—is that this rep ended the call, hit a key accessing the "form letter" function in his contact management program, selected letter "P1" that goes to people after his first call, it whirred out of D.G.'s laser printer on the opposite end of the building, who then signed and initialed it—along with hundreds of others that day—then crammed it into preassembled generic literature kits and rolled them all out the door on an overflowing mail cart. What a gross misuse of the mail in the sales process!

What to Do for Maximum Impact

As I've so often stated, when the sales strategy is for the sales rep to be the primary communicator in the sales process—as opposed to a direct mail strategy where the mail stands alone as a sales vehicle and seeks a response—the mail needs to complement what was discussed on the call. Here are a couple of ideas.

Prepare Them for What They'll Get. Tell them to look for the "two-page price list that will specifically detail their quantity discounts, and will have their specific model numbers highlighted."

Avoid Looking or Sounding Canned With Your Literature. Recall your feelings the last time a telemarketer called you at home, stumbling and stammering through a script that sounded as if he was reading it for the very first time. Letters can look and sound canned too, leaving readers with the same sour feelings. Form letter templates are useful time-saving tools, but should be used as a starting point to fashion a personalized letter with tidbits gleaned from the call.

Their Degree of Interest is in Inverse Proportion to the Weight of the Package. Less is better. Picture a harried, overworked and underpaid decision maker as his mound of mail is dumped on his desk. Among the pile is a padded envelope transporting folders of brochures, catalogs, and price lists for every product in your warehouse. He's thinking he'd rather have his teeth drilled than sift through this clutter. Contrast that with a concise letter essentially stating, "This is exactly what we discussed to solve your problem," attached to a brochure or catalog page that details the precise solution he can envision himself already taking advantage of.

Ideas for Making Your Follow-Up Literature Stand Out

✔ **Monotones are Boring.** Just like spoken monotones cause listeners to drift, readers can react the same way to your letter. Put variety in it! Use typographical tools to put inflection, warmth, and feeling into your correspondence. Use ALL CAPS to scream out a point. Try **bold face** for emphasis. Consider *italics* for words or short phrases. <u>Underline</u> occasionally. Even consider a different type style for a word or two.

✔ **Hand Write a Note.** What would you read first, a handwritten letter, or a crisp, perfect laser printed document? The hand written note implies "These words are from me to you," almost as if they were spoken directly. Plus handwritten letters tend to be shorter. You probably won't want to scratch out everything you mail, but it's a nice informal touch for something that needs to go out in a hurry.

✔ **Use Simple Language.** Write as you speak. Toss out strict conventional grammatical rules. Never say, *"Enclosed please find ..."*

> Say, **"Here's the price list we discussed. I've highlighted your special quantity discounts."**

✔ **Mark Up Your Letter.** Notice direct mail letters you get at home (or at the office). You'll likely see liberal use of underlining, and notes in the margin.

✔ **Use a "P.S."** Professional direct mail copywriters will confirm that the most read part of a letter (and sometimes the first, or only part scanned) is the "P.S." Mention a hard-hitting, memorable benefit or request for action ... something that'll stick. Maybe give the impression that it was an afterthought ... kind of an "Oh, by the way ..." point you wanted to make. Best yet, handwrite the "P.S." for lapel-grabbing impact.

Action Steps

Prospecting

Chapter 34

Prospecting Tips and Techniques

I've seen boxing matches where the assaults weren't as fierce as the verbal warfare candidates launched at each other during the most recent political campaigns. Nevertheless, it is fascinating watching the persuasion and campaigning techniques candidates use. Look beyond the negativity and there actually are some sales lessons to be learned.

For example, at local events such as community meetings, festivals, and craft shows I observed congressional wannabes working the crowds. The more astute ones—those leading in the polls—typically spent little time with those who were already supporters, those wearing the candidate's sticker. Oh, sure, to reinforce their supporter's loyalty, they did the obligatory hand-pumping, flashing the toothy smile, and repeating a zillion times per day, "Nice to meet you. Appreciate your support!"

But it was with the people who wore no stickers that they seemed to spend the most time with. (Those who were walking billboards for their opponents warranted a handshake, but not much more.) They wisely focused on the "undecideds."

Applies to Sales As Well

And the same should be true with our sales efforts.

Spending inordinate time with existing customers takes productive time you could spend with new prospects. It's like catching a fish, admiring, and coddling it, then spending about an hour securing it in the livewell so it doesn't get away. Unhook it and throw the line back in the water for gosh sakes!

If your job is solely to maintain and develop existing customers, fine. But I know many of you are also responsible for beating the bushes, bringing in the new stuff as well. So, spend the time you need with existing customers, make them feel special, and generate additional revenue by servicing them. But don't chat it up like two giggly teens discussing the latest fashions. Move on, and focus energy on bringing in new business.

Prospecting Pointers

Here are ideas from Lou Ellen Davis' book, ***"The Insurance Agents Guide to Telephone Prospecting"*** *(Financial Sourcebook Publishing, Chicago).*

❑ **Practice "multi-level" listening.** This refers to listening for the other person's timing. If you feel they hesitate before responding to you, they're likely weighing what you just said.

❑ **Pay attention to your own breathing.** Get in touch with how different it is when you are irritated as opposed to when you are comfortably in sync with what's going on around you. How are you breathing right now? What does it tell you?

❑ **Listen to the other person's breathing.** Ms. Davis says that breathing can tell her that prospects might not be listening—they have drawn a breath to say what's already on their minds before she has finished a sentence—or it can tell her they are listening, and wavering on just how much more time they'll give her, which defines her timing on when to expand an idea as opposed to zeroing in on the close.

❑ **For the very first word from your mouth,** consider using **"Hi."** It's shorter than *"Good morning."* Remember, you don't have much time to make an initial positive impression.

❑ **In the opening,** if your company name has a "turn-off" word, such as *"insurance"* or *"investments"* in it, replace it with "Company." As in, **"I'm with the Johnson Company."**

❑ **Some salespeople are reluctant to prospect** because they feel they're interrupting someone. They are! Interruptions are a part of life. Interrupting prospects is a perfectly normal, necessary part of the economic process. Assuming you are courteous and reasonable, if the person you are calling can't handle it, *they* have a problem.

❑ **To make cold-calling easier,** think about *liking* the people you call. For example, if you're calling pharmacists, recall one you've visited over the years, one who showed warmth and compassion. Keep that image in mind as opposed to a person whose goal in life is to get rid of salespeople, and your outlook will transfer into effective calls.

How to Avoid Cancelled Appointments

Harold Lindsay, an independent insurance agent, wrote about how to avoid canceled appointments in **"SELL!NG."** He said most cancellations are due to improperly set appointments.

1. Never set tentative appointments. They usually result in cancels or no-shows.

2. Always, always, always send a thank you/reminder card. A thank you for agreeing to meet, including a reminder of the date and time.

3. Make a courtesy call to let them know you are on the way. Lindsay used to think this would give them an easy way to cancel. Sure, some did, but most appreciated the call and were ready when he arrived. *("SELL!NG Newsletter," published by Dartnell, 800-621-5463)*

Let Them Tell You How Qualified They Are

The salesperson caught my attention with a pretty darn good opener, but I was right in the middle of moving day, and although I had some interest in what he offered, I wasn't prepared to discuss anything of substance at least for a few months, and told him so. He then asked me a thought-provoking question,

> **"So how would you rate yourself? Suspect, prospect?"**

It really got me thinking, both as a buyer, and as a salesperson—wondering how I could use the same question. I answered that I was presently a prospect, with the potential to be a good prospect after the dust settled and I began planning my next year's promotions in earnest. Examining my answer, I noticed that not only did I prioritize this guy's next call to me, I also told him what needed to happen between now and the next contact in order for me to become a better prospect, which is a sign that I was truly interested and not just trying to sweep him off the phone.

If appropriate, do the same with people who suggest that you call back another time. Here are suggested questions to use or adapt.

> **"How would you categorize your level of interest in this, from a scale of 1-10?"**

> **"Would you say that you're definitely in the market and will be purchasing within the next year?"**

> **"How would you suggest I rate you, in terms of interest in doing something like this?"**

After they answer, get commitment from them they'll contact you if anything changes.

"Just in case you do have some changes that would cause you to move up your timetable, could I be one of the first you'd call?"

If they rate themselves, it takes the guesswork out of it for you.

Get Them Talking When They're Not Interested

On an initial prospecting call, particularly one following a mail drop your company had done, or information requested by them which they've already received, or even in situations where they know of your company, you might occasionally hear, "I'm familiar with your company, and I'm not interested."

What should you do? Many reps mutter a "Thank you," and dejectedly move on to the next call. Granted, in some cases, it might be best to cut your losses rather than challenge the prospect's comment with a statement that forces them to defend their intelligence.

However, depending upon how much conviction the prospect displays when making their "not interested" comment, you might want to pursue things from another angle. Instead of attacking the decision in its entirety, you can test parts of his reasoning.

For example,

"I see, Mr. Prospect. Is it the product/service itself that caused you to reach your conclusion, or was it something else?"

In response they might state adamantly that they aren't interested. Fine. Pack up and move on. However, they just might respond with one of the following:

"Nothing wrong. We're just happy with our present brand/supplier/ other."

"Well after looking it over, I noticed you didn't have _____ like we need."

With the first response, you can reply,

"I understand. Tell me, what aren't you getting that you'd ideally like ...?"

For the second response, you can ask more questions to determine exactly how they arrived at their understanding. In both cases, you have them talking, which is better than simply hanging up in response to a lame "not interested" brush off.

147

In some instances it's best to not waste your time. However, other times you can uncover real reasons you're able to deal with, which may help you turn around the prospect. Don't give up too easily.

Ideas for Appointment-Selling

Here are some ideas from Bill Bishop's tape program *"Prime Prospects Unlimited"* on "selling the appointment."

"Is there any reason why we can't get together around 8:40 this Wednesday morning?"

"Is there any reason why your partner/attorney/Aunt Flabby can't join us?"

"Would it be a problem for us to meet around 9:20 Tuesday?"

"Do you have any objection to a 10 minute meeting so you can see our _____?"

The key words in closing these appointments are in **bold print.** Master the key words, and follow them with the words that are appropriate to your situation. Of course, if you aren't setting appointments, you could use these same key words to close the sale by phone.

Leaving Prospecting Messages is a Waste

I've suggested for a long time that leaving messages for decision makers to call you back on cold calls is a waste of time. My reasoning:

• when you place the call, you can be totally prepared with what you're going to say, as opposed to being embarrassed when you have to cluelessly stumble through files trying to figure out why you called this person,

• you should be on the phone when and if they call, therefore entering into voice mail ping pong, with them becoming frustrated. This isn't that much of a problem, though, because,

• few people will actually return calls, unless they recognize you. And forget about just leaving your name without a company, thinking you're being mysterious. Sure, they might be duped into thinking it's a customer, or the IRS, but when they find out it's a sales person they become annoyed.

Stephanie Anderson, Telesales Manager at the computer training firm, Mastering Computers, shared some numbers that back up this theory. Her 40 sales reps tracked results of leaving messages on cold calls for a couple of weeks. They found that for every 100 messages left, only 12% resulted in returned calls.

Now here's the real interesting part: in tracking cold calls where no messages were left,

- dials were **up** 10%,

- completed contacts were **up** 10%,

- sales were **up** 15% over the previous test where messages were left.

Stephanie's reps call to sell seats in seminars, and they are aggressive in going for the sale as quickly as possible, usually on the first call. And their compensation structure reflects that. Reps are paid $15 commission for a sale on the first call, $12 for a sale on the second call to a prospect, $8 on the third, $4 on the fourth, and $2 on the fifth. It's a unique, but common sense way to illustrate the importance of spending your time wisely only with people who can and will buy from you, and moving the buying process along as quickly as possible.

Are You Selling to VITO?

If yours is a big-ticket sale that strategically impacts the buyer's organization, you should be talking to VITO. No, I'm not talking about the head pizza chef at your corner delivery place; VITO is the "Very Important Top Officer," according to author and trainer Anthony Parinello. And I strongly recommend his book, *"Selling to VITO,"* which gives strategies and tactics for dealing with the top.

In just the first 75 pages of this 225-page paperback, I've dog-eared and marked up pages and ideas so much it looks like the book has been through a chipper-shredder. Here are just a few tidbits:

❏ **VITO's are different than most buyers.** Some lower-level contacts might worry about turf-protection, impressing others, or holding on to their own shaky position. VITO is straightforward. He/she wants to improve the company's bottom line by raising revenue, lowering expenses, or improving efficiency.

❏ **VITO's aren't necessarily the president of the company.** Focus on responsibilities, power, authority, and functions revolving around what you sell, not the title.

❏ **VITO's speak directly,** and will tend to be less patient than the rest of the business world.

149

❏ **On listening:** When you're listening to any prospect, do so as if you're hard of hearing. Visualize them, and listen as if you need to read their lips.

❏ **Have staying power.** Half of your energy in selling to VITO is in initiating the relationship. Did you know that half the fuel in the space shuttle's huge tanks is burned just to get the thing 1,000 yards off the ground?

❏ **VITO's buy from people perceived as having equal business stature.** Not necessarily title, of course, but people they perceive as professionals who can make things happen and deliver results.

❏ **You are not closing a sale.** You are applying for a job ... as VITO's partner. And just like any job interview, the more you know about VITO's situation, the more you'll shine. As I always preach, be a detective. Poke around the organization by phone. Talk to users. Question other departments. Do research in the library or on-line by computer. Sound like a lot of work? It *must* happen if you want a chance.

Get the book. Even if you're not selling to the top in an organization, the ideas are consistent with what you read in the book you're holding, and will help you in all your sales contacts.
("Selling to VITO," by Anthony Parinello, published by Bob Adams, Inc., $10.95. 1-800-777-VITO.)

Look at Every Lead as a Potential Sale

Maybe you've heard or uttered these comments regarding the sales leads at your office:

"We only get bingo cards from literature collectors."

"Most leads are from students or competitors' reps."

There is some truth in these remarks. It's frustrating to call a lead and reach an answering machine that says, *"I'm at my high school prom right now and can't come to the phone ..."*

However, the danger is that we sometimes generalize about all leads, which could cause the real gold to slip through the cracks. According to *"Sales Lead Management Made Easy,"* 45% of inquirers to industrial ads buy from *someone* within one year's time. But, sales reps typically follow up on only 13% of all inquiries, with a close rate just a fraction of that.

Scary stuff. So what's a sales person to do? Keep in mind that all it takes is one great prospect to make a series of calls worthwhile. Keep in mind you need to open a few oysters before you find the pearl. If you look at all inquiries with suspicion you will miss opportunities. Conversely, if you view every lead as your largest potential customer ever, you'll place calls with enthusiasm, sort the wheat from the chaff, and cash in big!

(SOURCE: "Sales Lead Management Made Easy," Thomas Food Industry Register, Five Penn Plaza, New York, NY, 10001)

Start at the Top, Then Work Down

When prospecting, ask for the name of the person at the highest possible level where the decision could take place. For example, if you're selling leasing services, you would ask for the name of the V.P of Finance. While speaking with that person's assistant, you could then gather additional information which would help you find the appropriate person to speak with. Plus, you're then able to drop in the fact that you've already spoken to someone in the V.P.'s office, who then suggested you speak with the new contact.

Prospecting Tips

Here are few tips I found in *Registered Representative* magazine. Although originally written for securities brokers, most are easily adaptable.

❑ **Prospect 24-Hours a Day.** If what you sell has broad appeal, don't turn off the prospecting machine when you leave the office. Robert Peddicord with Edward D. Jones in Las Vegas says that getting his car serviced or his clothes dry cleaned are just a few examples of where he has found business. "I look around and realize that almost everyone is a prospect."

❑ **Work the Good Relationships.** According to personal research data, Jeff Adelstone of Adelstone Financial says it costs a financial professional anywhere from six to 10 times more to land a new client than to hold on to an existing one. Prospect within your existing account base.

❑ **Don't Bury Dead Accounts.** Gene Gamble with Prudential Securities in Chicago asks his branch manager for the problem accounts of brokers who have left, or other accounts no one else wants to bother with. He calls, listens to their problems or complaints, and lets them know he would like to work with them. Some of his biggest accounts have come this way.

Call the Entire List

Call every name on your prospecting list. Jumping around, or prejudging based on some arbitrary excuse wastes time, and might cause you to miss that big sale.

Prospect Your Past Customers

Make a point to call one inactive customer per day. Mention the fact you've done business before, question to uncover needs similar to the ones that caused them to buy from you before, and then offer something of value. Calling 250 inactive customers in a year will likely get you FIVE TIMES more business than the same number of cold prospecting calls.

How Many Prospecting Calls Before Quitting?

A question that causes much debate is how much energy you should put into trying to reach someone before throwing in the towel. Shawn Sirgo with Intralox offered an interesting suggestion during a Telesales Rep College. He said that after three voice mails (good ones, where value is communicated), and they are still unresponsive, it's best to send a letter. Otherwise, you could be chasing nonresponders who have no intention of ever talking to you.

Works With Kids And Prospects

Shawn also mentioned a parenting technique that could be adapted to sales. He suggests pointing out the alternatives of actions available to kids, and letting them choose—within reason—the best option. For example, "You could continue throwing a fit here on the floor of the grocery store and not only cause everyone to look at you, be punished when you get home, and not get what you want now anyway, or, you can get back in the cart and we can move on."

Essentially this points out the negative implications of the present situation, and the positives of taking action (the action you want). For example,

"Mr. Customer, lets look at the options. Number one would be for you to continue with the old system, put up with the frequent maintenance calls and pricey service contract, or you could opt for the new system which would virtually eliminate maintenance and the advanced features you want. What do you think is the best choice?"

How to Get The Name

Ann Barr submitted a tip on getting the name of your prospect which could be useful with protective organizations. She suggests after identifying yourself, say,

"I'm sending information to your company about widget supplies. Who should I address that to?"

Then you can call back later to ask for that person by name (with the intention, of course, of eventually sending something).

Start at the Top, and Question

I've often written that when prospecting it's best to start at the highest level possible, then get referred to the actual decision maker and use the name of the higher-up who sent you. The theory at work is that Mr. Bigshot's name will carry clout with the underling. An add-on technique here is to ask Mr Bigshot (or his or her assistant) what role he plays—if any—in the decision-making process for what you sell. You might learn that he or she ultimately needs to sign off on decisions of that type, or they do become actively involved later in the process. This provides you an opportunity to ask questions and learn their needs, concerns, and desires. Or, you could learn that the subordinate is autonomous, which is also valuable information.

Not Asking, But GIVING an Appointment

When you want to set an appointment with a physician, they don't ask you, "When is a convenient time to come to the office?" They GIVE you a time instead. According to Dave Mather, sales people should do the same thing when setting up face-to-face visits, or even telephone appointments.

After progressing to a point in the call where asking for an appointment makes sense, Mather suggests saying,

"I have 10:15 Monday open ... will you be in your office 10:15 Monday?"

(This is much better than the goofy, *"Would 2 or 4 be better?"* technique that many sales reps begin with).

Their response then is either yes or no. If it's no, they're not turning you down, since you simply asked if they would be there on Monday morning. And Dave says here is where many salespeople lose it ... backing off or fading away, or worse, becoming indignant and pushy.

At this point, since you're not begging for an appointment—you're simply arranging a time to get together—here is a way to respond when you hear a "no," to "Will you be in your office at 10:15?"

"Well, then, is a morning generally good for you, or is the afternoon better?"

This is an appropriate time to use what's commonly referred to as the "alternate choice." You've taken the pressure off the prospect, and it gets them thinking about alternatives. They might say, "Mornings are good, but not this Monday." Therefore, you focus on coming to an agreement on a better day and time. And that positions you as the business partner you are—not some peddler desperately trying any technique he can to get an appointment.

How to Eloquently Dump a Prospect

Knowing how to move on when you realize a prospect isn't worth your time is just as important as knowing how to handle one who has potential. A positive technique—one that also leaves the door open for the future—is to explain the types or sizes of companies that are ideally suited to derive the most value from your company, and then invite them to get back in contact with you when they are in that situation. For example,

"Kathy, the companies that can show the best savings with us are those who have over 100 cars in their fleet. When you reach that point, I'd be happy to reopen a dialogue with you."

Confirming Appointments

Do you set appointments by phone for face-to-face visits? If so, by confirming the appointment you can ensure you're not left in the lobby while the decision maker—who either forgot or blew off your appointment—is elsewhere, unable to meet with you.

Nanci McCann, writing in *"SELLING!"* (1-800-621-5463), suggests writing a brief confirmation note after your phone call. She says not doing so is simply irresponsible. Showing up with no one to meet is entirely avoidable, and costs you time, money, and sales.

Here's her suggested format:

Dear John,

(Confirm the details) Thanks for taking my call today. I look forward to our meeting on DAY, DATE, TIME, and PLACE.

(Sales message) I believe my company has an excellent solution to your new package requirements that is still under budget. Can't wait to show it to you!

(Throwing ball into his court) Call if anything changes at your end. Otherwise, I'll see you as planned on DAY.

Mail, fax, or personally deliver your message. Vary the style of notes to keep them fresh, especially if you meet with the same customer or prospect often.

Also, consider sending news items, articles, or insider information you know will be of value to the person.

By confirming your appointment in writing, you immediately take charge. You leave nothing to chance. And you also put the onus on the client to get in touch with you if a change in plans is necessary. Writing is efficient. It's tangible (you both have a copy), and not open to misinterpretation.

Finally, these same ideas work even if you never leave the office for sales calls and are setting phone appointments.

Chapter 35

The Time, Place, and Method for Getting Referrals

An insurance agent called and after introducing himself, said, *"I'd like to come out and visit with you about your life insurance, and show you some of the products we have."*

After I quickly explained my coverage was more than adequate, he asked,

"Do you have any friends in your business that I could call?"

"No."

Call Analysis and Recommendation

I could spend several pages talking about his approach, which was horrible, since he gave me no reason why I should listen to him talk about "his products." Instead, I'll focus on his misguided efforts at getting referrals.

To increase your chances of getting referrals, you need to,

• ask the right people, and,

• ask in the right way.

Clearly, this guy failed on both accounts. First he asked for a referral from someone who just shot him down, then he used a question that virtually guaranteed a negative answer.

Let's analyze a much better way to maximize your chances of getting quality referrals.

Ask the Right People

Common sense tells you that people who already enjoy the benefits of what you provide are the most likely candidates to wish the same for their friends. Your happy customers can be a goldmine of sources of potential new business for you. Amazingly, this resource is vastly underutilized. In most cases, they're happy to turn you on to their friends and colleagues.

As for the insurance sales rep who called me, he had about as much of a chance getting referrals from me as an IRS agent asking me for names of friends he could audit. I'd be more likely to *warn* my friends about callers like these, callers who have only their best interests in mind.

Develop your own targeted referral strategy. Make it a point to contact your best, happiest customers, those who think you're the greatest.

Ask in the Right Way

And at the right time. Which is usually after the customer has experienced something pleasing. Remind them of how much they enjoy the results they get from what you provide, and then ask for the referral. For example,

Customer: *Thanks for getting that shipment to me so quickly. It really helped out.*

> **Sales Rep: You're welcome. Quick delivery is certainly something we pride ourselves on, and I always make a point to note that on our orders. By the way, who else do you know who has the same type of fast delivery requirements, that I could contact and discuss what we might be able to do for them?"**

Be certain that you're mentioning the benefit you deliver or the problem you help them avoid. After all, that's why they buy, and why they'll be interested in helping their friends.

Other than getting additional business from existing customers, selling to referrals from your best customers is one of the most effective, and inexpensive ways to increase your business dramatically. Consider that if 20% of your accounts bring in 80% of your business, if you can find more accounts that "look like" those high profit and volume customers, that's much more appealing than working the small ones.

Go and get those referrals, from the right people, in the right way!

Why Customers Do and Do Not Give Referrals

According to Ted Kurtz, a psychoanalyst and consultant in Cold Spring Harbor, New York, here are reasons why customers give, and don't give referrals:

Why Customers Refer

1. Some like the prestige of being asked. They view it as a compliment.

2. Some enjoy being "in the know." They feel they're viewed as the Consumer Reports of products and services.

3. They want to help you. They know your business depends on getting new business. They see you as a friend as much as a business contact.

4. They want to help their friends. They want their friends to succeed just as they have. The fact it is helping you is secondary.

Why They Don't Refer

1. Some don't want the responsibility. They don't want the responsibility of feeling their friends will hold them accountable if performance expectations aren't met.

2. Some are competitive. They don't want to give competitors the same edge they have.

3. They don't believe they can refer successfully. They feel others won't take their endorsement seriously.

4. Some are private. They don't want to get involved in others' business.

Kurtz suggests determining what type of customer you're dealing with, and using an approach that compliments them. Don't let the fear of the few who won't refer keep you from building your business through referrals.

Get Referrals from Within Their Company

If you have a customer within a company that has multiple locations, or many departments at one location, you probably haven't even scratched the surface of potential business. The hard part is beyond you—getting the company as a customer. Now that you're in the door, part of the family, ferret out other opportunities. Ask your customer,

> **"Who else within your company also uses/does _____, who could also take advantage of something similar to what we're doing together?"**

Prompt them a bit:

> **"How about other departments? Other locations?"**

Even if they come up empty, ask them,

> **"If I can find other buyers on my own, it wouldn't be a problem if I mention your name as a reference, would it?"**

Try a "Reverse Referral"

Naturally, referrals are one of your best forms of prospects. In addition to the standard way of getting referrals—asking customers for them—consider a twist: Compile the names of individuals and companies most likely to buy from you based on characteristics they share with your best customers, then get your customers' approval to use their names.

For example, let's say you sell to mechanical contractors. You get access to a list of members of a national mechanical contractors association. You isolate a few prospects based on size, geography, and so on. When speaking with your good customers you can then ask,

> **"By the way, I've targeted several members of your association as people we likely could help in much the same way we worked with you. I was wondering, do you know Joe Jones at Control Mechanical? How about Alice Donovan at Aircom Services?"**

If your customer does know them, ask permission to use his/her name. Also ask what he/she knows about them.

If the customer doesn't know them, ask for permission to use his/her name anyway, as a testimonial. Plus, you have a nice lead-in to ask for other referrals:

> **"Oh, who else do you know who you feel would benefit from our service much the same way you have?"**

Action Steps

Time
Management

Chapter 36

How to Squeeze
More From Your Day

Most of us would agree that we could sell more if we just had more time—or realistically, better control of our time. While on a plane recently, where I catch up on my mounds of reading, I came across a fine article by Dan Wallace in *"Home Office Computing"* magazine. It's called *"Do Twice as Much in Half the Time."* I've excerpted and adapted the ideas that apply to telesales.

❑ **Ask for the first appointment of the day.** Whether it be a phone appointment, or in person, it's the one least likely to start late.

❑ **Update your contact management program** and keep it current. Place a printout of your accounts/prospects by the phone, and make manual corrections on the paper when you receive mail back or otherwise hear someone has moved on. Then, when you're on terminal hold with someone, update them in the computer.

❑ **Rearrange your work space.** Use the "near-far" rule. Keep things you use frequently at arm's length, and things you don't use often far out of the way. If piles are cluttering your desk, invest in some shelves.

❑ **If you're right handed,** place your phone on your left and keep a pad and pencil nearby. If you're a lefty, do the opposite.

❑ **Use a telephone headset.** Not only does it allow you freedom of movement to express your ideas with your entire body, it also frees up your hands to clear the clutter when you're on hold.

❏ **When you have a backlog on your voice mail,** write or type the messages and delete them from your system. You won't waste time scrolling through them the next time you check your system.

❏ **Don't waste time on unproductive chit-chat,** either on the phone or with others in your area.

❏ **Use the lunch hour to return calls** that require only a short answer, or when you're posing a simple question. Many people will be away from their desks and you'll reach voice mail.

❏ **When you do leave a question on voice mail,** be specific. This way they can leave you a complete, detailed answer.

❏ **Group your calls.** Place a flurry of calls in the morning, then block out time to do the busywork created by the calls, such as mailing, chasing down answers, and so on. Do the same in the afternoon.

❏ **To discourage interruptions,** if you have an office, stick a sign on the door that says, "Important sales calls in progress." Or, hang one on your cubicle that reads, "Door closed."

❏ **Ditch low-potential prospects,** or low-performing customers. Cut your losses. You need to make the tough choices about what your time is really worth.

❏ **Associate with time-conscious,** organized, highly-motivated salespeople. The feeling is contagious, and your desire and actions to get the most from your time investment are a natural result.

(Source: Ideas adapted from an article by Dan Wallace in "Home Office Computing Magazine," 411 Lafayette St., New York, NY, 10003)

More Time Efficiency Tips

➡ **You have a lot more time than you think**. If you added up all the nuggets of idle time during the day ... the brief intervals between other activities ... you might be surprised. Take those two or three minutes of down time between activities, the four minutes of idle time before a sales meeting, the time spent on hold with a vendor or customer service, or the time you must wait for anything, and put it to use. Keep a folder close by at all times labeled "items to scan." Put in memos, newsletter or magazine articles, brief reports, anything you can devour and dispose of quickly.

➡ **Apply the ACTION philosophy** to paperwork and other tasks just as you should on your calls. This means that there should be movement after you've handled a piece of paper or project, and you're closer to your ultimate objective than you were before. Therefore, every time you read something that ultimately requires action, do something proactive with it then and there. Make it a personal rule to not handle paperwork twice unless something has happened to it in the meantime. Do it, delegate it, or toss it.

➡ **Perhaps the most ignorant statement** I've ever heard is, "I don't have time to do a lot of preparation before calls." That's like saying, "I don't have time to do it right the first time." The result is never as good as it would have been with the preparation, and always creates more work later. Call preparation helps you be more efficient on your calls, therefore getting more accomplished. If you don't have a clear idea of where you're going on a call before you place it, you'll likely wander about like a lost dog on a city street. With a focused objective you know where you want to be, and consequently, what it will take to get there.

➡ **Know when and how to say "No."** I've seen far too many sales reps who feel obligated to jump through hoops at the request of prospects who want to pick their brain, or otherwise would like obscure product information or other research done. And they do so without even knowing if they'll get something in return. As it relates to investing inordinate amounts of time with prospects, be sure they're truly worthwhile. There's nothing wrong with asking,

> **"I'll be happy to do this for you. I'm assuming you want it because this is something you're interested in, and that we'll be working together on a purchase?"**

➡ **Flush your account files.** I'm astounded by the rubbish that resides in many reps' follow-up files, some of it not even as valuable as garage sale leftovers. Read the skimpy account notes and you see a long list of comments like, *"Not ready now, check back in 6 weeks."* Simple math tells you that time you spend trying to push a two-ton rock up a hill would be better invested looking for someone you have a chance with. Set an objective for a decision of any type on your next contact with these people. Ask,

"When do you feel you'll move forward with a purchase?"

You save time on your calls, and the results are more pleasing.

Get It Done

Don't make a "to do" list at the beginning of the day. Make a "To Get Done" list. View your plans as something you'll accomplish, not as an activity you'll try to perform.

Start Another List to Better Control Your Time

Most of us have too much to do and not enough time. We jot down tasks on our "To Get Done" list, or worse, little scraps of paper that litter every place we inhabit. According to author and certified management consultant, Jeff Davidson, there's a better way. First jot down what you want to get done today. Categorize the tasks under "urgent" and "not-so-urgent." Ok, that's easy. Then, as unexpected hassles blindside you during the day, start a second list, the stuff you'll get to tomorrow (after all, it's normally the little fires that ignite during the day that steal our attention from even the best-intentioned plans, and upon close analysis, much of it truly can wait). Then, right before leaving, transfer today's unfinished business to tomorrow's list so you're back to just one list.

Is It Really Worth It?

For those of you who control who you call, do you have a "Is this worth it?" benchmark? It's a measurement you can apply, or calculation you can perform in order to decide where and how you should allocate your time.

First, you need to arrive at a dollar figure that represents a sale or account size that is worth your time pursuing or servicing. For a simplistic example, your revenue goal for the year might be $500,000. That breaks down to approximately $10,000 per week. Keeping in mind how long it typically takes to pursue and land a new customer, and the average customer's reorder rate, you know that a prospective customer must be able to represent at least $500 in sales per month in order for you to justify spending time chasing them. Otherwise, you might be investing time with a minuscule return. Therefore your "Is it Worth It?" benchmark would be a $500 monthly volume customer, or a $6000 annual customer.

This sounds simple on the surface, but not always practiced. Sometimes reps follow the path of least resistance, choosing to call prospects representing small margins, one-time sales, or low volumes. By agreeing to call back or spend time with a low- or no-potential prospect/customer, you are actually saying "no" to spending time with someone who has more potential ... someone who does meet your "Is this worth it?" criteria.

Get Obstacles Out of the Way First

Ever notice how those dreaded tasks never go away on their own if you ignore them? They set there, staring at you, reminding you of your procrastination every time you take a glance at them. This is an incapacitating habit, because every time you're reminded of what you're avoiding, it saps energy from you. You have to put additional thoughts into coming up with another irrational justification for putting it off further. Instead, start the day by tackling the tasks you'd normally dodge. Place that tough call. Write that proposal or report. By clearing it out of the way first thing in the morning you kick the day off with a success, you have a mini-burden lifted from your shoulders, and your positive momentum catapults you into your subsequent tasks.

Prepare a "Not to Do" List to Manage Time

Every time management manual will tell you to prepare a "to do" list. Harold Taylor, Editor of *"Time Management Report"* suggests that a "not to do" list is just as important. Since managing time is a "zero-sum" activity, every item of secondary importance that you pinch from your schedule frees up that much more time to be invested in revenue-generating activities. Therefore, refuse to let yourself get caught in time-wasting meetings or committees that aren't mandatory, and delegate clerical work whenever possible. Also, put this on your "not to do" list: don't chase prospects who won't commit to anything.

(FROM: "Time Management Report," 2175 Sheppard Avenue E, #310, Willowdale, Ontario, M2J 1W8. Cited in "Bottom Line Business," 55 Railroad Ave., Greenwich, CT, 06830)

More Tips

Here are some tips to help you more effectively control your time and squeeze more production out of every day.

➥ **Help people get to the point.** Those who just want to chit-chat with you are pick-pockets. They're robbing you of your ability to employ that time in a productive way. Regardless of whether they are customers, peers, or vendors, politely help them explain the reason they're talking to you:

> **"So how can I assist you?"**
>
> **"What can I do for you?"**

➥ **Talk in the past tense.** To signify the end of the call you can say,

> **"It's really been great speaking with you ..."** Or,
>
> **"I'm glad we had the chance to talk.**

➥ **Reschedule personal interruptions.** When friends call to chat, let them know you're busy, but still want to speak with them.

> **"Mike great to hear from you. I want all the details about your vacation to North Dakota. I've got some business calls I need to make here, so what's the best time tonight for me to call you back?"**

➥ **Use "Power Blocking."** Set aside blocks of 45-minute time blocks for activities, and do nothing but that during those times. For example, you might have two blocks of prospecting, and three blocks for follow-up calls during the day. This helps you focus and avoid spraying your activity in all directions.

➥ **Take the "Why am I doing this?"-test.** When engaged in a questionable activity, like stuffing envelopes, or writing a proposal to a marginal prospect, ask why you're doing it. If you can't honestly say it's either making you or the company money (or saving money), don't do it, or delegate it.

➥ **Analyze and adjust your work hours.** You might be physically present for eight hours, but how much work do you get done during that time? Perhaps by coming in a half-hour earlier each day, you can accomplish what would normally be two hours worth of work later in the day. That would be like squeezing out another ten hours worth of production per week!

➥ **Never write internal memos or E-mail again.** Got something important (and is it really *that important*, anyway?) to say to someone internally? Say it as you walk by their desk. Or call them for goodness sakes! I know, I know, some situations require that you cover your behind with a memo, but most are just plain time bandits.

➥ **Go public with your intentions.** If you must do something for someone else, commit to having it done by a certain time. Saying, **"I'll have that price quote to you by 2:00,"** forces you to get right on it and complete the task. Many people waste time by procrastinating.

➥ **Turn wait time into productive time.** If you think it's dumb to waste money, it's even crazier to waste time. After all, you'll make more money. You couldn't buy more time if you wanted to. Think of all the places you wait ... in traffic jams, at the airport, doctor appointments, mechanics, and so on. Always carry with you a file of reading or light paperwork you need to get done. Doing it during this idle wait time eases the frustration of waiting, employs that time productively, and frees up your work time for more important tasks.

➥ **Have a purpose and a plan.** No tips on time control will do any good unless you desire to be a lean time machine. Do you? And from that desire flows your plan ... your monthly, weekly, daily, and hourly plans for accomplishment. There's no magic here. It's back to the basics.

Analyze Your List

After completing your "to get done" list for the day, whip out your editing knife, and slice out one activity. Ask, "Which of these is not directly contributing to my success?"

Another Question

Ask yourself this question: "What takes up more of your time (or your staff's time) than it should?" Why? Minimize, delegate, or cut the activity.

Find a Negative Example

Think of someone who wastes a lot of time (and is likely not success-ful). Consider what they do that squanders time. Then ask yourself, "Do I do any of those things?"

Minimize the Mail

You can sell without sending out bushells of brochures and letters. But, can you sell by just sending out literature? Not much. The point is, you won't sell unless you're TALKING TO PEOPLE. Drop all non-essential activities from your day and spend more time performing the one function that puts more money in your pocket.

These Tips Aren't For "Dummies"

Jeffrey Mayer, author of the book, "Time Management for Dummies." (Order it at 312-944-4184) shared a few tips.

❑ **Review your "Master To Do" list throughout the day.** This ensures you don't spend time looking at one pile after another, trying to decide what to tackle next, getting depressed in the process, and then saying "screw it" and getting up for another cup of coffee or a chat with your neighbor.

❑ **Do the important stuff first.** That's what you're paid for. Make the bigger calls, work on the larger proposals, the more difficult projects ... all early before the inevitable little annoyances begin chipping away at you.

❑ **Don't let the arrival of e-mail messages, voice mail messages, or postal mail interrupt you.** You know that when you're engrossed in something you're on a roll. Discipline yourself. And when you do review these interruptions, sort out the items that need immediate attention and add them to your Master To Do List. The others can be left for later.

Action Steps

Self Motivation

Chapter 37

Motivational Tips and Techniques

Anyone Can Be a "Natural" With Practice and Desire

Very few top performers are "naturals," if such a thing even exists. They reach their levels through work and determination.

An important part of my life has been coaching my daughter's basketball teams, and my son's basketball and baseball teams over the years. I also work almost every week with sales professionals. Between these very diverse groups I find many parallels relating to the "game" performance of the highest achievers, which really is just the result of the work they do away from the game. Sure, there are people with some genetic gifts that allow them a head start and the ability to not have to work as hard to reach a certain level, but in the long run it's what is done with those tools that dictates the result. Desire, attitude, and hard work evens the playing field every time.

Practice = High Performance

So how much time do you spend on self-development? There is a direct correlation between practice and results.

Research reported in the *"New York Times"* stated that scientists believe that peak performance in any area, whether academic, artistic, or athletic, usually comes from those who practice the most. They cited studies including champion divers from China who had already logged as many hours of practice time by the age of 11 as their American counterparts had by 21. World-class violinists had put in 10,000 hours by the age of 20 while those at the next level down had practiced 7,500.

Quite often in seminars a recent college-grad, fresh to sales, will say, "You make it sound so easy," after I smoothly whip off an opening statement or response to a difficult question. What they see, though, is just the end result of thousands of hours of research, thought, and practice. Anyone can be smooth, after being rough first. Everyone can be better. You can too—if you want to.

Characteristics of the Top Performing Reps

Without a doubt, a common characteristic among the top performing sales reps I've seen in my years of telesales is a positive attitude.

I'm not referring to an all fluff and no substance person who simply walks around with a smile all day. I'm talking about the person who not only believes good things will happen ... *he expects them to happen.* And because of these beliefs and expectations he takes action to ensure the result. A positive attitude is more than a smile and a perky voice. It's an outlook on *every* facet of life that transforms into actions. Let's look at some ideas.

☐ A positive sales rep doesn't whine about the quality of sales leads. He either locates an alternate lead source or finds a way to manufacture sales from the existing leads, knowing that other, not-so-positive souls will moan about them and give up.

☐ A positive rep isn't devastated by a lost sale she worked hard to win, but missed out on. She learns from the experience, seeks out information regarding why the other choice was made, decides what she could have done differently (and what she will do in similar situations next time), and quickly moves on.

☐ A positive rep views every moment of each day as a ticking-away opportunity that can never be reclaimed. He recognizes time is too valuable to squander by meandering down the aisles of cubicles, small-talking with anyone who will join in.

☐ Positive reps think and act **BIG.** They expect to chase and close large pieces of business. Therefore they work from an assumptive perspective, as if they've already achieved. Then they map out their plan. They're not limited by self-doubt that ties their feet to the ground.

☐ Positive reps take every situation, especially the ones that don't go their way, and ask themselves, **"What can I learn from this?"** Negative reps always say, "Of course I was dumped on again. It always happens to me."

It's All How You View the Situation

Speaking of attitude and outlook and how it affects your sales performance, consider the story of two shoe sales managers who were assigned to develop territories in remote parts of Africa.

One came back dejected, with nothing to show for his time. His excuse: *"It's no use trying to sell down there. People don't wear shoes."*

The other returned, jubilant, with record-breaking sales. He exclaimed, "It was a salesperson's dream. No one had any shoes down there!"

So what's your outlook and definition of your territory, job, and resulting effort? Looking at it from another perspective can often give you the push to reach new heights.

Learn From Your Mistakes

We all flub up occasionally. How you deal with it is what charts your success or demise.

The great, late, college football coach, Bear Bryant, said about mistakes: "You should do three things with them. Admit them. Learn from them. Make sure they never happen again."

Dr. Martin Groder, writing in *"Bottom Line Personal"* said, "You won't learn anything from a mistake if you refuse to admit your error in judgement to yourself." You'll just commit the same mistake over and over again. Like using an opening that elicits more resistance than interest, or using a worn-out closing technique that only serves to "close" the door.

Groder offers further advice we can relate to objections: "When someone tells you you're wrong, resist the urge to defend yourself or deny that a problem exists. Assume your critic is right until he/she is proven wrong." Except, with objections we don't want to *prove* them wrong, we use questions to help them come to a better conclusion.

Motivational Ideas

Here are self-improvement and motivational ideas from Art Mortell, in his book, *"World Class Selling."*

❏ **Use "Forced Scheduling"** to push yourself into success patterns. Set before-hours telephone appointments, or brainstorming sales-idea breakfast sessions with others to build successful habits.

❏ **Exaggerate.** Take what you typically avoid, and get outrageous with the activity. If you avoid prospecting, hold a marathon prospecting day, doing nothing but cold calling. Comparatively, the one or two hours you should prospect regularly will seem like child's play.

❏ **Emulate.** Look at the people who are achieving at the levels you aspire to. Study their positive characteristics and emulate them. Don't try to *become* them, just practice their success behaviors.

(SOURCE: "World Class Selling," by Art Mortell, Dearborn Publishing, 520 N. Dearborn, Chicago, IL, 60610)

A Quick Pick-Me-Up

Ever feel down after a call? Put things in perspective. Ask yourself,

- "What humor can I see in this situation?"
- "Does this experience really affect who I am?"
- "What can I learn from it?"

Replay the Calls

Successful reps never experience failure. They always take a situation where they didn't accomplish their primary objective—the "no's"—and pick that situation apart to learn why. They therefore don't fail; they succeed at learning from the experience. Football coaches and players regularly view hours of film of previous games. Then, they work on correcting any deficient areas, and also improving their strong points. Telesales reps need to conduct a similar "replay" of their calls. Viewing "no's" as pure failure is a precursor to ultimate failure. Conversely, perceiving "no's" as a component of the learning process will lead you down the road to success.

How to Beat Call Reluctance, and Become More Positive

Want a way to beat call reluctance, start a freight train of momentum for the day, and start every day with a feeling of accomplishment? After compiling your "To Get Done" list for the day, select the most formidable, perhaps the least desirable call you need to place and start your day off with it. Make it a habit each day. You'll find that once this becomes part of your routine the remainder of the day flies by like a swift breeze, and you no longer spend time in call avoidance behavior which only brings down your attitude and production.

How to Increase Your Sales By 50%

What would you need to do in order to increase your sales volume by 50%. Think again if you said, "I need to get 50% more customers."

About 5% of your customers likely generate 50% of your current sales. So why not try to clone that 5%?

Take the top 5% of the customers you sold within the past year ... those responsible for the bulk of your sales volume and income. Ask yourself these questions:

How did you find them?

What do they have in common? (size, location, type of business, personality of decision maker)

What problems did you solve or needs did you fill that initially caused them to buy?

What else can you learn about these customers that can help you sell others just like them?

How can these existing customers help you find more customers just like them? (referrals)

Increasing your sales dramatically is probably not possible if you do the same thing over and over, because up to this point, even though you've been successful, you've spent time generating customers who don't contribute the bulk of your business. Not that those are bad customers, but to make the quantum leap, you need to replicate the larger ones.

How to Avoid Rejection

Here are some additional specifics regarding how to view situations, therefore avoiding rejection.

Instead of thinking, *"I got rejected,"* say,

"At least I received a decision."

Instead of thinking, *"They criticized my product,"* say,

"I learned something about how some people view our product."

Instead of thinking, *"I lost the big deal I was working so hard to get,"* say,

"What can I do next time to ensure this doesn't happen again?"

Instead of thinking, *"This is devastating,"* say,

"What positive can I take out of this?"

Chapter 38

View Your Fears As Absurd

Have you paged through your computer account records or flipped through your file folders while planning your day and intentionally bypassed one particular account? And did you continue doing the same thing for weeks ... maybe months?

If so, you're not alone. Many of us can trace this reluctance to fear. Fear we'll get blown off the phone. Fear we'll sound like a blubbering fool to this intimidating prospect. Fear we won't know the answers to his questions. Or, fear of *anything* for that matter. And if we do muster up just enough courage to place the call while in this state of mind, isn't it interesting how our fears become reality?

A fascinating psychological phenomenon is that the more we dwell on what we fear, the more difficult it is to forget it, and the longer it stays in our minds, imbedding its visual manifestation, ultimately turning into negative behavior.

To overcome fear, Dr. Victor Frankl, an Austrian psychiatrist, suggests that you turn fear into a ridiculous, absurd event in your mind, and then allow the natural human reaction to absurdities turn it off completely. For example, when you hear of something that is totally off-the-wall, you shrug it off, saying, "No way."

Try this: Take what is hindering your success, and exaggerate it to the extreme.

"I am scared silly of calling the Big Fish Company because my contact, Mr. Mackeral, is actually a demon with supernatural powers. He has on occasion actually transformed himself into digital signals, sending himself back through the phone lines, through the headsets of sales reps, into their ears and has attacked their brains, in most cases turning their minds into useless protoplasm, leaving their bodies slumped at their desks. In some cases, their managers couldn't tell anything was wrong for hours some cases, their managers couldn't tell anything was wrong for hours before the decaying carcasses were discovered."

Absurdities are so ridiculous the human mind immediately rejects them. And once we can ridicule our fears, these problems lose their power over us. Harvard psychologist Gordon Allport wrote that any person who can figure out a way to laugh at his problems is well on his way to solving them.

So, what's anchoring your ability to excel? Create an absurdity through which to view it, and you'll find it truly was ridiculous to begin with.

(SOURCE: "High Performance Sales Training", Lee Boyan & Rosalind Enright, Amacom books.)

More Self-Improvement Ideas

❑ Customers don't care about what you need—making a sale—they only care about what *they* need and want. So the key to increased sales is pretty clear: focus all your energy on the other person. Put whatever you want aside, and you'll find yourself naturally enjoying more success.

❑ Most people spend more time worrying about what needs to be done than actual **doing** it. Time is wasted, stress sets in, and the problem or task is still there. A motto we all should follow to get more done in less time is the theme of the old NIKE ad campaign: Just Do It! Start right now. Think about something you've been putting off. Write that letter. Make that follow-up call. Send out the price quote you might have been delaying. Complete that report. Act on the memo before it collects dust. Set those goals, and most importantly, take ACTION!

Action Steps

Chapter 39

Assumptions Usually Are Dangerous

How does that old saying go? *"Never assume, because it makes an 'ass' out of 'U' and me"?* If you're regularly making a lot of assumptions, I assure you that you're also harnessing your real potential.

I returned a call to a fellow who simply left his name (no company) on my voice mail with no other message than to phone back. His voice tone sounded as if he was suffering through a thunderous hangover, slurring words like his mouth was full of oatmeal. *"Probably a non-customer who either wants to pick my brain and not buy anything, or a salesperson who likely will end up as fodder for my newsletter; what a waste this will be,"* I thought as I dialed the number.

WRONGO.

About a minute into the call I was stunned to learn that he actually was a high-ranking decision-maker in a large company that potentially wanted to hire me to do some training. Luckily I recovered nicely to salvage the call. The experience also got me thinking about all the potentially disastrous assumptions we make as salespeople.

Assumptions are dangerous because they place you in a frame of mind where you've already made a conclusion ... one based on incomplete information. And after you've made that conclusion you likely won't go out of your way to contradict it. Worse, your actions serve to validate and reinforce the assumption.

For example, picture the rep who says, *"Oh, this list of chiropractors is no good. They don't want to talk to us, and when they do, all they want is to beat us down on price."* And whaddya know, on the very next call he gets a question on price, filters it (erroneously) through his negative mindset as someone who wants something for free, and consequently acts indignantly and loses any chance at a sale. He turns to his cubicle-neighbor and says, *"See, just got another cheapskate."*

179

Beware of These Areas

Let's look at some areas in which I see reps make assumptions.

❏ **Company names.** What do you think of when you see an individual's name followed by the word "Enterprises," or "and Associates"? Some feel it's just a wannabe business operated out of a briefcase. You can't be so sure. I've closed some big sales to substantial operations with these types of names.

❏ **Location.** This doesn't really even make sense, but reps will make crazy comments like, *"Oh, the South isn't a good territory. They're not good buyers."* Or, you might have heard this before: *"People on the East coast are rude and intimidating."* Sure enough, when they do reach a prospect who happens to have a direct—not rude— personality, they crumble, getting exactly what they expected.

❏ **A job title.** Don't assume that a "Research Assistant" can't buy from you, or that a Vice President can make the decision on her own. You still need to ask the questions to learn the buying process.

❏ **Negative call history notes from others.** If you've ever inherited the meager remains of account records from reps who've moved on, you know what I'm talking about. I've seen account notes containing, *"She's a real witch, and won't give any information."* So what would *that* do to your call preparation and attitude? View with skepticism everything negative you see in notes that weren't your own, especially if the rep was fired, or left because he wasn't doing well. After all, if he was doing superbly, he'd likely still be there, making a fortune.

❏ **Time of day, week, month, year.** *"Mornings are bad for decisions," "People are on vacation in the summer," "Everyone leaves early on Fridays,"* whine, whine, whine. Funny, I never hear these assumptive excuses from top producers. That's because they're too busy on the phone, proving the assumptions false, leaving others coughing in their dust.

If you must assume anything, let it be that this next call, and your next month will be your best ever.

Chapter 40

Find a Coach

My golf game last month had degenerated to such a low point of ugliness that I finally gave in and contacted the teaching pro who gave me a few brush-up lessons two years ago.

And within 15 minutes, by simply watching my disjointed herky-jerky swing and having me do a few exercises, he performed what I considered magic. I was once again striking blazing rockets 300 yards down the center of the fairway. Well, maybe 280 yards. Ok already, 250 yards with the wind and a good roll, and a bit to the right.

The point is, that even though I felt in my mind I knew what I should do with my swing, the muscles doing the work were saying "Huh?" The results I wanted just weren't there.

And I see the same things happening with sales professionals. Sure you can get somewhat better on your own if you have the desire, are willing to research new ideas, and put in the work on your own. But we all have those blind spots in our rear view mirror that we don't even know exist.

Therefore, to make a quantum leap, get a coach.

You should seek out the best you can find. Typically it's your manager or supervisor, or maybe it's an accomplished sales rep you respect. Ask them to review your calls—either on tape or live—on a weekly basis. If it's not a manager and you have a choice, select someone whose personality is compatible with yours and will coach in a positive, constructive way. Although the "tear 'em down, build 'em back up" style of Bobby Knight might be effective with some college basketball players, most adults wouldn't respond favorably to that type of abuse.

Why You Need Coaching

We don't know what we don't know. You might be doing something wrong and not even realize it. A friend has had similar golfing problems as mine, but had never, ever taken lessons. He said, "I don't know what I'm doing wrong, and wouldn't know how to fix it if I did."

Practice does not make perfect. Practice can be a dangerous thing. Because, if you continue committing the same mistakes, they become habits. **Perfect** practice makes perfect.

Suggestions for Productive Learning Sessions

Maximize your time together. The best use of time is to have a coach listen to tapes of calls. Dead time between calls and non-contacts can either be edited out or fast-forwarded through. (Our Recorder Link product plugs into your phone and your tape recorder, clearly taping both ends of the call. Call us at 800-326-7721 to order, or call from the handset of your fax, press "1," then select document "112" to see a brochure.)

Discuss positives, then suggested changes. When I coach—whether it be telephone calls of sales reps making over $100,000 or junior high basketball—I use the same format. Praise the person and the positive performance first to reinforce it, then make any suggestions, explain why, and demonstrate personally or give examples. After calls calls I start by asking what they liked. I then state positives I observed. Next I ask what they would have done differently. Finally I'll make my suggestions. I suggest you and your coach work something similar.

Reflect on the coaching session. Learning takes place after an event, when you ponder it and break down its components. Discuss for several minutes what you covered.

End with an action step. Be certain you receive an assignment to work on during the time between sessions.

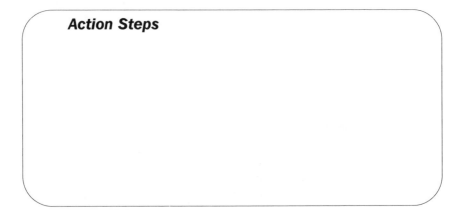

Action Steps

Chapter 41

Avoid Choking Under Pressure

If you're a golfer, you can probably empathize with Greg Norman. If you don't golf, you can relate to the experience I'm talking about, certainly on a salesperson level: Choking. Clutching up. Losing it. Going blank. The wheels falling off. A train wreck. Verbal and mental gridlock. Performance paralysis. Whatever descriptive term you choose, I'm talking about collapsing under pressure.

Greg Norman, arguably the best golfer in the world at the time, did it at the Masters in front of 100 million people in 1996. Jeff, in the cubicle down the row, did it with the prospect who would have represented two month's worth of quota.

How to Prevent Collapse

So what causes this and how can we prevent it?

Jack Stark, sports psychologist for the University of Nebraska football team, in an interview with the *"Omaha World-Herald,"* said that activities such as golf, place kicking, free-throw shooting, job interviews (and let me add, sales calls) that require a burst of activity after down time are fertile breeding grounds for negative thoughts that can cause a polished pro to turn into a Jello-legged babbling Elmer Fudd.

Self-destructive thoughts (*"Please don't hit it into the water, again, dummy," "I hope I don't say something stupid."*) cause an adrenaline rush, according to Stark, that result in 1,200 chemical changes in one-tenth of a second. He says these changes inhibit our finer thinking and natural motor activity. That means instead of just doing what we're otherwise capable of expertly and repeatedly in a role play situation, or when no one is watching at the driving range, we lose it when it counts.

So what should we do to avoid turning into Gumby when faced with money situations?

Stark teaches players a system that also works in any life circumstance. He calls it **FOCUS**, an acronym to help remember the steps.

Forget. Start with a blank sheet. The past doesn't exist. Do not, I repeat, DO NOT let negative images or thoughts enter your mind.

Organize. Get your notes, product info, whatever you need in front of you. Position your body properly.

Concentrate. Visualize the call in a positive light. See the ideal call. Hear the words being spoken—by you and the customer—as you want them to occur. Matt Oechsli, author of the "Inner Game of Selling," suggests using affirmations in the present tense: "I sell huge accounts," instead of future or wishful thinking: "I will sell this big account." And as King Soloman said, "As a man thinketh in his heart, so is he."

Unwind. Take a slow, deep breath. Loosen your shoulders.

Shoot. Dial the phone. Place the call. Don't worry about how you're going to succeed. Let it happen. Thinking about how it will happen at this point is sure to throw you off. A long-jumper doesn't think about his jump when he's in the middle of it—he's thinking about the other side, the result.

Work and Preparation is Key

Up to this point, we've talked about avoiding choking at the moment we're engaging in the activity. And all of this presupposes that we're capable of performing at the level we'd like to be. But there is no magic here. Greg Norman hits 7,000 practice golf balls per week during the off season. We must train our minds so that we know what questions we'll ask in given situations, what answers we'll provide to tough questions. So how much time do you spend on your own self-development? As Zig Ziglar says, "What you do off the job determines how well you do on the job." And that makes performing under pressure so much easier.

Chapter 42

Challenge Yourself

Quick, give two examples of how within the past month you've knowingly and willingly—or even volunteered—to enter a situation that caused you to feel scared, inadequate, challenged, anxious, or in over your head.

If you can't, you're likely not testing your limits. You're probably coasting along and not growing. (If you answered, *"I feel like that every time I place a phone call,"* you might want to reevaluate your career choice!)

Sure, it's rewarding to work so hard that you become a smooth sales rep, asking and answering questions with ease, never inserting a long *"Uhhhhh"* where words should be ... confidently and routinely handling every call. But if you start thinking you're too good to improve, ignoring what propelled you to your level in the first place, you're slipping down the backside of the mountain and might not even realize it.

The path of least resistance usually leads to mediocrity. Regardless of how good you are, to continue growing you constantly need to invite— even seek out—fresh, more difficult challenges. The scarier, the better.

Here are a few ideas for tackling new challenges and risks.

❑ **Channel your anxious feelings into positive energy.** This is critical. Worrying is an emotion that handcuffs you mentally. If you fear something, you can either let it possess you, or you can take action to control it. It's amazing how action exorcises anxiety.

❑ **Tackle your most intimidating, dreaded task right out of the starting gate each day.** We tend to put off what we fear most, then our energies turn into avoidance instead of action. This cripples our other activities.

❑ **Laugh at, but learn from your mistakes and shortcomings.** And naturally, we all experience them. Why do you think they call them "growing pains"? Just like muscles, we grow personally when we're pushed to the point of failure. Look at these instances humorously. It's said that we can look back on most every mistake and humiliating experience we've ever encountered and laugh. I chuckle at the times I experienced mind vapor-lock on past calls. But in every case the short-term pain was the motivation that compelled me to do whatever necessary to do so it wouldn't happen again.

☐ **Recall the quantum leaps you've made, and how you grew.** You walked for the first time, talked, rode a bike, and drove a car. Those were major accomplishments—at the time. Then it became second nature. Everything that is routine for you now was likely a major deal before you did it the first time. And that's also true for everything you've yet to do. Does asking for larger orders cause your anti-perspirant to kick in ... causing you to avoid asking at all? Do it more often, get some successes, make it a habit, and then it's routine. It's expected. You pooh-pooh it as no big event. And think about how proud you've felt after tackling a tough task, win or lose. I'll bet sloughing off never gave you such a triumphant feeling.

☐ **Say "Yes" to scary situations.** Don't be afraid to venture out on the highwire without a net. It's not as bad as you think. Mountain climbers say that looking at a mountain from the base can be quite intimidating, but once they're halfway up, it doesn't seem nearly as scary.

Sure, you're good, but not nearly as good as you can be. Live closer to the edge regarding your challenges. You'll be more motivated, and your growth will be perpetual.

More Motivational Tips

☐ **Recall your most motivated moments.** When were you last fired up, storming toward something you desired with the intensity of an out-of-control freight train thundering down a mountain? What were you pursuing? This gives you a clue to what you really want. Can you—and are you willing—to repeat the desire and the tactics again?

☐ **Expect to excel.** Ask winners and they'll tell you, matter of factly, that there was never a doubt that they'd achieve their lofty levels. Sure, they ran into road blocks along the way, but progress has a way of masquerading as problems, and they prodded along.

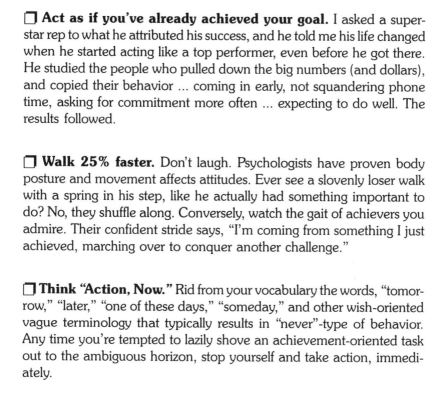

❏ **Act as if you've already achieved your goal.** I asked a super-star rep to what he attributed his success, and he told me his life changed when he started acting like a top performer, even before he got there. He studied the people who pulled down the big numbers (and dollars), and copied their behavior ... coming in early, not squandering phone time, asking for commitment more often ... expecting to do well. The results followed.

❏ **Walk 25% faster.** Don't laugh. Psychologists have proven body posture and movement affects attitudes. Ever see a slovenly loser walk with a spring in his step, like he actually had something important to do? No, they shuffle along. Conversely, watch the gait of achievers you admire. Their confident stride says, "I'm coming from something I just achieved, marching over to conquer another challenge."

❏ **Think "Action, Now."** Rid from your vocabulary the words, "tomor-row," "later," "one of these days," "someday," and other wish-oriented vague terminology that typically results in "never"-type of behavior. Any time you're tempted to lazily shove an achievement-oriented task out to the ambiguous horizon, stop yourself and take action, immedi-ately.

Become—and Stay—Motivated By Targeting Goals

You've experienced it. I have too. A slump, a rut ... one of those "Every-thing/everyone is dumping on me," attitudes.

The key to success is how you deal with it. How you get and keep yourself motivated. That's right, I said how *you* motivate *yourself.*

No one can motivate you. Just like no one can stress you out, or reject you, you alone can *allow* yourself to be affected by outside influences. There-fore it's critical—especially in this profession—that you have a never-ending plan that keeps your outlook—and correspondingly, your performance—at sky-high levels. And there's one proven way to do that consistently.

Goals.

Everything of significance that you've ever achieved was likely first visual-ized by you as a goal. Great stuff just doesn't automatically happen.

To get more motivated, and stay that way, you need targets to shoot for.

Here are tips for setting and reaching your goals and staying motivated.

☐ **Pick goals that you desire passionately.** If you just mildly wish for something you won't muster the drive to pursue it and weather the storms you'll encounter along the way. For example, if you just *wouldn't mind* dropping a few pounds, that's not strong enough. If you feel you **must** lose 15 pounds because you absolutely refuse to go up another clothes size, and you've had it with feeling sluggish all the time, you'll do what it will take to shed the excess baggage.

☐ **Pick goals you can see yourself attaining.** Before you begin, you must be able to visualize the end result. Otherwise your subconscious will never buy into the notion you can accomplish it. People never rise above their own self-perception. If you can't see yourself earning $20,000 more than you do today, you'll never get there. Conversely, if you visualize yourself already there, you'll think of what you'll need to do to actually reach your destination

☐ **Pick goals you're willing to work hard to achieve.** Everyone would *like* to make more money. A small percentage are willing to do what it takes to make it a reality. That's why lotteries are so popular. Whatever you select as a goal has trade-offs attached. Only if you're willing to toil and sacrifice will you reach that goal.

☐ **When setting your goals, remove your doubts.** Most of us fly too close to the ground. Doubts are not the result of rational thinking, but habitual thinking. Write out some of the self-limiting beliefs that are like sand-filled weights strapped to your feet, and rewrite them in a positive, possibility-thinking way. For example, *"I've never been able to close the large accounts where the big commissions are,"* could become, **"What I need to do is analyze what other people do who consistently close the large accounts, and work up my own strategy."**

☐ **Take risks.** Sure it's a bit spooky treading into territory you've never traveled, but it's also motivating. Plus, the only risks that aren't a bit scary are the ones you've outgrown.

☐ **Don't let details get in your way.** Fussing about the details burdens your thinking and fuels the fires of doubt. After setting your goal, immediately fire your machine in motion. It's easier to view the possibilities when you're moving, plus it eliminates worry. Don't worry about what happens in the middle of a jump—focus on the end.

How to Avoid Rejection And Keep Your Attitude Up

A sales rep asked me, after I had listened to a few calls (which weren't as bad as he thought), "Why am I getting rejected all the time?" My answer: "Because that's what you're viewing it as."

Only you can allow yourself to feel rejected. No one can reject you. We all have standards we use to measure ourselves. Most people are way too liberal when defining rejection (therefore they tend to avoid the behavior that causes it—calling), and much too conservative when measuring success. Loosen up your collar a bit, step back, and consider a few ideas I'll comment on from Frank Grazian, Executive Editor of *"communication briefings."*

➡ **"Find rewards in the process of doing your job."** Don't be infatuated just with your end result. Enjoy the moment-to-moment absorption in the activity of talking to, and helping people. I remember years ago when I was on the phone eight hours a day, talking to 40 different people, in various industries. It was a gas just learning about so many unique businesses and their needs.

➡ **"Take pride in how well you do your job."** Strive for, and expect excellence, but also take a time-out occasionally to soak in what you've accomplished along the way.

➡ **"Avoid depending on others to tell you how well you're doing."** Let's face it, no one is told enough how much they're appreciated, how good they are, and how much they're loved. (And most of us are guilty of not doling out the accolades as well.) Therefore, if your depends on stated public approval from others, you grant them immense power over you and your attitude—and it makes you vulnerable to gut-wrenching disappointment if you don't get it. Develop an internal set of checkpoints to guide you. When you reach them, reward yourself. Bathe in the shining light of your accomplishment.

➡ **"Understand how your sales efforts contribute to a greater good—the need-fulfillment of others**." People only buy from you because the results you deliver help them. Look at your ten largest accounts, and dwell on what buying from you really means to them in terms of profits or other results. (If you can't answer this, you've got some serious questioning to do during your sales process.)

➡ **"See yourself as a problem-solver.** If not, you'll be stymied every time you run into an objection.

➡ **"Don't be afraid of risk, and potential setbacks."** Robert Schuler asks, "What one great thing would you do if you knew you could not fail?"

(Ideas were adapted from communication briefings, 700 Black Horse Pike, Blackwood, NJ, 08012)

Action Steps

Case Study Examples

Chapter 43

What to Say When They "Buy it Locally"

Mona Roth with CBS Inc. in St. Louis called me about a specific situation she encounters, as do many of you: the objection, "We prefer to buy it locally."

The details: CBS Inc. sells supplies such as ink and other copier items to quick print shops nationally. Her products are usually the very same brand the printers buy locally. The owner of the shop is typically the decision maker (many are Ma and Pop operations).

Reasons for Resistance

As with any objection, I started by asking Mona why she feels the buyers say, "We prefer to buy locally." She narrowed it down to three primary reasons:

1. Fear of not buying from the manufacturers of the equipment. The printing press and copier companies apparently have trained the owners into believing that unless they purchase their supplies from the manufacturers, they might have a problem with the terms of their service contract (or the service person will give non-buyers last priority when scheduling repair calls). Mona says that by law, manufacturers can't force the buyers to use their supplies or treat them differently if they don't buy. She indicated she usually answers this one without a problem.

2. Keeping the Money Local. An honorable, but somewhat illogical reason, as we'll point out later.

3. Habit. Print shop owners are just like you and me. They get in a habit and it's easier to continue it than change it. And part of buying locally means they're in the habit of buying something only when they need it and having it delivered the same day or the next. Naturally, they're also paying for the convenience. This is the one she has the most trouble with.

With these reasons established we looked at the next step: determining what value Mona's company, CBS Inc., offered. What is it that these buyers want, what do they want to avoid, and how could CBS provide it?

We came up with two main points.

1. One-stop buying solution. Local suppliers are often quite limited in what they can provide, compared to a larger, national company like CBS. Therefore, the printers who buy locally must typically deal with several vendors for different items. That means taking time to place orders, receive orders, handle multiple invoices and checks ... which all takes valuable time. CBS' existing customers like the fact they can get it all from one source, saving time that can be re-employed more profitably.

2. Price. CBS can offer lower prices on virtually all items. It's pretty clear: they can save the printers money.

With our background preparation done, now it's time to plug it all into the objection-answering scenario, and brainstorm responses and questions.

1. Isolate the Objection
Prospect: "We prefer to buy locally."

> **Caller: "I see. So what you're saying is that your preference for buying from companies in your own city is the reason why you haven't considered using us yet?"**

2. Get them Talking, Find Out Their Reasoning
> **Caller: "Let's talk about that. What is it about buying locally that you feel strongest about?"**

If they say, "We like to keep the money in our local economy," we'll want to point out it's **costing** them profits. They're giving away money they could indeed keep in the local economy—in their *own* bank account. Continue with,

> **"About how many cases do you buy per month?"**

Mona said they typically can beat most local vendors' prices by $4 per case. On average, most printers buy four cases per month. Find out specifically, then point out their loss.

> **"Bottom line, it looks like you're paying almost $200 per year more just to buy locally. I guess the question now becomes whether you want to contribute to the profits of your vendors, or keep that $200 yourself, which would be pure profit. So really, you would keep that money local, in your own account by buying from us."**

Or, put it in terms of what that lost profit is costing them:

> **"That's almost $200 per year extra you're spending.**

193

And don't look at it just as $200 in revenue; how many of your average print jobs would you have to do to generate $200 in profit?"

A Different Response

Let's explore what we would do if they told us, "We like the convenience of buying from someone down the street so we can get it quick."

Again, run the numbers, and help them come up with their missed profit. Other possible questions could deal with the time they spend on their last-second purchasing practices, and dealing with multiple vendors.

"How often does that happen?"

"How often do you have to hold up rush printing jobs while you wait for supplies?"

"How many different vendors do you have to handle paperwork for and write checks to each month?"

Based on the answers, you could come up with a recommendation similar to,

"Would it be possible for you to anticipate your needs, consolidate your orders, or buy two at a time instead of one so you're not in a bind, so you can take advantage of the extra profits, and save time ordering and when paying your bills?"

As with most objections, we need to understand them, and figure out how to ask questions to deal with them conversationally. We've just scratched the surface of possibilities with this one. Take time to do this with your own.

Action Steps

Chapter 44

Selling Books in Bulk by Phone

You might have heard of the book, *"The Wealthy Barber,"* (Prima Publishing), a best-selling financial self-help book written by David Chilton in an entertaining, "novel" form. Rosanne Johnstone handles Special Sales of the book—bulk copies to companies such as mutual fund and brokerage firms who would distribute the book to clients as a show of goodwill to educate them, with the hope of them investing more as a result.

Rosanne asked for assistance. She sent me a copy of her script and the package of materials (book, letter, other promotional stuff) she pre-mailed to lists of prospects at mutual fund companies.

Here is the initial script:

"Hi ... It's Rosanne Johnstone, I'm calling from The Wealthy Barber Distributors. I'm calling to follow-up on the package we sent to you a few weeks ago. It included the book, The Wealthy Barber and a Wealthy Barber Calendar."

"Do you remember receiving it?"

"Have you had a chance to review the material or read the book?"

IF YES

"How did you like it?" OR *"What did you like best about the book?"*

IF NO (they didn't remember receiving it)

"Who tends to distribute your funds?"

(Based upon the answers here, there are just a couple more questions, and then suggestions as to how the various groups could use the book, and then an offer for bulk copies of the book, and several attempts at a close.)

Analysis and Recommendation

Rosanne told me that her boss didn't believe in cold calling, so they sent out the material to the cold list to warm up the call. The problem she discovered was that many of the people she called were not the correct decision makers. Quite a costly proposition considering the quality and quantity of materials she sent prior to knowing anything about the company. (By the time I spoke with Rosanne, she had figured this out, and corrected the problem by first sending a lead-generating post card offering a copy of the book to interested prospects, which was working quite well. For the purposes of our discussion, we'll discuss a phone approach that would work as well.)

My suggestion is to call *before* sending the material. In addition to getting the real decision maker's name, collect as much information as possible from other people. For example, she'd find out about the mutual fund company, who they sell through, what type of sales support they provide their distributors, and other relevant information. If questioned as to why she needs the information, she could use a benefit-oriented justification:

> **"We distribute a best-selling financial book that mutual fund companies provide to their dealers to help generate fund sales, keep their name in front of clients, and ultimately strengthen client relationships. I wanted to learn more about your fund company to determine how appropriate this might be for National Funds."**

This sleuth-like approach gathers valuable info that can be used on the call to the decision maker.

Mail-Call vs. Call-Mail

A strategic decision needs to be made at this point. Mail first, then call the decision maker, or call back later, then mail? My opinion is to call first. Better yet, save time and ask to speak with the buyer while still on the information-collection call. Here's why.

1. An unsolicited mail package arriving at the door of a busy executive competes for his/her attention not only with every other unsolicited package, but with all of the other important day-to-day distractions such as urgent mail, faxes, e-mail, phone calls, whining employees, cranky customers, and demanding bosses. Many of us believe that when we send out that letter we crafted so diligently, it's unconscionable why someone wouldn't camp out nights by their phone waiting for our call—if they didn't call us first. Get real. Obviously, when you detach yourself emotionally from your creation and think about it objectively this is why asking *"I sent you a* *letter/package, didja get it?"* is so inane.

2. By calling first, you can prequalify the prospect, generate interest, move the sales process forward, and when you ultimately do send the material, you can prepare them for what they'll receive, building anticipation in the process. There are several by-products of this approach:

- you don't waste time and money mailing to people who have no need or interest;

- you have a great reason for placing follow-up calls (assuming your initial call went well), and,

- your package rises above the clutter.

The Opening

Because the call is unsolicited and therefore is also competing with all of the other factors mentioned earlier, we need to be sure it seizes attention instantly and buys the right to move to the questioning (which by the way, are the two objectives of an opening statement).

I asked Rosanne for the primary result/benefit buyers would realize from getting bulk copies of this book. She said increased business for the fund. When the fund company distributes the book (with the fund's name on an attached sticker) they would keep their name in front of the broker/planners who sell the funds, and provide them with a useful tool they could provide their end-clients, increasing the business of the broker/planner. So let's weave that into an opening. It would be similar to the justification we used earlier to help us get information.

> **"Mr. Fund, I'm Rosanne Johnstone with The Wealthy Barber Distributors. We specialize in helping mutual fund companies by providing a resource to their dealers and brokers that generates fund sales, keeps their name in front of the brokers, and also helps the brokers ultimately strengthen *their* client relationships. *(pause)* We distribute a best-selling financial book with high perceived value, and I'd like to ask you a few questions to see if this is something that could be a fit with your dealer communications."**

Questioning

Rosanne felt she wasn't asking enough questions, and I agreed. After all, we're not selling one copy of a book here, therefore it can't be peddled like the magazine solicitation calls we receive at home. The key is in getting the buyer to believe several things:

- that they need to increase their fund sales, and maintain and enhance their relationship with their broker planners;

• providing resources to broker/planners is a way to accomplish that, and,

• that *"The Wealthy Barber"* book would be a way to accomplish that, and that the investment in the books would return more than the expense.

Then, and only then would a presentation have the greatest chance at being viewed favorably. It makes all the difference between throwing the long bomb for the touchdown, or simply punching the ball into the endzone from the goal line.

Action Steps

Chapter 45

Avoid Telling Prospects What to Do

My assistant, Tricia, announced. "It's someone from Forbes magazine on line one,"

"Cool," I thought. "They're calling to let me know I've made their list of America's Richest, like my buddy, Warren Buffett (well, maybe not buddy, but we live in the same city).

Realistically, I thought—and hoped—they were calling to give us some publicity. I get calls all the time from niche publications like Waste Water Times looking to reprint our sales tips. But this was big time. Maybe Forbes wanted to do a story on "Telesales: The Real Big-Dollar Career Choice of the Future."

The rep started, *"Hello, this is _____ with Forbes magazine. Are you familiar with us?"*

I didn't know whether I should play dumb and say, "Hmmm, Forbes, I do recall seeing it at the club," or replying with a resounding, "Of course!" I chose the latter.

"I'm calling today to let you know about a special subscription offer to Forbes. Do you read the magazine?"

My excitement quickly deflated. "Yeah, I pick it up on airplanes, and I fly frequently, so I read it pretty regularly."

"Well, I want to tell you how you can get your own copy."

"Let me save you some time. My postman has to wear one of those lumbar-support straps to lug all the periodicals I get every month, and I'm lucky to get through the ones I must read, and that is not including the online stuff I peruse. Since I do read *Forbes* now, at my leisure, I don't need my own subscription."

"Well," he replied, *"if you were to only read one or two magazines per month, one certainly would have to be Forbes."*

That went over like a steak dinner at a PETA convention.

"Who are you to tell me what I should be reading?! You don't know a thing about me!"

Unfazed, he continued, *"Every issue, Forbes magazines gives you ..."*, and I could almost hear him paging through the screens on his "Objections Rebuttal" script. What a joke.

"Hey, save it," I told him. I've got to go read some magazines." (Couldn't resist.)

Analysis

This guy's wheels started falling off when he didn't question me more, and instead stuck to the rigid script he had in front of him. (I'm sure the list they had wasn't just of a bunch of schmoes off the street. How does Forbes— or its service agency—expect to live up to the image its magazine creates by having callers **read** from scripts?)

He should have asked questions in response to my statement, "I read it on the plane ..."

He could have gotten me thinking about why I liked the magazine:

> **"Oh, what features do you normally turn to in the magazine?"**

> **"How do you use it?"**

> **"How often would you say you're not getting to see a copy?"**

Then he could have picked up on the answers to get me thinking about my good feelings of the mag. Then, his best chance would have been to tailor a presentation of benefits. For example,

> **"Based upon what you told me about the value you're getting from Forbes, particularly in the areas of ____, I've got a special offer for you that will ensure you have that information delivered to you regularly, so you never miss it."**

Instead, he prematurely fast-forwarded into his pitch: *"Well, I want to tell you how you can get your own copy."*

And the worst of all his evils, telling me what I should be reading! It's an insult, and a sign of ignorance. No one likes to be told what to do by people they don't respect.

The lessons here,

❏ pick up on prospects'/customers' comments in order to question more deeply,

❏ use that information to make your recommendation,

❏ never use the inane statements, *"Well of course you should be doing this ...",* unless someone asks you for, or pays you for your opinion.

Action Steps

Chapter 46

A Prospecting Call That Should Have Never Been Placed

The pink message slip said to call "Patti with Printing Services." Hmmm, a prospect wanting to buy something from me, or a salesperson? I returned the call.

"Hi Patti, it's Art Sobczak with Business By Phone, returning your call."

Silence ensued, then, in a tone used by kids caught with hands in the cookie jar she giggled nervously and said, *"Who are you with again?"*

After I repeated my company name, she said, *"Well, I was cold calling and got your name somewhere ... OK, well, I'm a new salesperson and was cold calling and would like to come in and talk to you about your printing needs and what we can do."*

"Why?"

"Why what?"

"Why should I talk to you?"

"Well, do you do any printing?"

"All kinds of printing."

"Sounds like I should come out and talk to you."

"Sounds like you need some of my training materials on prospecting."

Error Analysis

It's sad. I've got to be typical of business owners and decision makers getting calls like these. No wonder people already have a negative attitude when they answer the phone, suspecting a telephone salesperson. Let's pick this thing apart to highlight the errors.

❏ **Leaving a Haphazard Message Without Preparation for a Result.** The sales rep wasn't prepared for the return call, and didn't remember me. Therefore she fell into a gaping hole within the few seconds of the call.

☐ **Awful Opening.** *"Well, I was cold calling and got your name somewhere ..."* Give me a break! Boy, that made me feel special.

She further compounded the dreadful opening with, *" ... like to come in and talk to you about your printing needs and what we can do."* Skimming through just the local Yellow Pages I notice about seven pages of printers. Because she happened to dial my phone number didn't seem like enough justification for me to consider her any differently from the hundreds of other printers locally and thousands nationally that I'm not using. Bottom line, there was no reason to stay on the phone with her, much less *meet* with her.

Recommendation
Seems like I'm always repeating myself when I analyze this type of call. Here goes again.

☐ **Get Information First.** A few simple questions of my assistant would have garnered her some great information about the types, amounts, and frequency of printing we do, and probably what we pay. An easy way to position the gathering of this information is,

> **"To determine if what we do would even be worth talking to him about, there's probably some information you could help me with first."**

The subsequent message (voice mail or written) then could be highly tailored to my situation.

☐ **The Call Back Message.** The caller could have left this one:

> **"I understand you do quite a bit of direct mail, and depending on what your plans are for the next several months, we might have an opportunity to help you save money because of some recent price discounts on paper ..."**
> (I made that up—although it always seems paper prices are either going up or down. Nevertheless, some type of interest-creating point needs to be there.)

And then, she must be prepared to instantly recognize everyone for whom she left messages.

❑ **The Opening.** The purpose for the opening is twofold:

1. put the listener in a positive, receptive state of mind, and,

2. move to the questions.

You don't, I repeat **don't**, want to ask for a decision or an appointment here. It's too early. I would have listened to something like,

> **"Art, I'm Patti Stevens with Printing Industries. I understand that you do quite a bit of direct mail, and typically have some big marketing projects around the first of each year. Depending on your plans and types of pieces you send, we might have ways to help you lower your costs, while increasing your quality or even the quantity in some cases. If I caught you at a good time I'd like to ask a few questions ..."**

It's foolish for a sales rep to ask for an appointment within the first 10 seconds on a pure cold call, especially when they don't know how qualified the suspect is. A purchasing manager at a client company told me he agreed to let a sales rep who sold rolls of steel meet with him. When the rep got there, he said, *"Well, I sell rolls of steel, how do you use steel?"*

The purchaser said, "I don't use rolls of steel."

The rep left, having just wasted a good percentage of the day.

It seems so simple: have a customer-oriented reason for calling, one they likely would have some interest in hearing. Communicate it succinctly, and at least you'll have a chance to get to the questioning.

Action Steps

Chapter 47

Preparation Always Pays

T he caller started out with, *"I'm with Cherry Communications, and I have your name on a list here as a telemarketing service company. Is that right?"*

"No, we're not."

"So what do you do there?"

"What do you do, and what are you looking for?"

"Uhh, we're in the long distance business. We sell T-1's, stuff like that?"

"Uh-huh. Well we're a sales training resource company that helps people sell by phone more effectively."

"Oh really? (laughter) How am I doin'?"

"Do you really want to know?"

"Sure!"

"First, I wouldn't start out a call by saying, 'I have your name here on a list ...' Especially when it's bad information."

"Oh, so have some fluff or somethun at the beginning, right?"

"No. Not fluff. Something of potential value that would give me a reason to spend time with you."

"Yeah, well, you don't want to sound rehearsed."

"No, you've got to sound conversational, but you still need to have something prepared ..."

"Like I said, you're saying you need some kind of phony line at the beginning."

Ahhhhhg! This guy was hopeless.

Analysis and Recommendation

Let's look at just a few of the mistakes this guy made in just the span of a couple of minutes.

❏ *"I have your name on a list ..."* Now **that's** personalizing a message, isn't it? (And it was erroneous to boot!) I say this repeatedly, only because it works: get information before talking to the decision maker. If your information is bad—or if you have none—get educated by someone other than the buyer, because the tuition is steep with him ... it costs you any chance of a sale.

❏ *"So what do you do there?"* Ditto the previous comment on getting information. What really torques me, though, is when people like this call and assault you with questions before even hinting at why you should answer. That's why I turned it around so quickly to get him to explain his purpose.

❏ *"Fluff."* Is that what a good, solid, prepared opening is?

❏ *"You don't want to sound rehearsed."* What does *that* mean, anyway? If you rehearse, you sound natural. So doesn't sounding rehearsed mean you sound conversational? He probably meant "canned." I'd like to think he believes preparing for a call is better than winging it—but I doubt it.

Do your homework, on the phone and off, and prepare your results-oriented opening so well that it "sings," and you're certain to move to the questioning (with them in a positive frame of mind) a high percentage of the time.

> ### *Action Steps*

Chapter 48

Get to the Point Quickly With the Opening

M ichael Moore works as a sales support rep for Graphic Controls, selling consumable medical supplies such as cardiology chart paper and electrodes. Michael's job is to work with established accounts to regain lost business or stimulate additional business in particular product lines. He also works closely with an outside field rep.

The following is an opening statement that Michael sent me for suggestions.

"Good morning Sally, my name is Michael Moore from Graphic Controls, how are you doing today? Great.

"I work along with your local representative, Mark Goodman, as a Sales Support rep. My primary job is to help Mark's district by calling on hospitals that currently purchase products from Graphic Controls and talk with them about consolidating vendors on a by-department basis. My secondary job is to be available for customer questions and concerns with an 800 number that goes directly to my desk.

"Sally, Graphic Controls is now an ISO 9001 registered manufacturer and distributor of recording charts and electrodes which means that we have an ongoing process to ensure the quality of our products to our customers. What I would like to do today is ask you some questions about the products you are currently using from other vendors and then I will send you equivalent product samples for you to evaluate. How does that sound?

"Just to let you know, the pricing you will receive will be discounted because you are already buying from Graphic Controls."

Analysis and Recommendation

To clarify, these calls are going to existing customers, and they are familiar with their outside rep. The purpose here is to get them to compare Graphic Controls products with some of the competitive products they're using now.

My first reaction to this opening was that is was rather lengthy, a bit too formal, and really doesn't address what the customer really wants anyway: getting the best performing product at the best price. After all, they don't care that Mark's job is to talk with hospitals about consolidating vendors. And although getting into the ISO 9001 stuff about quality control might be a real bonus later on, it clutters things up now.

My suggestion here was simple: after the intro and saying he works with Mark Goodman,

> " ... **and because you are now buying** (whatever they're getting) **from us, you're also authorized to receive discounted prices on other items we carry that you're likely buying from other vendors. I'd like to ask you a few brief questions, and then send you out equivalent samples for evaluation.**"

The Result

Michael faxed back a revised opening with these suggestions incorporated, and then listed the remainder of his plan on the call, which was very good:

❑ ask questions about current products, likes, dislikes, etc.,

❑ based upon the answers, explain the benefits of appropriate Graphic Control products, and mention that literature and a quote will be enclosed with the samples, and then ask,

> **"Sally if these products perform well, and the prices of our products will save your department money, will you switch to us for these items?"**

If "yes," he then proceeds with explaining when the samples should arrive, discussing the details of the next contact.

If "no," then he needs to find out why through further questioning. This is a very smart move, since it's silly to mail samples out haphazardly like someone throwing candy to the crowd from a parade float. This way, you've received commitment they will evaluate the samples with the intention of buying.

I do have a couple of other recommendations. It would be good to determine specifically upon what criteria they'll judge the samples. If someone says, "Yeah, we'll take a look at it," their judgement might be based upon how they feel that day, or maybe they'll use a comparison that isn't truly accurate. Let's help define the rules, in advance. Ask,

> **"Sally, what do you typically look for when you test a sample?"**

Or simply ask,

"How will you determine if you like it?"

Listen for the answer, and then help them:

"How important is _____ to you?"

Naturally this question would focus on an area of strength for you.

And finally, get a time frame for the evaluation and next contact. This not only firms up their commitment to do the evaluation, it also attaches a time frame to it: Ask,

"Sally, when do you feel you'll have the evaluation done, so we can arrange a convenient time to speak again?"

Action Steps

Chapter 49

A One-Call Close Example

I received a request to review a sales presentation from Loren Kofsky, a trainer with Software of the Month, a service that provides just loads of quality shareware every month to its members. Loren sent a copy of their opening, and the main presentation part of the call.

The opening started with,

"Hello, is Mick Jagger available? I'm Seymour Stalls with Software of the Month Club. I have you listed as having an interest in computer software. The reason for my call is that I have something here that could potentially help you save a lot of time and money. If I've caught you at a good time I'd like to ask you a few questions about how you use your computer to see if this would be of any value to you, OK?"

Next there are some basic qualifying and need-uncovering questions, and then a presentation that explains the program, offer, and then attempts a close.

Analysis and Recommendation

Here were my suggestions to Loren:

Instead of *"I have you listed,"* which can come across as cold, and could create the image of someone simply calling zillions of people from a list, I suggest trying something a little more personal:

> **"I understand you have an interest in computers and soft-ware ..."** (maybe pause at this point).

Or, let them know HOW you know about their interest, which is based upon the list you've obtained:

> **"I understand that you just purchased a new note-book computer and you also have an interest in soft-ware ..."**

Regarding the "save you time and money," (which can come across as trite; see the material later in this chapter for alternatives) is there anything else that can be added or changed to dress this up a bit? For example,

> **" ... and depending on your specific interests, and how you normally get your software, I have something here that could potentially help you get more of the types of software you have interest in, while saving you the time of looking for it, and reducing what you normally spend for it."**

Then I suggest using the last sentence in the original opener, which is very good.

As for the main presentation, I suggest always tailoring your benefits to what they tell you in the questioning. That's what gives presentations so much more impact.

"We'll Save You Time and Money." Yeah, Right.

Everyone says they can save time and money. And it's not very effective.

"But wait, Art," you might be thinking, "Isn't that what you always say? To have a benefit/results statement in an opening?"

Yes, you should. You must—if you want to start out with an open-minded prospect who willingly participates in a conversation as opposed to one who shifts into his let's-get-rid-of-this-pest mode. But the phrase "save you time and money" has become as hackneyed as "How are you today," and therefore doesn't carry much weight. Problem is, it doesn't conjure up a picture and feeling of the end result the prospect is looking for. My feeling is that the phrase actually causes the listener to think, "Uh-oh, a salesperson. Let's see how I can get rid of him."

Therefore, your job is to get creative. To come up with jazzy, unique, mental picture-painting, emotion-stirring words that semi-hypnotize the listener into a state of mind where he's thinking about the potential result. You need to be descriptive and tailor your phrase to the situations he encounters—ones you can help with.

For example,

➡ instead of *"save you money,"* a sales rep might say,

> **" ... and we might be able to help you reduce the amount you spend every month on interest and penalties."**
>
> Or, " **... help you cut down on the expenses for short-run printing jobs."**

➡ Instead of *"help you increase sales,"* consider,

> " ... **help you get new customers, and keep them buying from you.**"

➡ Instead of *"save you time,"* think about,

> " **... reduce the number of hours your staff now spends on manually researching rules and regulations.**"

At your next sales meeting have reps describe the physical pictures and emotional feelings customers experience when they have the problems you solve, and also their feelings after you solve them. Then work on ways to creatively describe them.

Action Steps

Create Call Script relative to reducing expenses related to what correspondences send to internal & users customer - process for adoption. →

Chapter 50

Examples From a Well-Prepared Call Guide

I thought the huge packet of material I received from the Sheraton Colorado Springs was unsolicited direct mail, like I often receive from hotels approaching me to hold the Telesales Rep College at their location.

Wrong. (I'm glad I opened it!)

It was page upon page of opening statements, questions, and sales presentation ideas sent for evaluation by Gibson Hazard, Manager of Business Development. Pick out and adapt the ideas you could use in your calls.

First, a brief background. The sales reps at the Colorado Springs Sheraton call on meeting planners with the purpose of booking meetings, conventions, and sleeping rooms at the hotel.

Call Objectives

Let's start at the beginning, with the call objectives. Gibson listed three.

Primary Objective: (what to accomplish, at minimum) speak with the meeting planner, determine if Colorado Springs would be possible as a future meeting site, and learn when that meeting would be.

Ultimate Objective: (what to accomplish, ideally) to collect all the facts on a specific meeting, and persuade the planner to accept a proposal for it.

Secondary Objective: (the fallback position) get as many meeting planner referrals, with permission to use the contact's name.

Opening Statements

The sales reps call on leads from a variety of sources.

Lead from Newspaper Article

"Mr./Ms.____, I'm ____ with the Sheraton Hotel in Colorado Springs. I just read in ____ that you will be (fill in with nature of news item, i.e. building a new facility, holding a convention, etc.) in Colorado Springs. Congratulations! The reason I'm calling is that we specialize in providing (market type, industry) with meeting space and hotel accommodations with great service at an affordable cost. (pause) When do you anticipate needing hotel accommodations for your Colorado Springs project?"

Related-Situation Opener

" ... the reason for my call is that we were able to help the (related market type with a satisfied history) with their extremely successful (meeting type), and help them come well within their budget, and we might be able to help you enjoy similar results. (pause) Please tell me, what upcoming meetings/conventions do you feel would fit the Colorado Springs area?"

Cold Call Outside of Colorado Springs

" ... we specialize in helping (market/industry-type) hold successful conventions and meetings in a beautiful Alpine setting, with the comforts and amenities of a truly World Class city, all at an affordable cost. I'm calling to discuss the upcoming meetings you have to determine if we might be able to help you get similar results."

Questioning

And the next step, naturally, is to get them talking, in order to first qualify them, learn their requirements, and hot buttons. These are just a sampling of the questions used after the prospect is qualified.

"When are you accepting proposals on this meeting?"

"Who besides yourself will be involved in the decision process?"

"When are you looking at doing the site inspections for this meeting?"

"When will you make the final decision on the hotel

you'll use?"

"What are some of the most important factors you'll consider when choosing a city and hotel for your meeting?

The Sales Message

After sufficiently identifying and developing needs and interest through questioning, it's time to present benefits of how the Sheraton could fill those needs.

A. Transition: "Based upon what you told me, I believe we would be a perfect fit for help you put on the successful meeting you're visualizing."

B. Paraphrase their needs: "Let me be sure I have a good understanding of your situation (review hot buttons, meeting dates, and decision dates). Is that all correct?"

C. Bridge to recommendation. Present at least three benefits.

> **"Let's look at ...** (present feature/benefit they're interested in, and then trial close). **How does that sound to you?"** (Continue with a couple more.)

D. Make a summary statement, painting a word picture of them coming to Colorado Springs, enjoying the hotel and benefiting from it.

E. Commitment question. "May I go ahead and send you a proposal today for your meeting?"

Here are a few other tips I pulled from the material.

Question to Ask if they are Only Lukewarm, and Simply Asking for Literature: "I'd be happy to send you information. Let me ask you, assuming you like what you see, what is the probability that you would accept a proposal from us at that time?"

Decision Question: "If you were to make the decision right now, do you feel you have enough information from me to do that? What would that decision be?"

Of course, these are just pieces of the picture, and they still need to be delivered in the right way, at the right time. But a pretty nice job overall!

Chapter 51

Beware of
Fuzzy Phrases

For many years I've warned sales people to watch out for—and clarify—"fuzzy phrases." On one of my own calls I heard a number of these which was the impetus for this chapter. (Fuzzy Phrases are statements that on the surface can give either a positive or negative impression, but upon close examination say absolutely nothing. For example, "We'll give it some consideration, and then we'll go from there." Or, "There's a possibility for the future. We'll get back in touch.")

On an initial call with a prospect who inquired about training, I had done a thorough job of qualifying, questioning, and presenting. This guy and his company seemed for real. He told me he was the main decision maker, was sold on doing an in-house training program based on our conversation, and would take a proposal to the president with his recommendation that they move forward with it. He led me to believe there would be no problem getting approval. (Ever have the feeling some things are just *too easy?* I had that suspicion here.)

The Suspicion Came True

On my follow-up call, he abruptly said they've decided to "hold off" (a great fuzzy phrase itself). He gave an excuse about it "not being in the budget," which I always read as a cover-up for some other reason. Then he tried to scoot me off the phone with more fuzzies:

"Put me in your follow-up for a few months down the line and we'll see what happens."

"Time will tell."

"It's one of those things."

He was as evasive as a butterfly in a windstorm in response to my attempts to decode the "not in the budget" statement.

Then I tried to clarify the other fuzzies.

"When you say *'time will tell,'* does that mean you are still committed to doing this training, but for some reason it can't take place for a few months?"

"When you say *'it's one of those things'* what are you referring to?"

This guy was as slippery as a wet bar of soap. He continued ducking the issue by uttering additional abstract answers.

Getting frustrated at this point, finally realizing I needed to shift to my secondary objective and salvage something from the call by getting a commitment for the future, I directly asked him,

"Do you feel, realistically, that you will ever do this training with me?"

"Like I said, time will tell. You can check back with me in a few months to see what develops."

Recognizing I had done everything I could, still coming up empty, I responded,

"Let's do this instead. If something does change with your situation, you call me, since I'm confused as to why I'd be calling other than to check the status of your situation. If things 'do develop,' I'll be happy to continue our discussions."

Like Kenny Rogers said, "You've got to know when to hold 'em, and when to fold 'em."

Other Fuzzy Phrases And Responses

Fuzzy Phrase: "Let's stay in touch."

Response: "Great idea. So you eventually plan to move forward with this? When?"

Fuzzy Phrase: "We'll give it some consideration."

Response: "Great! Which aspects will you weigh most heavily?"

Fuzzy Phrase: "I'll look it over and we'll go from there."

Response: "Upon what criteria will you base your decision?"

Fuzzy Phrase: "I'll bounce the idea around."

Response: "Good. Does that mean you personally are sold on it?"

Chapter 52

A Call Destined
For Failure

My assistant, Tricia, answered the phone, and requested the caller's name and company as always. She announced the call to me, and since the name wasn't immediately familiar, I didn't know if it was a customer, prospect, or salesperson. It turned out to be a sad excuse for a salesperson.

First, upon accessing the flashing line, I was greeted with the caller already talking—very loudly—obviously to someone else in his area. After waiting for a pause in his sentence, I interrupted, "Hi, this is Art."

"Uhh, good morning, umm, good afternoon, this is _____ with In-land Printing, howareyou?", he stammered all in one breath. (About this point I could tell I was about to collect some great newsletter material.)

"I'm doing great, thank you."

"Art, you talked to someone here last week and had sent us a package of materials ... a catalog, brochure, sell sheet, newsletter, and I was wondering if you want us to quote on this?"

"You're mistaken. I didn't talk to anybody there about printing."

"Just a minute, (he then yelled to someone else in his area) Terri, is this who you talked to? What? Ok. (then I guess it was my turn to be talked to again) *Well she talked to someone there who sent us this stuff."* And then in a who's-the-real-decision-maker-there tone, probably because I was questioning him, he said, *"Should I be talking to someone else about this?"* Big mistake.

"Let me get this right. You misrepresented yourself and asked us to send you all of my sales material, which cost me money for the printing, the postage, and the time to stuff and send, just so you could place this sales call?"

"Uhh, well we identified ourselves and said that's why we wanted it ."

At this point I was forced to give him the benefit of the doubt, (although I thought that was unusual because I talk to most of those sales reps myself). He proceeded with, *"So do you want us to bid on this?"*

"Where are you?", I asked.

He responded, *"I'm in New York, and we have a plant in St. Louis."*

I lobbed out an objection to see how he'd react: "I do all of my printing locally."

Then—get this—he said, "OK." CLICK.

That *was him* hanging up.

Call Analysis

I'm writing this just seconds after talking to this moron, so excuse me if I sound a bit harsh. Not only were his marketing tactics cheesy, his sales skills and approach were abysmal.

After this nitwit hung up on me, I checked here, and his company did not represent itself as a printer looking to get our material so they could bid on it. Therefore, he lied about his shady marketing tactics. With that you might be saying, "But, Art, you always say it's good idea to get as much information as possible about a company before speaking to a decision maker. What gives here?"

Yes, it is good to learn as much as you can before speaking with a buyer. I would not have had a problem if that was stated when they requested my material. (It would have been likely that at that time he would have gotten nowhere with me, given the sad state of his sales skills, but I would have probably sent the material anyway, suggesting that he buy and use some of the items to retool his approach and tactics.)

The ethical way to collect information about an organization is to fully identify yourself, and justify your reason for asking questions—and certainly for anything you request be sent—with the value for them doing so. For example,

> **"There's a possibility that, depending on your future direct mailing plans, and your requirements, we might have something worth at least taking a look at. I'd like to find out just a little about what you do to see if our company might have something to offer regarding either a more attractive price or total value."**

Sure that's a bit vague, but all we're trying to do at this point is pique curiosity to the point where they'd answer a few qualifying questions. Remember, we're not talking to the ultimate decision maker yet, but we likely would need to "sell" this person on the fact that we might indeed have something to offer.

The Caller's Other Mistakes

OK, let me calm down a bit and address his other mistakes on this call.

• **Talking to someone else while waiting for the prospect to pick up the line.** This screams out to the person you're calling, "I'm not focused on this call. I'm smilin' and dialin' and spewing the same spiel to everyone who picks up." When you're waiting on hold, concentrate with the intensity of a sprinter in the starting block. Go through the opening statement in your mind, and think of the possible responses you might hear, and what you'll say next.

• **Poor opening.** To review and paraphrase, he said, *"I've got some of your materials here and was wondering if you'd like a bid on them."* I looked at this several times and maybe I'm myopic, but I couldn't locate even a shred of a reason in there to listen to this sap. Instead, to create interest, he could have said,

> **"The reason for the call is that we specialize in working with direct mailers, typically helping them lower their total price per thousand, while always working within their scheduled mailing dates. I'd like to ask a few questions about what you mail, and the quantity and frequencies to determine if there is anything you're doing that might be worth having us bid on."**

• **He didn't move to the questioning phase of the sales process.** That's because he blew both his feet off before he had any chance to move forward. Even if he hadn't alienated me so badly with his sleazy lead-generation tactics—and subsequently lying about them—his opening was so bad it still wouldn't have salvaged this call.

Action Steps

Chapter 53

"Calls of Shame" Candidate

This caller could be the poster child for everything you shouldn't do on a sales call. Let's listen in.

As you read the caller's part, imagine a voice and tone similar to a cocky, know-it-all, smart-aleck who calls everyone "buddy."

Caller: *"Hi, I'm ___ with ___ Computer Products ... hey, you're familiar with us, aren't you?"*

Me: (I did recall signing a few checks to them over the years.) "Somewhat. You sell toner, don't you?"

Caller: *"Yeah, that's us. Well I'm calling because I've got some good news for you."*

Me: "Oh?"

Caller: *"I'm your new account rep."*

Me: (Trying to hold back my elation.) "Uh-huh."

Caller: *"According to our records here, you haven't bought in a while. I see you have, hmmm, what, a Laserjet 3 and 4L?"*

Me: "4L and 4P."

Caller: *"Hmmmm, do you know if those take the same cartridges?"*

Me: (Getting a little annoyed at myself for spending time with someone who clearly didn't state any reason of value why I should speak with him at all, let alone this long) "Let me get this straight. You sell this stuff all day long, and you're asking ME for the specifications on them?"

Caller: (nervous laughter) *"Well, you're right, I should know. Let's see, yep, they take the same one."*

Me: (By this time I had looked up his company in *our* database, and saw they were a subscriber to my newsletter, and have been for a few years, although a couple of years ago they used to get multiple copies and just get one copy now.) Do you know what we do here?"

Caller: *"Heh, heh, hmmm, Business By Phone. Somethin' with phones?"*

Me: "Among other things, we publish the *TELEPHONE SELLING REPORT* newsletter. Have you ever seen it?" (I seriously doubted he had, based on this call.)

Caller: *"Oh yeah, you know what? They're photocopied and posted at various places."*

"Photocopied" is a nasty word for any type of publisher. I proceeded to explain copyright laws when he jumped in again.

Caller: *"Well anyway, I want to get this account reactivated here."*

Me: "That's what YOU want?"

Caller: *"Yeah, I recommend we go with two of those cartridges ... will that be enough?"*

Me: "Let me propose something. Since your company is already buying something from me, but obviously violating copyright laws, I'd like to suggest a deal to your boss where I could give your company multiple copies of the newsletter every month without having to pay for them, and you could improve the quality of your calls and sell more. We could trade out."

Caller: *"You know the problem with that, don't you?"*

Me: "What's that?"

Caller: *"I don't get any commission on that."*

Can you believe that response! Given what had transpired up to this point, I guess I shouldn't have been surprised.

Once he realized he wasn't going to get any commission on this call, he backpeddled for his quick exit.

But first, get this, he said, *"So you probably work with a lot of salespeople. How'd I do?"*

What do *you* think I said?

Call Analysis

I believe that even the most casual observer could point out the faults with this call. Let's highlight them.

❏ **Poor pre-buyer conversations.** He should have found out the details on my printers before speaking with me personally. Then he could have researched what cartridges we use. He also could have found out how many we use now, how often we buy, from whom ... details very valuable to a salesperson.

❏ **Horrible opening.** *"Hi, I'm ___ with ___ Computer Products ... hey, you're familiar with us, aren't you?"* Where's the value here? A better one would have been,

> **"We had the opportunity to provide you with toner cartridges in the past, and if you're still using laser printers, it's likely we'd be able to offer you the same type of values you received from us before ..."**

❏ **Stating *"I'm your new account rep."*** It's not a valid reason for a call, especially with an inactive account. What are customers supposed to say upon hearing this announcement? "Oh, fabulous, thanks for letting me know that. Well, let's start out with a large order, OK?" Give me a break.

❏ *" ... you haven't bought in a while."* Phrasing it this way sounds accusatory, as if the customer hasn't been doing the company a favor by giving its regular order. A better way to address this is what I mentioned in the suggested opener above:

> **"We had the opportunity to provide you with toner cartridges in the past ..."**

❏ **A me-oriented attitude.** One of the worst things I could think of saying to a potential customer is, *"I don't get any commission on that."* Not only do customers not care if you get commission, they question your motives if they suspect you're on commission. This guy just flat-out removed any doubt regarding his intent.

This one certainly goes into the Calls of Shame. Hopefully it's not representative of the typical call from that company.

Chapter 54

Avoid Phrases That Create Liars

Here's the setting: A sales rep travels nowhere on a prospecting call. The call is about to end. And because either he doesn't realize he's making a mistake, or he's in a rush to save face and get off the phone, he utters one of these laughable phrases,

"Well, keep us in mind, OK?"

"Here's my number, write it down just in case."

"How about I give you a call in six months or so?"

When on the phone as a prospect, I really do feel quite guilty (OK, maybe only slightly. All right, not the least bit of remorse) when I respond with an "OK, I will keep you in mind," or when I do my best imitation of copying down their phone number while I'm actually doodling abstract farm animals.

These phrases make liars out of people. They usually have no intention of "keeping us in mind," let alone writing down our number. But let's look at what's really important here. These phrases don't accomplish anything positive, and give no reason for the listener to *ever* want to consider "keeping you in mind" or calling you. Here's what you should do and say instead.

1. Determine if There Ever Would Be Potential

Too many reps either hang on to prospects when they have no shred of evidence that the person is a prospect, or they let them go, when, indeed, there might be some potential. Find out for sure. Ask,

> **"Ben, under what circumstances would you ever see yourself considering another vendor?"**

Notice the wording here. It's a question that not only asks if they ever would use someone else, but it also asks for the circumstances that would surround it. For example, I've heard prospects respond, "Well, I suppose if

I ever got into an emergency situation where they weren't able to deliver, I'd have to look elsewhere." Then you have an opportunity to pick up on that and continue questioning.

On the other hand, if they say, "Look, you're wasting your time buddy. Quit calling me," write them off and move on. Chalk them up as someone you won't waste time with.

2. GIVE Them Something to Think About

To reiterate, *"Keep us is mind,"* is a worthless phrase. If you truly do want someone to keep you in mind, give them something to think about that will trigger a memory of you. And tie it into a problem they might experience—a problem you could solve. That might prompt them to not only think of you, but to call you.

Let's say you know you can help a company lower their property taxes, but they either don't see the need at this point, or don't believe you. You might end the call with,

> **"I still feel we can help you. Here's something to consider: when you review your property tax itemization, take a look at the specific valuation and charges for your out-of-state properties. If you feel those taxes are high and question them, keep in mind we are specialists on the tax laws in every state, and know the best way to challenge, and eventually lower the bill. I'll send you a card with my number on it, so keep it in your tax file, and give me a call then if you feel it would help."**

The process is simple. Tell them what to look for, and associate it with the problem you can solve. When they do experience it, you'll have a greater chance of them thinking of you.

Action Steps

Chapter 55

Examples of a Fine Opening and Questions

After attending a Telesales Rep College seminar, Clay Mahle, with Contractors Labor Pool, sent me his opening statement for review, along with a few need-development questions. They were excellent, and I'll share them with you just as he wrote them.

First a little background: Contractors Labor Pool provides electricians, plumbers, and other tradespeople on a temporary basis to building contractors. Clay calls on the contractors to qualify them, generate interest, place workers immediately, or, at least get agreement that the contractor will use CLP when the need arises. Here is Clay's opening, and questions.

Opening

"Mr. Prospect, this is Clay Mahle with Contractors Labor Pool. We specialize in providing skilled tradesmen on demand, when your need arises. A number of physical plant managers use our service to increase their service capacity and flexibility, without the hassle and expense of hiring extra staff. My purpose in calling is to ask a few questions about your operation to see if our service would be of value to you."

Questions

"How does your department currently handle peak loads?"

"The last time you were short-handed, how did you handle it?"

"What is the biggest headache you have with day-to-day operations?"

"How does your current complement of mechanics compare to your needs?"

"What are your priorities?"

"What is your biggest roadblock to meeting your goals."

"What do you do when an emergency outstrips your in-house capacity?"

"What criteria do you use to evaluate personnel services vendors?"

"Under what circumstances would you consider using another labor source?"

You did well, Clay. Nice job!

Action Steps

Chapter 56

Be Certain to Position Your Value

Trish Walsh sells compression garments for The Tulip Company, in San Diego. In nontechnical terms, these are girdle-type stretch pants that cosmetic surgeons give to patients after liposuction.

She told me she usually talks to nurses in the office, and occasionally secretaries. Her main problem is that she is typically rushed off the phone since doctors' offices are busy places and they don't have time to talk to a lot of salespeople.

Her opening statement is,

"Hello, this is Trish Walsh with the Tulip Company. We specialize in light weight, compression garments. Is this something you would be interested in or use? Do you stock garments? What are the most important features you look for when buying a garment?"

She said she then listens, and points out the three outstanding features of hers, and how they might fit the doctor's needs. Then she asks if they would be interested in trying one for their next patient, and offering an opening-order discount.

Analysis and Recommendation

The main objective I see here is to position herself not as a bothersome salesperson, but as someone with real problem-solving value to offer the doctor. There really isn't enough reason in the first few sentences of this opener for the listener to get excited, therefore they don't see a valid reason to answer questions.

We first discussed what these doctors really want most, what they want to avoid, and how she could deliver those results as it relates to her type of products. Our conclusions:

• Doctors want the best surgical results possible. The Tulip Company compression garments help the contouring and sculpting process better than anything else available.

• Doctors always want patients who are happy, and all the side benefits that go along with that. Tulip garments are lighter, and more comfortable than typical armor-like, clinical-looking garments. Patients really like them.

The Opening Statement

I suggested a new opening that appeals to what doctors want, which would at least generate initial interest, buying time for questions:

"Hello, this is Trish Walsh with the Tulip Company. We've come out with a new line of compression garments that patients love because they're lightweight and comfortable, and doctors tell us they've been getting better results with them, especially for contouring. If I've caught you at a good time, I'd like to ask just a couple of questions to see if you'd like more information on these garments."

Questions

Now that we have the listener in a positive, curious frame of mind, we begin questioning, starting with a basic qualifying question:

"Do you stock garments?"

Then a question to get competitive information which will be used to help frame the next need-development questions:

"What kind are you using?"

Now we want to ask questions focusing on specific needs we can fill, or problems we can solve. Asking, *"What are the most important features you look for in a garment?"* forces the listener to think too much, and assumes that they have conscious buying criteria, which they might not have. Therefore, we normally don't get substantive answers we can use from this question.

Instead, we want to ask need-development questions. These are formed by taking your strongest benefits, and coming up with questions which will uncover a specific need your product fills, or problems it solves.

Keeping in mind what the doctors want most, here is what the Tulip Company garments do:

• help the patients feel more comfortable after surgery, therefore they're happy, and that reflects well on the doctor, and,

• aid in the sculpting and contouring after surgery, ensuring better results for the doctor.

Additionally, Trish mentioned that if doctors don't stock garments, they typically need to order them, one at a time, normally overnighting them the day before a surgery, experiencing the extra stress of the rush, and incurring the added cost. Therefore, we took this into consideration in developing the need to keep a few on hand.

Here are the need-development questions I suggested:

"How often do patients mention the discomfort of their garments?"

"How much would you say the present garments help in contouring or sculpting?"

(If not stocking garments) **"Do you find you're typically rushing to order single garments, and having to pay extra for overnight delivery?"**

You can see that these questions get the listener thinking about—almost experiencing—their needs or problems; we're not forcing them to think of them.

Now the doctor/nurse is in a more receptive frame of mind to hear about the benefits Trish can provide since they're thinking about how their present garment may be inadequate, and she's better able to position and present her garments based on the needs they just told her about. And she does it all with questions.

Action Steps

Chapter 57

Here's a Call That Won the Sale

The call on hold for me was a person with US West, my local telco. The friendly, articulate caller said,

"Hello, I'm _____ calling for US West. Since you now have Call Forwarding, we wanted to let you know about a new enhancement to that service that potentially could make your life a little easier, depending on how you're now using it."

She captured my interest, which is exactly what the opener should do. I responded, "Oh?"

"Let me ask you a few questions to see if this is something you'd be able to use."

Great so far. She was asking questions before presenting. If she presented the new enhancements at this point, she would have talked about hope-to-be benefits, rather than precise items of value.

"First, when do you use your call forwarding?"

This was the question that began unlocking precisely what she needed to know to help me buy.

"The only time we use it is when we're not in the office, after-hours and most of the weekend."

"And where do you forward your calls?"

"We send them to a voice mail system at my other office."

"I see. How often have you had situations where you've left the office but didn't put the call forwarding on?"

That was the pain-reminding question that caused me to immediately re-live the times where I was already home, having forgotten to activate call forwarding. Or other times, calling into the office after hours, realizing it wasn't on, thinking of the calls and orders we might have been missing.

Her next question:

"So what do you normally do in situations like that?"

"Well, either drive back to the office and activate it, or wait until the next day, potentially missing important calls." (I really made it easy on her with that last answer. But that's what brilliantly-composed questions are designed to do, aren't they?)

Now it was finally time for her to present. Notice the appropriateness of the timing as compared to if she would have presented earlier.

"Well, based upon some of the inconvenience you experience now, I've got something to tell you about that will eliminate those drives back to the office, and get rid of the worry that you're missing calls. US West has just introduced an enhancement to Call Forwarding that will enable you to activate your service from any touch tone phone anywhere ..."

And she went on to tell me about the service. She really didn't need to. I was sold as soon as she mentioned it. Although she did handle the remainder of the call well, asking for the order, confirming all the details.

The Call Structure

To review, let's look at what she did, and why it was effective.

1. Pre-Call Planning. This was obviously built into the program, but she was calling people who were existing customers, and had the Call Forwarding service. Her primary objective was to get the order on this call.

2. Opening Statement. She created interest with the opening and moved me to the questioning part of the call:

"Since you now have Call Forwarding, we wanted to let you know about a new enhancement to that service that potentially could make your life a little easier, depending on how you're now using it."

3. Questioning. As all good sales questions do, hers were based on getting me thinking about the problems that her service could solve. And they were right on target.

4. Presentation. This is child's play if the right job is done with the questioning. She simply told me how my problems would go away.

5. Commitment. She asked for the sale and got it.

Overall, a fine call, and I'm a happy customer.

Chapter **58**

How to Build Relationships

(NOTE: This chapter was written by my friend, Cary Zucker, President of Neutron Industries.)

When we train salespeople here at Neutron Industries, we always use the phrase, "People don't care how much you know until they know how much you care." This illustrates the essential point that customers want you to know them from a human standpoint as well as from a business perspective.

It's the little things that turn customers on. It's understanding them as human beings—not as just the decision maker for industrial cleaning chemicals in our case.

The Three P's

Incorporating the human, personal angle is a major part of our sales process. We teach the three P's:

Personality: learning about them personally, letting your own personality shine through.

Product: being able to present the benefits and results of the products that best meet their needs, concerns, and desires, and solves their problems. This is where the consultative sales skills are essential.

Promotion: as a direct marketing company, we often run promotions and special offers. Skilled reps know when they can and should use these.

Ideally, we want to have a balance between the Three P's ... 33 1/3% of each on every call, and in every relationship. When one gets out of kilter, it raises the chances of the competition coming in and knocking us out. For example, if 80% of the sale is based on product, and only 10% each on personality and promotion, then the savvy competitor with a more balanced menu of personality, promotion and product can steal the business. I've seen it happen time after time.

How to Build the Personality "P"

The Personality "P" is perhaps the most difficult one to teach if it's not already present in the rep. What we have done is provide a tool for our reps that makes the process easier. If you haven't yet read *"Swim With the Sharks Without Being Eaten Alive,"* by Harvey Mackay, run down to your bookstore and get a copy right now. Among the hundreds of useful ideas is the "Mackay 66," a list of 66 questions Mackay suggests you get the answers to in order to truly know your customer. I won't belabor the value and results of having and using this information, Harvey does it quite well in the book.

We whittled the list down to a very manageable 17 questions for our industry and telesales process. We don't necessarily get the information from the decision maker; screeners, assistants, and others in the organization are good sources. And every question has a purpose. Someone outside of our industry might find number 14, "Do they smoke?", a bit unusual. We don't. We sell air fresheners.

If the "personality" component of your sales calls and relationships is lacking, I encourage you to develop and implement your own version of the Mackay 66. The result will likely be more loyal and repeat customers. As Marshall Field said, "The person who comes back to you is the one you made to feel important."

(Cary Zucker is President of Neutron Industries in Phoenix, a supplier of industrial maintenance chemicals and cleaning products. He started Neutron with seven employees, growing it to over 200 presently, and has made the INC 500 twice in the past 10 years. As a telemarketing company, Neutron is widely known for its programs on employee recognition, goal setting, motivation, and pride in one's work.)

Neutron's Version of "The Mackay 66"

1. Nickname and Title:
2. Birthday and Birth Place:
3. Where Did You Go to School?
4. Were You in the Military?
5. Marital Status:
6. Name of Spouse:
7. Anniversary:
8. Children—Names and Ages:
9. Special Interests:
10. Clubs:
11. Sports:
12. Hobbies:
13. Recreation:
14. Do They Smoke?
15. Vacation Interests:
16. Achievement They're Proud Of:
17. Does Your Competitor Have Better Answers to These Questions Than You Do?

Additional Notes:

From: "Swim With the Sharks Without Being Eaten Alive."

More Great Stuff

Chapter 59

We Should Act and Think Like Kids

Starting in December each year we often hear "Christmas is for the kids." That's just one more reason I try to be more like a kid. You should too. We all should. All year around. We'd be happier and would achieve more. Here's why.

1. No's don't bother them. My kids react to no's as if they are hearing-impaired, relentlessly firing off their next salvo of requests. Certainly they're not always successful, but they achieve more than if they'd buckled in to the initial "no." And, most kids aren't afraid to go to different levels within the decision-making hierarchy to get what they want.

2. Kids take risks. I about had a calf when I saw my son, Eric, roller-blading up and off a plywood ramp! "Oh, that's nothing, Dad," was the response when I asked if he wasn't just the slightest bit scared of crashing. In retrospect, most grown-ups are too risk-averse, traveling the warm, safe, beaten path. What's the last risk you took? If you're reluctant to live on the edge, consider one thing: Do you regret more of the risks in life that you took, or those that you didn't take? So why not throw caution to the wind once and awhile?

3. Their imaginations run wild. Admiring the abstract explosion-of-colors-on-paper my daughter, Amy, proudly displayed to me, I sheepishly asked, "What exactly do you call this?" "Well, of course it's a city, Daddy," she stated matter-of-factly. Oh. Many of us fence in our imaginations by saying (and therefore believing) "I'm just not creative." Bull. Unharness your imagination, and let your ideas run wild. You'll be surprised.

4. Kids have high ambitions. I remember when my son, Eric, was younger. His toughest decision was whether he was going to play in the American League, or the National League when he became a Major League Baseball player. Ask any kid, and they'll also tell you they aspire to be something great. Sadly, many adults lose this desire, and are content if they can cover this month's checks. Have you set your goals yet for the next week, month, and the rest of the year? If you haven't, do so today. And regardless of where you are right now, aim higher. You can get there.

5. They have great attitudes. A trivia question on the radio asked, "What do kids do about 400 times a day, that adults do less than 20 on average?" The answer: laugh. (I've seen some adults who have really contributed to pulling that number down to 20!) We should lighten up more.

6. Kids are constantly active. The word "walk" isn't in the vocabulary of most kids. They dart wherever they go. Yet, it's sad that the sedentary lifestyle and attitudes of a lot of people contributes to a poor self-image, and lack of ambition. You can spot the people in your organization with the poor attitudes ... normally the ones who shuffle from place to place. Put a spring in your step, move more quickly like a kid, and that really does translate into a better attitude.

7. They're curious. I'm often exasperated trying to explain things that I've always taken for granted, like, "Why is there frost on the grass when you wake up in the morning?" In sales, we need to have that child-like curiosity because it helps us to understand everything we should know before we make a presentation.

So, don't grow up think young. And if you'll excuse me, I need to go strap on my roller blades. Where is that plywood ramp ...

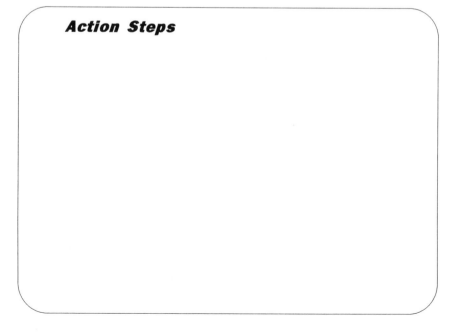

Action Steps

Chapter 60

It's Not Just a Numbers Game

L istening in as a few sales managers discussed sales philosophy as it relates to the phone, I heard what is likely the most inane statement someone can utter, yet, surprisingly, it's not questioned too often:

"It's just a numbers game. Make so many calls, and you know you'll get so many successes."

I cringe when I hear stuff like that.

Sales is not, I repeat, **IS NOT**, just a numbers game.

The lottery is a numbers game. So is keno. Roulette, for gosh sakes, is a numbers game.

Sales is a **quality** game.

When someone refers to sales, particularly telesales, as a pure number game, it's an indication that the person is likely looking at their sales effort from a quantitative standpoint rather than a qualitative one. They feel they can pull anyone off the street, have them make the calls, and some success will result. Like plugging raw materials into a manufacturing process and getting finished products at the end. (And I can predict with reasonable accuracy how well these people train, compensate, and motivate their reps.) They believe sales success is like flipping a coin. Flip it 100 times, and it's likely you'll get close to 50 heads and 50 tails.

I don't buy into the "just numbers" theory. If it were true, 10 sales reps, all working from the same list, making the same number of calls would get exactly the same results. Any manager who has ever yanked his hair in frustration as to how to motivate someone knows that isn't true.

There's no doubt about it, telesales is a game *of numbers*. But it's like baseball is a game of numbers. Like hitters, the salesperson who is able to be successful just a few more times out of their total attempts will make the big money. And it's the people who are most concerned about **improving** their numbers who are most successful.

Yes, you are going to hear plenty of "no's" if you're going to hear "yes's."

But the problem is, too many people reactively accept the "no's" as an undeniable given. "You're that much closer to a yes, keep calling," they're told. Oh, now *that's* motivating. It's like saying if you run across the Kennedy Expressway in Chicago during rush hour often enough, you might eventually make it across without getting hit.

Instead of counting up the no's, blindly accepting them, hoping that a "yes" has got to come up eventually, like an addicted gambler who feels it's got to be his turn to hit the big one next time, it's much better to focus on what we need to do to improve our chances of getting a "yes." And THAT's the difference between being quantitative versus qualitative: Realizing you're going to hear "no's," but figuring out whatever you can do to minimize their occurrence.

That means doing what's necessary to ensure you're saying the right things, in the right way, to the right people, at the right time. A numbers-oriented person has no problem burning through names at a torrid pace, knowing that at some point he/she will stumble upon a person who is primed to buy. What they're also doing in the process, however, is inviting some unnecessary rough treatment, while likely alienating prospects in the process. More than once after getting a call from a rep obviously just putting up numbers I've said to myself and anyone within earshot, "I can't believe they'd let a salesperson like that on the phone representing their company, calling hundreds of businesses per week, making that kind of negative impression."

Accept the fact, yes, that you need to place the calls to be successful; of course you must put in the activity to see a result. And also be convinced that **you**, not random chance, control your results.

Action Steps

Chapter 61

You Can Do It
By Phone

Columbus must have felt this same way, convincing doubters the earth is round. Even after he proved it, people still believed otherwise.

I get exasperated when I hear or read people saying, *"You can only use the phone to set appointments. You can't sell* (fill in the blank) *by phone."* Just in the past two weeks I read this drivel twice in well-known business publications, got into a heated on-line discussion about it with a sales manager still living in the Mesozoic period, and another one with a manager who had seen an article of mine in a magazine and called me with the same feelings. Someone correct me if I'm wrong, but if it's being done now, that means it's possible, right?

The Truths of Sales Communication

Here's my take on the issue:

1. Sales is a *process* where we use several methods of communication in order to achieve our objective: the sale and continuing relationship.

2. Face-to-face selling is the most effective way to sell because we're able to use all methods of communication; by phone we mostly lose the visual.

3. Face-to-face selling is by far the most costly way to sell.

4. Most face-to-face calls are a waste of time, whereby the same result could have been achieved by phone more quickly and less expensively.

5. About 5%-30% of a face-to-face call is spent on business, 70%-95% on small talk. Inverse those numbers when applied to phone calls.

6. Most face-to-face sales reps could increase their sales by cutting

240

their number of visits and increasing their number and quality of telephone calls, by moving the sales process closer to the end objective on the phone, so that by the time they meet with someone, they've ensured they have someone who is qualified, interested, has authority, has money, and has an immediate need.

7. Most prospects and customers would rather not see a salesperson; it takes too much time to get down to business. As I wrote this, I fielded a call from—and quickly got rid of—a financial planner-type whose basis for the telephone call was to "set up a time to sit down with me for 20 minutes." Since he was referred by a friend, I would have spoken with him by phone (maybe), but I wasn't about to invest face time with the guy since he didn't mention anything of real interest on the phone. He was just trying to set an appointment. Probably subscribed to the "the phone is just for appointments" theory. As a result, he got nothing.

8. Some prospects and customers do need—sometimes demand—to see salespeople (not as many as outside sales rep like to think, though).

9. For every sales rep or manager who says, *"You can't sell our product/service by phone,"* there is someone already doing it.

10. Anyone who has a predetermined "leaping off point" regarding how far they'll take the relationship by phone, or how far they'll take the initial call (*"We only want to introduce ourselves and send out a catalog on the first call."*) is living by a self-imposed limitation that is based on false assumptions. Here's my advice to anyone who believes this theory: take *every* phone call as far as you possibly can. Makes sense, doesn't it? Ending a call prematurely wastes an opportunity with a captive listener you've worked hard to get to, and is interested in what you're saying. Why let him cool down considerably, meaning you have to work just as hard to bring his emotional temperature back to this point and beyond on the next contact?

Sales is sales. Period. Those who enjoy the greatest success use their time the most efficiently: mostly by phone.

Chapter 62

Treat Your Inquiries Like Gold

Virtually every business receives inquiries of some sort ... by phone, mail, or online. Some are generated by advertising, others by word of mouth. What's tragic is that some salespeople simply pick up these inquiries, sense no feeling of urgency, and with indifference in their voice phone the inquirer and say, *"You wanted some information from us?"* As if they are doing the inquirer a favor by calling!

They Want Satisfaction, NOW

Let's think about the state of mind an inquirer is in when they initiate the contact. Just recall the last time you were thumbing through the Yellow Pages searching for a product or service. You selected a number, dialed, and voiced your question or need. If your question was answered satisfactorily, and the company left you with a feeling that they could do the job and wanted your business, you probably gave it to them. On the other hand, think about the times your call was answered and you were made to feel that you were actually bothering someone. Their tone of voice screamed out, *"I don't care about you."* Maybe they said, *"There's no one here now. You'll have to call back."*

Did you call back? Probably not. You likely moved on to the next name. Your prospects will do the same if not treated properly. Someone who contacts your company is most interested at the precise time they call. Their buying temperature is highest at this moment. They have taken the time to contact you, and have likely thought about their needs. If you don't give them some satisfaction, they will find it somewhere else. Therefore, when handling inquiries, here are some suggestions:

1. Make sure that all phone inquiries are handled by *someone.* If you can help them on this call, it could prevent them going to several other competitors, perhaps losing any chance at a sale for you.

2. Give immediate attention to mail inquiries. These have already aged a few days by the time they reach you.

3. On follow-up calls to inquirers, determine their immediate interest. Follow this format: **"Mr. Smith, I'm Gail Spencer with ABC Plastics, distributors of high quality plastic widgets. First, I want to let you know we appreciate your interest in our products, and I want to provide you with the information you called in for yesterday afternoon.** (pause) **Please tell me, what is it that prompted your call...?"**

Businesses spend tremendous amounts of money to prompt people to contact them. Treat every single inquiry as a sale waiting to happen.

Upsell on Incoming Orders

Speaking of inquiries, here's an idea that can be adapted for incoming order calls.

My plane didn't leave for another hour, and I was fried after giving a day-long seminar. Wanting to decompress and not expecting to do any sales research, I bellied up to the airport bar and ordered a beer. **"A buck more gets you a large one,"** suggested the bartender. **"That's like two for the price of one."**

That worked for me, given that they were gouging people for about eight bucks a small beer anyway ($3.50, actually). The extra dollar sounded like a deal, percentage savings-wise.

Sipping from my frosty vat, I watched the bartender/salesman repeat his offer to over 15 people. *Every one* accepted!

I complimented him on his sales success, and asked how many people typically go for the larger size. "About 95-99%," he said. Think about it: around $200 a day extra revenue with marginal product expense. The guy is more than paying for himself, and getting larger tips because of bigger sales.

Here's what makes his approach successful.

1. He's ASKING. Few people would voluntarily order the larger size. He confirmed that, since he's watched others who didn't ask.

2. He minimizes the *incremental* expense, instead of presenting the __total__ price. Saying, "A buck more gets you a large," is better than saying, "You can get a large for $4.50."

3. He reinforces the value. "That's like getting two for one," helps you think about the great deal you're getting. And we all like a deal.

Everyone can apply these three, simple principles. Think about how you're asking, incorporate these ideas, and I know you'll increase your order sizes.

Action Steps

Chapter 63

Do People Like You?

One common-sense principle of building relationships and prompting people to take action is being likable.

According to Bert Decker's book, *"You've Got to Be Believed to be Heard,"* George Gallup has conducted his Personality Factor poll prior to every presidential election since 1960. In every election, only one of three factors—issues, party affiliation, and likability—has been a consistent prognosticator of the final election result: the likability factor. And just like in politics, likability plays a major role in our everyday lives, especially sales.

Joe Girard, famous car salesman, named 12 times by the Guinness Book as the "world's greatest salesman," said likability was the secret to his success. Each month Girard sent out over 13,000 greeting cards to each of his past customers with nothing more than whatever holiday occurred that month (Valentine's Day, Thanksgiving), his name, and on the inside, the inscription, "I Like You." As hokey and impersonal as that seems, it worked for him.

Compliments Help Your Likability

Dr. Robert Cialdini, the author of *"Influence: Science and Practice"* cites an experiment conducted to measure the effectiveness of likability stimulated by flattery and compliments. Men in this study received comments from another person who needed a favor from them. A few men received only positive comments, some received negative ones, and others a mixture of positive and negative comments. The result: the people who provided only praise were liked best by the men. What's interesting is that this was the case even though the men fully realized that the flatterer *stood to gain* from liking them. What is quite surprising is that pure praise did not have to be accurate to work; positive comments produced just as much liking for the flatterer when they were untrue as when they were true!

Here are a few ideas regarding compliments.

Be Sincere. Despite what the scientific evidence shows, I wouldn't want to take a chance on the transparent flattery. Common sense prevails here.

Appeal to the Person's Self-Perception. King George V of England said, "Flattery is telling the other person precisely what he thinks of himself." We all have skills or traits we pride ourselves on. If you can identify and reinforce their self-perception, chances are you're adding to your likability factor. In preparing a presentation for an association of sales pros, I interviewed a number of members whose names were provided by the association. After speaking to just a few, I recognized a pattern of extreme competence. I commented to one,

> **"Based on the answers you're giving, and what I've heard, I'd say I've got a list of top producers here. Is that true?"**

The rep melted, modestly admitting, "Well yes, I do quite well." My comment was mostly observational, and it just happened to also be complimentary. Since she likely viewed herself as a top performer, the remainder of the interview went even more smoothly.

Base Your Compliments on Evidence. If you can comment on your perception of an event, a project the person is working on, the job they did ... then your compliment obviously seems more sincere. And listen for "compliment invitations," for example, when they say something like, "... and we just had our best quarter ever ...", they've served up a perfect compliment opportunity.

Personal Compliments Have Impact. As the old managerial adage says, "Praise the performer, coach the performance," do the same with your compliments.

> **"*You* have a knack for that."**

> **"*You* know how to motivate people."**

By the way, YOU are a fine salesperson.

Chapter 64

Use Conference Calls to Sell to Multiple Decision Makers

If there are multiple parties involved in the decision-making process, it's to your advantage to speak with them all at once. And you don't need to burn an entire day on the road, running up travel bills to do so. Conduct a conference call.

Here are ideas on leading up to, and holding the call.

Identifying the Other Players

"Who else will be involved in the decision process?"

"Who will you consult with in discussing this?"

"What will have to take place before you make this decision?"

Getting Agreement They Like What You Have

This is a key any time there are multiple contacts. If your contact isn't sold, you can bet they won't go to bat for you.

"So are you personally sold on this?"

"Is this the best option you've seen?"

"I assume you're comfortable recommending my program to the committee?"

How to Suggest a Conference Call To Your Contact

You don't want to make it sound like you're going over your contact's head. Let him still feel like he's playing a major role.

"Would it be worthwhile to discuss having a conference call where we all can discuss the issues together?"

"Would it be easier for you if we arranged a conference call, so that I would be available to answer any questions directly, instead of you having to take the time to relay them back to me?"

"If we had a conference call, do you think that would help you save time of having to speak with each person individually?"

Tips for Conducting the Conference Call

• If their phone systems allows it, have them all get on separate phones instead of one speakerphone. The conference feature with individual phones ensures much clearer communication.

•Have a list of the names of everyone participating. Get it in advance, and ask your contact about each individual, and their particular needs and outlook as it relates to what you're offering.

• Send to everyone participating a copy of your proposal, sample, brochure ... whatever you refer to during the call so you can utilize the visual element.

• During the introductions, ask people if they would identify themselves when they speak, since it helps in your note-taking.

• When you make statements or ask questions, address them to individuals by name. It helps them pay attention, plus it personalizes the communication.

More Conference Call Tips

Here are more ideas *from* *"The Electronic Etiquette Guide,"* (Paging Services Council, P.O. Box 32229, Washington, DC, 20007.)

■ **Identify yourself** before getting into your topic. This will eliminate confusion, particularly when there are several people on your end of the phone.

■ **Never interrupt** another speaker.

■ **Keep noise on your end to a minimum,** especially when using a speakerphone.

■ **If you need to leave the call, don't place the line on hold.** If you have background music or a message-on-hold, it will disrupt the call.

And just like any telesales call, be sure you have an objective going in, work toward it during your call, ask for their commitment and action, and make sure everyone knows what the next step is after the call. This will ensure your success.

Chapter 65

How Well Do You Know Telephone Sales?

Here's a quiz for you. Read through the questions and pick the one that most closely describes your feelings, or the way you'd act in that situation.

Questions

1. Regarding my telephone voice and rate of speech, I should,

a) mirror and exactly match the other person's rate and tone.

b) adopt a radio announcer-like voice and delivery.

c) use my normal rate and tone, adjusted slightly closer to that of the other person.

2. After making a sales point by phone and encountering silence, I should,

a) remain silent until they speak, because the first one to talk, loses.

b) jump in and continue pitching more benefits.

c) pause a second or two longer, and then ask, "What are your thoughts on that?"

3. When a screener asks, "What's this in reference to?", I should,

a) answer with a persuasive message that mentions the potential value I might be able to deliver to the boss.

b) insist that "It's a business matter, will you please tell him I'm on hold?"

c) avoid giving any information at all, and say I'll call back later. The screener can't buy from me.

4. When setting appointments by phone, I should,

a) introduce myself, and my company, and use the "alternate-choice" close to set a time and date, all within the first 15-20 seconds.

b) introduce myself, ask if I could send literature, and ask if I could call back in about a week.

c) get them interested, qualify them, and take the sales conversation as far as possible by phone before asking for the appointment.

5. Regarding asking someone for his time at the beginning of a prospecting call I should,

a) identify myself, then immediately say, "Do you have a few minutes to talk?"

b) never mention time.

c) identify myself, present a potential benefit, then say, "... and if I've caught you at a good time I'd like to ask a few questions ..."

6. After sending out literature to a prospect, I should,

a) call back in five days.

b) wait for them to call me.

c) ask them by when they will have had a chance to review the material, and schedule the call back then.

7. The phone

a) isn't effective when selling tangible products, since customers need to see the product.

b) isn't effective when selling intangible services, since customers need to see me explain it.

c) can be—and is—used to sell and/or service customers buying virtually anything.

Answers on next page.

Answers

1. c) Adjust your tempo and tone slightly in the direction of the other person's. If you try to make a drastic change, you'll force an insincere, phony impression.

2. c) Only by getting them talking will you get a precise reading on their reaction to your point. Silence can be positive or negative. Find out for sure with a question. If their mood is negative, "pitching benefits" will only build on that negativity.

3. a) The screener determines who is worthy of taking the boss' time, and who will just waste it. You therefore need to communicate the potential value you could deliver, and tack on the contingency that, "... **and to determine if this is something he'd want to take a look at, I'd like** to ask him a few questions."

4. c) Close for an appointment before they see a reason to meet you, and you create resistance. And if you think you can only go as far on the first call as the introduction, you've created a false, self-limitation. Take them as far as you can by phone, and you'll save time, disqualify prospects by phone instead of with a costly face-to-face call, and when you do visit them, spend more time with hot, interested, pre-sold prospects.

5. c) Asking for their time when they see no reason to comply isn't a high-percentage play. But, show no respect for their time, and you might annoy them. The safe bet is get them interested, and use the implied-consent phrase, **"if I've caught you at a good time..."** They'll let you know if they're busy, but still will want to talk to you later.

6. c) Tie the timing of your callback to their performance of some action, and let them tell you when that will be. Therefore, they agree to look at the material, and set a call back time all in the same sentence!

7. c) Many salespeople waste far too much time behind a steering wheel, in airplanes, in lobbies, and in front of people who would rather not see them. Rid yourself of excuses about why you don't use the phone more, and think of HOW you could use it to increase your sales effectiveness, efficiency, and income.

Chapter 66

Everyone Sells the Same Thing

C an someone please answer a question for me? What in the *world* is the difference between selling a product and a service?

I did a survey to past newsletter subscribers who chose not to renew. Upon reviewing the comments, one said, "You deal too much with selling products. I sell a service."

OK, with that in mind, consider another comment: "We sell a specialized product. You don't cover how to do that."

My first reaction to these was outrage at how misguided these people are, and that they obviously just don't get it ... how they haven't been reading carefully. Then I calmed down and objectively thought it through: the blame really is mine. Their perception is their reality, as it always is in sales, and life in general. The real problem is I apparently haven't done a thorough enough job (for some) of communicating one very basic, but yet critical point:

Regardless of the type of physical product or intangible service you provide, everyone's customer buys only one thing, and that's the end result of having or using that product or service.

I've strained to come up with examples—products or services—that contradict this.

I can't.

My conclusion is that people place so much emphasis on what they're trying to sell, they lose focus—or perhaps never had it to begin with—regarding what the buyers want.

Selling the Result

Sometimes it pays to revisit the basics, and what should be obvious, in order to make a point. Let's look at the difference between selling a product or service itself, and the ultimate result.

For example, a business-development rep for a consulting firm isn't selling "consulting engagements," even though I've talked to plenty who had that attitude. What they're trying to do is help prospects see and feel—in advance—the result of having specific problems solved.

A rep selling a machine of any type won't have much luck by describing large hunks of metal with moving parts that takes up space on factory floors. They are actually helping buyers who want to be able to finish jobs 33% more quickly, with less labor expense in doing it, and to virtually eliminate maintenance on the machine used in doing it.

You get the picture.

Is this Sales 101? I guess so. Without understanding and building on the basics, nothing else matters. Like I have told the basketball and baseball teams I've coached over the years, the fundamentals are what wins games—the fancy stuff is just for show.

An Exercise for You

Regardless of whether you sell a product, service, or widget, take 30 minutes with a pad of paper to answer a few questions.

❑ What problems do people experience that you solve with the results of your product/service?

❑ What specifically do people hope to gain that is—or can be—delivered by your product or service?

❑ In dealing with your type of product/service, what do people want to avoid?

❑ And what do they want?

❑ What are precise reasons people have purchased from you in the past?

❑ What results did they realize?

The answers are the reasons people buy. Regardless of what you sell. If you still think people are buying the product or the service, go back and do the exercise again. Think results.

Chapter 67

Tips from Fellow Salespeople

Richard Crebs and Doug Calkin with CIA both shared quite a few useful ideas during a San Francisco Telesales Rep College, and I'll devote this chapter to many of their great tips.

To put things in context, CIA (no, not *that* CIA; Commercial Insurance Alteratives) specializes in providing low-cost insurance to hospices which are members of the National Hospice Society. Their sales process is to generate interest, get commitment that the decision maker will complete a faxed form (giving essential info such as current insurance expiration date), and then follow up to ultimately close the sale. Here are just a few of their ideas.

Working With Screeners

On a prospecting call, while still gathering preliminary information from an executive assistant or office manager, Doug likes to ask, **"Should I be speaking with you on this?"** This question typically prompts the person to respond with the name of the actual buyer. Plus it flatters the person.

Faxing the form to the screener directly, personalized with that person's name, helps get the screener on Doug's team. He has success with screeners who will walk the fax into the decision maker's office, have him or her fill it out, and then handle faxing it back. Doug stresses that he personalizes it with the screener's name. This way it's not an unsolicited mass-fax, plus he had received commitment that the screener would take care of getting it completed and faxed back.

Phone Appointments

When you set a phone appointment, confirm that appointment after your call with a fax. Reiterate in the fax some of the key points of interest discussed. Also confirm the phone appointment by fax the night before the actual call.

To make the phone appointment memorable, Richard said that he likes to pick days that stand out, for example,

"How about if we speak again on Groundhog Day?"

Naturally, if you're setting a lot of follow-up calls, you won't want to set them all just on one particular day. Therefore, you could say,

"How about the Monday before Groundhog Day?"

Know When to Be Quiet

Doug stated that one of the purposes for attending the College was to work on talking *less* on the phone—while **listening** more. One of his valuable quotes we all should follow is, "Don't answer questions they weren't going to ask." For example, some sales reps are compelled to talk about everything *they* think is important. When, in fact, some of those things could be of no value—or worse—be perceived as potential liabilities.

Ask Again. Why Not?

On closing and getting commitment, Richard says, "If you ask and they say 'no,' ask again. All they can do is *really* say 'no.'"

Call Before the Meeting

When the prospect must go before a committee or discuss the proposal in a meeting, he always asks,

"Could I call you back right before your meeting?"

This gives the opportunity to further coach the prospect on making the best recommendation during the meeting.

On Saving Them Money ...

A common claim by sellers is that they can save people money. Standing alone, it's like a politician's State of the Union address: nice to hear, but people are skeptical it will actually happen, since there aren't any specifics to back up the claim. Therefore it doesn't carry much impact. Doug suggested a question that makes the money savings come to life:

"What would your organization be able to do with that extra savings each month?"

Speaking of money, Doug has a background in retailing and offered an idea about presenting price when you're selling to anyone who resells your products. He said that if you're selling a new line, or a display, a program (or any type of "grouped" offer), instead of giving the total cost such as $1000, first position it in terms of the bottom line profit to them. For example,

"With this new display, your profit will be $200."

Action Steps

Chapter 68

The Redeeming Quality of Election Season: Sales Ideas

The political campaigns seem to get more expensive and nastier with each election. And with them comes the rhetoric; most of it is downright laughable, but some can provide valuable lessons for salespeople.

What I find particularly interesting are the questioning techniques used by the media and the way politicians deal with them. Let's first look at some questioning ideas.

Questioning Techniques

Listen carefully and you'll find reporters posing questions to candidates (or their assistants) with the intention of placing words in the politicians' mouths—words that might not reflect their real feelings at all. You'll hear such questions as,

> **"So, what you're saying is ..."**

> **"What's really happening here is ..."**

> **"Isn't this, then, really a matter of ...?"**

Of course our objective as salespeople is not to trap someone into saying something they don't really mean (like many reporters do so they can get a good sound bite for the news). What we can do, though, is help the person clarify, in his mind and ours, something they do believe but have not yet clearly articulated, or perhaps even given much thought to. For example,

> **"Really, what you're telling me is that you've lost over 50 hours worth of production time just within the past month because of line problems. Is that accurate?"**

> **"So what you're saying is that you could have had a slight profit, instead of losing money last month,**

257

only if you would have ...?"

"What I'm reading here is that you are leaning toward making a change. Is that accurate?"

It's also interesting to note how politicians respond to questions. This
can make the difference between being perceived as a knowledgeable, sincere individual, or an incompetent goof you wouldn't even trust to wash your
car. Likewise, the way we respond impacts the way we're perceived. Here
are some techniques for answering.

When You Need to Buy Time to Collect Your Thoughts

❑ Compliment the Questioner. "That's a good question ..." or "That's an excellent point ..."

❑ Comment on their Questions. "I must have
touched on an area of interest, based on the number of questions you have."

❑ Defer the Answer. "To give you the best answer,
I'm going to need a few more pieces of information
from you about the ..."

When You Want to Avoid the Question,
Or Shift Emphasis

Here's where the politicians are masters at tap dancing around the
issue. Not to suggest you should avoid their direct questions, but there are
ways to answer difficult ones without doing too much damage to yourself.

❑ Enlarge the Perspective. "Really, that issue reflects the state of the entire industry, not just our
company alone."

❑ Narrow the Perspective. "I can't comment for every one of our over 20,000 customers, but the most
recent survey completed by 1,000 customers shows
a 99% approval rating regarding the chemical's performance."

❑ Shift the Emphasis. "I'm glad you asked that,
because it gives me the chance to point out ... "

❑ When Their Information is Inaccurate. If you detect their question is based on a false premise, say, **"To answer that, I must first fill you in on what's going on with …"**

The next time you watch the politicians, don't just shake your head in disgust at how much of your money they pour down the drain every day. At least listen to the questions and responses so you can use similar ideas to be a better salesperson and make a lot more money … even if they'll get more of it!

Action Steps

Chapter 69

Don't Impose Your Feelings; Learn What *They* Hunger For

Think about the last time someone forced their feelings upon you by making a recommendation about what you should do ... a recommendation that wasn't based upon anything you wanted, but rather what *they* felt you should do or think.

For example, take the person who says, "You should go see this movie." Or someone who gives you an article of clothing (that you think is hideous) such as a tie or scarf, expecting you to wear it. Or the assertive person who goes even further by stuffing a book into your mitts saying, *"Here, you need to read this. It's great."*

Granted, these recommendations are well-intentioned, and some might be on-target. But many cause us to smile politely through gritted teeth while we think, "How can I tell this person that I wouldn't even waste my time reading a review of that movie, let alone watching it."

Typical on Sales Calls

This happens to all of us. Annoying, and sometimes embarrassing, isn't it?

And realize it or not, most of us are even guilty of it! In the sales world, that is. You see, every time we "pitch" our products or services without knowing precisely what the other person is likely interested in, we're simply imposing our feelings on them. The most productive, positive approach to take is to question first. This has several benefits to us and them.

1. It ensures they're interested in what we have before we suggest it.

2. It tells us specifically where we should focus our recommendations so they have the greatest chance at acceptance.

3. It moves the person into a positive, receptive, even desirous frame of mind so that when they hear your suggestion, they'll view it through the problems or desires you've discussed with them.

Let's look at a simple situation we all have likely experienced. In doing so, examine the psychology and principles, and think of how you can apply them to your calls.

Scenario One

Around 10:30 a.m., a supervisor walks over to a sales rep and says, *"Hey, I know one of the best Chinese restaurants in town that just opened a few miles from here. The Kung Pao Chicken is so spicy it'll make your eyeballs sweat. I've made reservations for lunch. Let's go there."*

The rep looks up, smiles politely, while his stomach is already starting to feel like the inside of an industrial laundry dryer running at full speed. Chinese food not only makes him gag, anything spicier than ketchup sears his tongue.

Scenario Two

Two different people this time. The supervisor saunters over to a rep and inquires,

"Hey, have plans for lunch yet?"

"Not yet."

"Are you up for going out?"

"Yeah, sure."

"Great, what are you hungry for?"

"Oh, I dunno, just about anything I guess."

"Do you like Chinese?"

"That doesn't sound bad."

"What do you normally like to get?"

"Ummm, I like most of it. A variety."

"Do you like spicy dishes?"

"Yeah."

"I do too. The spicier the better for me. How about you?"

"I get extra chile oil sometimes."

"Me too. How about Kung Pao Chicken?"

"Love it."

"Well, let me tell you about a place that just opened up that you'll just love. The reviews so far have not only called it the best Chinese place in town, but I can personally vouch for the Kung Pao Chicken. It's so deliciously hot it'll make the back of your eyes sweat! And the brown sauce, it's to die for."

"I can't wait. Let's go!"

Notice that at any point in the questioning, the inquirer might have heard a response that would have implied the person either wasn't hungry or available for lunch, didn't like Chinese (or spicy), or perhaps had another preference. And based on those responses, the questioner could have either given up—before making a useless pitch that would have no chance—or could have gone with the flow and readjusted, making a recommendation on the quality of the Chinese restaurant, as opposed to the spicy aspect if that wasn't of interest, or worse, was viewed as a liability.

So what in the world does this have to do with you selling by phone? Everything. Use the same principles illustrated here, based on your call objectives. Determine what action you'd like someone to take. Then prepare your questions, and their possible responses. Start with general questioning, transition to more specific questions, and once you've moved them emotionally, *then* make your recommendation.

Action Steps

Chapter 70

How to Handle Prospects Who Need Info Right NOW!

D o you ever have prospects or clients who are in a "panic mode" when they call you? These are the people who urgently need information, and want you to leap through hoops to fax it, overnight express it, or even get it on the next flight out, because their need is NOW.

This type of a request can set off a wild chain of events ... such as the sales rep scrambling for brochures and price lists, hurriedly scratching out a letter and/or proposal, frantically calling other departments checking on inventories, production and shipping capabilities, and overall causing the rep to cast aside all other activities, turning his world and everyone's around him, upside down to handle this urgent panic request because they are ready to "buy now."

Oh, realllly?

The Big Letdown

Most telesales veterans can share war stories of their experiences with the "panic mode" prospects. They burned trails throughout their organization to get the material to the harried requester, and then experienced one of the following:

1. The "prospect" never returned calls.

2. The "prospect" wasn't heard from in weeks.

3. The project was put on the "back burner."

4. They decided to go with someone else. (In some cases the contract was already awarded and they just needed one more bid.)

How does a prospect get in the panic mode? In many cases, his boss probably walks into his office and says, "How are you doing on that new project? I need the figures on my desk tomorrow."

The overworked and underpaid middle-manager, with a feigned look of total control says, "Just wrapping up the last details, boss," while inside his heart has plummeted to his toes faster than the express elevator at the Sears Tower.

Consequently, he burns up the phone lines, frantically calling salespeople to bail him out. His panic is misinterpreted by the sales rep as an immediate opportunity, therefore setting off the fury of activity at the rep's organization.

Some ARE Hot Prospects

Granted, some of these panic requests are valid, and will result in an immediate sale. The key to success is weeding out which ones. Ask questions in the areas of timing, their decision-making criteria, and competition. You might, indeed, identify people in deep muck whose hide you'll be able to save, make a sale in the process, and begin (or solidify) a relationship with.

Others, however, are a complete waste of time and money. And they deflate your morale. Further, like the "boy who cried wolf," others in your organization may treat subsequent "gotta get this out rightaway!" requests with rolled eyes and a sigh of "Here we go again."

Treat these crisis situations as medical emergency personnel would: Calm the person down, get complete information, assess the situation, and react accordingly. You'll save time, money, headaches, and your internal reputation.

Questions to Ask Frenzied Prospects So They'll Qualify—and Maybe Sell—Themselves

The way to handle panicky prospects is through good questioning and qualifying.

Decision-Making Criteria

Never get caught in the goose chase unless you know there is a decision that truly will be made, and that you have a shot at being the choice.

> **"Is this something the company has definitely decided it is going to do?"**
>
> **"Who else is involved in the buying process?"**
>
> **"Upon what criteria are you basing the decision?"**
>
> **"Assuming you like what you see in our information, will you buy from us?"**

Timing Questions

> **"When exactly will the decision be made?"**

"When do you absolutely have to have this material? What will happen after getting it?"

Competitive Information

"Who else are you looking at?"

"Based on what you know and have right now, are you already leaning more towards one vendor?"

Keep them on the phone and handle the call skillfully so they will lean towards you. Give them questions to ask other vendors, if that's part of their plan. I've had many situations where after speaking with me, they decided they didn't need to look around elsewhere. It was a relief for them, and a sale for me.

Action Steps

Chapter 71

How to Keep Customers After the First Sale

Here's a statement uttered by customers every day: "We're perfectly happy with who we're buying from and we wouldn't consider switching." But if you're thinking this is a chapter on how to overcome that objection, it's not. It's about how you can get your customers to *say it to your competitors.*

A newsletter subscriber sent me a note suggesting we address how to build relationships and retain customers once we've opened accounts. That topic could fill an entire book, but we'll cover a few tips here as idea-starters for you to build upon.

☐ **First impressions are lasting.** How many times have you walked out of a restaurant shaking your head in disgust and amazement at the horrific nonservice and indifferent attitude, vowing to never come back, and to tell everyone you know about the experience? Likewise, how about being "wowed" by the overwhelmingly pampered treatment you might have received elsewhere? Those feelings linger with your customers also. Go out of your way to leave a pleasing memory after the first sale. Underpromise and overdeliver when it comes to delivery times. Throw in something free as a "welcome" gift. Mail a handwritten thank you note. Call after the order has been delivered with additional useful information. Reinforce their wise buying decision.

☐ **Learn their business as if it were your own.** The bottom line is the bottom line. There's a lot to be said for building relationships on a personal level (which we'll talk about), but the best way to become truly indispensable is to be an integral part of their business. The more you know about them, the better-equipped you are to make profit-building recommendations. If you're looked at as a sales-boosting consultant—as opposed to a salesperson—customers will never consider listening to the overtures of competitors attempting to stick their foot in the door with promises of lower prices.

☐ **Provide value every time you call.** Don't call to *"just touch base,"* to *"check in,"* or, *"to just stay in touch to see if they need anything."* Customers could potentially view these reactive, no-substance contacts as a nuisance. Make it policy that every time you call you have a value-added reason for doing so. And don't even think about whining that you can't come up with value each time you phone. Reps who cop-out like that remind me of my preteen daughter when she says, "I can't clean my room—it's too hard." No, you just haven't *tried* hard enough yet. Answer this question: What information can you call with that would cause the customer to say they were better off after taking your call than they were before it? Any kind of industry or product news they might find interesting, notification of sales or promotions, or ideas you feel they could use are all value-added reasons for calling. Come up with your own.

☐ **Ask them why they continue buying.** This is so incredibly simple, yet it's rarely used by companies. What you might *think* is a great benefit of doing business with your company could be meaningless to your customer; they might buy for a totally unrelated reason. My dry cleaner might like to believe she gets my business because she does superb work and has competitive prices; I use her because she calls me by name and is close to my office. She has never asked. Ask your customers, **"Pat, I want to make sure we continue providing you what you want. What is it you like best about doing business with us?"** And, **"What else would you like to see?"** Not only will this help you build your relationship, it's information that can help you with your other customers.

☐ **Build personal relationships.** With new customers, at appropriate points during calls (such as the end), ask innocuous questions about their plans for the weekend, or for the summer. Listen carefully to the answers, and react accordingly, sharing of yourself as well. If they mention they're going to curl up in a beach chair with a good book, find out more about what they like to read, and what else, if anything, they do at the beach. Again, common sense stuff, but this works. ***One word of caution***: I've seen reps who were best buddies with everyone, but rarely sold anything. Likeable, yes. But also very *easy* to get rid of by customers, and reluctant to directly ask for business, fearful of being too "pushy." Build relationships, sure ... in the context of business.

❏ **Keep your name in front of them.** You don't need to call every week—indeed you shouldn't—if you don't have a valid reason for doing so. However, in between your calls stay in touch in other ways. I've received postcards from sales reps' personal vacations. Well-read reps clip industry-specific articles from any and every appropriate source and photocopy and send them to customers with a note attached. Send a fax to customers with confidential news of an upcoming sale. E-mail them. Advertisers call this strategy getting your piece of "mindshare," meaning they'll think of you if they have a need before your next contact or when a competitor comes courting.

❏ **Romance them after the marriage, and be fanatical about making it work.** Some sales reps are passionate about chasing the business, but lose interest after the marriage. You need to be committed to the relationship, and be fanatical about service. Otherwise, nothing else matters.

Action Step

Chapter 72

Position Yourself as the Least Risk Vendor

When you shop, do you always look for the least expensive item? Most people don't—including your prospects and customers.

When I was researching and evaluating home theatre equipment I realized that doing the whole deal correctly involved much more than hooking a few speakers to a stereo unit and big screen TV. I visited vendors who specialized in this custom design and installation. Budget was a concern, but not the primary one in the short term. I wanted to minimize or eliminate my longer-term risk of, 1) getting the wrong equipment for the room, overspending for it; 2) setting it up myself which would be undoubtedly painful (I have trouble hooking up a VCR, let alone a cabinet full of circuitry joined by a spaghetti-like web of cables); 3) setting it up incorrectly, which would not only produce undesirable results but cause more grief and expense later, and, 4) avoiding countless other pains that typically happen when I try to do something like this myself. I'm like Tim the Toolman Taylor Times Two when it comes to my ineptitude in such matters of mechanical dexterity.

I heard a great term used to describe exactly what I was looking for, and it applies to most of our own sales prospects as well: the "least risk vendor." Jim Pancero, author of *"Selling at the Top,"* (Dartnell, 1-800-621-5463) explained this concept in his tape program. He points out that when a patient is considering surgery, he doesn't look for the lowest priced vendor and base his decision on the price issue. Finding a bargain isn't the point; lowering the risk of surgery is.

According to Pancero, you can become the least-risk vendor by maximizing your strengths in a few key areas. Let's look at a few of these and what you can do to position the safety of choosing you.

Expertise and Experience. Know everything about why your company's (or maybe your own) expertise and experience makes you the least-risky choice. And when you're talking about your experience, do more than say the word "experience," since by itself, it's meaningless to the listener. Give examples of *results* of the experience:

> **"We have worked with four companies in your industry, and have helped every one beat production quotas."**

> **"Our service department has seen virtually every situation that can occur, and they get people back up and running within an average of five minutes of hearing the problem, usually by phone."**

References. Every time a customer tells you how much they've gained as a result of working with you, ask permission to use them as a reference with your other prospects. Open up a file in your word processor under "Testimonials," and write out their quote, company, and phone number so you can access it later. Better yet, ask if they'll write a letter for you singing your praises. Use these when you have prospects who can easily relate to the customers' situations.

Initiative. This means persistence. Companies spend money on marketing to position a message and create "mindshare." At the sales rep level you do this with frequent, quality contacts. Be sure they understand they'll get the same level of attention after you begin working with them.

Don't lower price. Lessen their perceived risk instead, and you'll increase sales.

How to Handle Specific Least Risk Situations

❑ Make certain your prospects know that you're the least-risk vendor. When a prospect complains that there are others less expensive than you, Jim Pancero, author of *"Selling at the Top,"* suggests responding with

> **"Of course they are. That's part of our company philosophy."**

You can then turn your vulnerability into a strength. And your competitors will unwittingly reconfirm your philosophy every time they call on the prospect and highlight the price issue. The competitive reps will try to sell the fact they have a lower price, while at the same time the prospect will likely view that as a riskier choice, based on the strategic position you've already carved out.

❑ When the price question arises, ask the prospect,

"How long do you plan on keeping it?"

Or, **"How long do you project you'll use it?"**

A person who only plans on keeping a copier for a short time might be willing to risk the consequences of a cheap model. But someone looking for a longer term investment might be happy to pay the extra few bucks.

❏ If the prospect tries to test you with the price issue, or whines about not having too much in the budget, don't apologize for price or be tempted to drop it. Instead, let them know tactfully that you could adjust the price, but they would have to reevaluate which aspect of the offer they could do without. In other words, equate a lower price with not as much value. Not *bad* value, just not as much. For example,

Prospect: "How can we get the price down?"

Sales Rep: "Well, we can look at all of the components I proposed, and decide which ones we could take out."

Action Steps

Chapter 73

Telesales Lessons from The O.J. Trial

L ike much of the country, I was fascinated by the O.J. Simpson ordeal. What particularly struck me were some of the happenings during the preliminary hearings. My interest was specifically in the techniques used by the trial lawyers, particularly Simpson's, and how their methods are similar to sales.

Preparation

For example, Robert Shapiro probably prepared for part of the hearing by thinking, "My objective is to get the judge to understand and conclude that the cops hopped the wall and collected evidence illegally; they did it for reasons other than that they felt there was immediate danger present at Simpson's mansion as they had stated."

As sales reps, we too, set objectives by thinking, "What do I want the prospect/customer to think or do at the end of this call?"

Methodology

Shapiro could have certainly stood before the judge and lectured, "C'mon judge, you and I both know these cops were like most football-lovin' guys, and took advantage of an opportunity to scale O.J. Simpson's wall just like he used to hop over airport terminal chairs in full gallop in those Hertz commercials, just so they'd get a chance to meet him. And unexpectedly they happened to stumble across some strange but innocent stuff that could incriminate my client if you really stretched your imagination, and they later made up stories to cover their behinds. Therefore you should throw the evidence out."

But no, like a good sales rep, he understood that when you **tell** someone what to think, they typically resist. Instead, the best way to help someone accept your beliefs, either initially or in response to objections, is to ask questions.

I particularly remember an impactful exchange on the stand ... when

Shapiro was grilling one of the detectives. To paraphrase,

Shapiro: When you feel there is imminent danger, do you wear bullet-proof vests?

Detective: *Absolutely.*

Shapiro: Did you wear bullet-proof vests at O.J. Simpson's property?

Detective: *No.*

Shapiro: When you feel there is imminent danger, do you enter with your guns drawn?

Detective: *Most definitely.*

Shapiro: Did you enter with your guns drawn?

Detective: *No.*

By simply asking questions, Shapiro aired his points brilliantly ... letting others do most of the talking!

A Call Example

Think about how to do this on your calls. For example, here's one a sales rep for fax-on-demand technology might prepare.

Objective: To help the prospect understand she needs a fax-back system to cut costs and increase sales, and get her to agree to test our system.

Strategy: Ask questions to define how much time and money she's spending, and to realize the hassle she's incurring in fulfilling simple literature requests that can be handled automatically.

Tactics: These are the specific questions to ask during the call.

"What types of common requests for information do you receive regularly?"

"How many per day?"

"How are they handled?"

"By whom?"

"How much time does each take?"

"What are the labor, printing, and postage costs incurred per request?"

"Ever have to fax the material because inquirers need it right away?"

"How much time does it take to fax?"

"Would it be advantageous if every inquirer could

have their material instantly?

"Would that help close more sales?"

"Do you have other pieces of information you would make available to inquirers if they could access it immediately with virtually no extra investment in time or money on your part?"

"What documents are those, and how would it be beneficial to make them accessible?"

These questions basically scratch the surface, but I think you see how the answers get them thinking about the results the system delivers. And it does it without prematurely presenting the "benefits," before she realizes it's something she indeed could use.

A Format for Your Calls

Use a similar format on your calls.

Objective: What do you want them to understand and do as a result of this call?

Strategy: The specific needs and problems you'll need to point out, and how you'll do it through questioning.

Tactics: The specific questions you'll ask. And, spend just as much time anticipating their answers, your next response, etc.

Just like a skilled trial lawyer, your mission as a sales rep is to help people reach conclusions. You do this with thorough preparation, and questions that help buyers understand that what you have is in their best interest.

Action Steps

Chapter 74

Have Strong, Clear Objectives on Every Call

I find that most unsuccessful calls started out with no clear objective. And that's to be expected when you think about it. Embark on *any activity* without first having a precise end result in mind, and it's likely you'll wander aimlessly like a balloon caught in a windstorm.

With a focused objective you psychologically are fixated on achieving the end result, consequently devising and deploying tactics to accomplish it.

And the more specific your objective, the greater your chances of being successful. Look at these vague objections, and their more specific alternatives.

Vague Objective: "To send them out our price list."

Stronger: "To get agreement they will compare our price list with that of their present vendor, find out how close we need to be to get a shot at the business, and to get commitment they will allow us to bid if we're within their requirements."

Vague Objective: "To introduce our company and send out literature."

Stronger: "To generate interest, qualify according to my criteria, and get agreement they will read my literature, check their existing inventory, and discuss a trial order the next time we speak."

Vague Objective: "Follow up on the literature and see if they'd be interested in seeing a proposal."

Stronger: "Define specifically what criteria they will use to select their vendor, present my appropriate

275

> benefits verbally, and ask if those were in a pro-
> posal if they would lean towards picking us. If so,
> writing a proposal, and asking for the prospect's
> commitment that he will recommend us in the se-
> lection meeting."

If your results aren't what you'd like, analyze your call objectives. It could very well be that you're actually achieving exactly what you're setting out to do.

Secondary Objectives Salvage Potential on Each Call

Cherie Dahl sells filters for industrial dust collection machines. When prospecting, her ultimate primary objective is to sell filters, or move the call as close as possible to that end, and schedule a follow-up. Like many of you, she encounters people who are fairly satisfied with their present vendor. Instead of simply ending the call and saying something useless like, "keep us in mind," her secondary objective is to get commitment from the prospect that he will start a file on competitive filters, just in case the need arises to shop around or change. This keeps alive an opportunity for the future and helps her achieve something from a call that otherwise might be considered by some people as a "rejection."

Pre-Call Checklist

Before you place that next call, take just a few seconds to go through this checklist:

✔ **Have you mentally separated yourself from whatever activity you were previously engaged in?** You should block out all thoughts of the previous call, the paperwork, etc. Focus only on the person you are about to speak with.

✔ **Put yourself in a prospect/customer-oriented frame of mind, and be sure that a feeling of warmth and enthusiasm is ready to be projected in your voice.** Make a conscious effort to do this since sometimes our voices can reflect a "down" attitude even when we're not aware of it.

✔ **Concentrate on what you are about to say.** Rehearse it in your mind so that it sounds spontaneous and conversational.

Don't be Paralyzed by Perfection

Although preparation is one of the critical ingredients in a successful call, over-preparation can be stifling. Some people go to extensive lengths studying files, memorizing product specifications, and writing notes and letters. As a result, they don't spend enough time selling. Preparation pays, but don't be paralyzed by the pursuit of perfection.

Have a Secondary Objective

Contractor's Labor Pool provides construction and trade labor to contractors on a temporary, as-needed basis. The primary goal on a call is to identify an immediate need and place people on the job. Naturally, in every situation there may not be an immediate need. Clay Mahle, a sales rep with CLP, then reverts to his Secondary Objective, which is to get agreement and commitment that the contractor could and would use CLP's service when they do require fill-in labor. The action he wants them to take at that point is to fill out the necessary paperwork to register with Contractor's Labor Pool, which solidifies their stated intentions, and makes it much easier for the contractor to fill his need when it arises, which typically occurs on a moment's notice. What could you set as a Secondary Objective ... something you could attain on virtually every call which would ultimately move you closer to a sale at some point, if not today?

How to Eliminate the "D.A.H. Factor"

I often joke in my seminars about avoiding the D.A.H. factor ... that's the lonely, embarrassing moment when a prospect fires a hardball question, objection, or comment at you, and you're absolutely unprepared for it. Your mind locks up like a garbage disposal with a spoon stuck in it, and the only sound you're capable of uttering is *"Daaahhh."*

For the most part, you can avoid—or at least minimize—the occurrence of this experience. It's in being prepared for prospect and customer responses and questions.

For example, assuming you craft a stunning opening statement, the desired response from them is, "That sounds great. Let's talk about it." However, you need to be prepared for the other, not-so-pleasant responses of, "I don't want that," "I don't need that," "I'm already using ..."

Likewise with your questions. Don't simply prepare questions; prepare questions along with all of their possible answers (both desired and otherwise), and then your next questions or responses.

Sounds like a lot of work, doesn't it? It is. Notice I base all of my recommendations here on *preparing* your opening, *preparing* your questions, and *anticipating* what resistance you'll get. We can only become better at an activity through knowledge, preparation, and experience. Invest the time, and your rewards on the phone are well worth the effort.

Action Steps

TeleTips

Chapter 75

TeleTips You Can Use

Would You Rather Be Popular, Or Rich?

Do you have those friendly prospects who welcome you every time you call? The ones you chat with on a personal level, those you wouldn't mind living next door to ... but at the same time haven't ever bought from you? Some phone relationships reach such a ridiculously personal level—often with prospects who are too wishy-washy to volunteer any type of decision—that reps get timid about bringing it back to business and move toward a decision. Popularity won't put beans on the table. Ask for a decision when things get too cozy with no business to show for it.

> **"Steve, I've really enjoyed talking to you lately, and we've determined we can help you in all the ways I've listed. Is there anything stopping us from moving forward on this?"**

This Idea Is Like Printing Your Own Money

Sales trainer Bryan Mattimore writes in his book, *"99% INSPIRATION"* (AMACOM, New York) about how he gets sales reps to transform product descriptions into visuals that prospects can picture.

He passes out old magazines and has reps create a collage of cutouts of all their favorite things: cars, sports, food, outdoor scenes, etc. Then they assign words to each picture.

This puts them in the proper frame of mind for their next exercise, which is to create one big metaphorical word picture to describe their product or service by completing the sentence,

> **"Our product/service is a lot like _____** *(insert a word)* **because it _____."**

For example, a sales rep might say,

> **"Our product is a lot like a filet mignon steak be-**

cause we've trimmed all the fat from it.

Try this. It will help you think of creative, visual ways to position your product/service. *(SOURCE: The Competitive Advantage, P.O. Box 10828, Portland, OR, 97210)*

If You Really Cared About Them, You'd Sell Them

I see reps leave all kinds of money on the table because they fail to ask for commitment, or larger sales. They don't want to be pushy, they rationalize. Consider one thing: If you really care about these people, you'll help them make a decision. Because, when you know buying from you is in their best interest, and they don't volunteer the sale, their anxiety sets in. Think about a decision you knew you needed to make, but you kept putting off. Then recall the relief you felt after finally taking the action. Take away their anxiety and help them make decisions by asking them to buy.

Handling the Literature Request

Don't be afraid to find out if it's a stall, or a sign of interest:

> **"So I assume you want the material because you're definitely interested in buying something like this?"**

> **"If you like what you see in the literature, what would be the next step?"**

Take a Warm Bath (Ok, Just Your Throat)

Drinking warm liquids tends to bathe and soothe the vocal cords, putting less stress on them when you're speaking. Cold liquids constrict the vocal cords, exposing you to potential damage. Also, dairy and cola products can produce unwanted matter in the mouth and throat, hindering your speech clarity.

Make a Big Deal Out of the Deal

Everyone likes to feel like they've made the best deal possible. Conversely, we despise the thought we might have been "taken." That's probably why most people hate the traditional dickering and game playing when buying a car. So reinforce the good feelings people get when buying from you. If you give concessions, do it painfully so they feel you don't do it all the time (which you shouldn't.) Compliment them on their negotiating skills. Let them know what a great deal they made:

> **"You're really getting a bargain here. Our margins are cut to the bone."**

Will They Buy From *Anyone*?

Spending too much time chasing elusive prospects who seem interested, but yet aren't buying? One way to refocus your efforts and be more productive is to ask yourself these questions about the prospects you pursue: "What are the chances they will buy from *anyone*?", and, "What are the chances they'll buy from **me**?" If you're not certain they'll make a purchase from anyone, the percentages in your second answer become somewhat moot. Therefore, spend your time with people you know are buyers and work to ensure they'll buy from you.

Marketing Tips

Barbara Leff shares some great tips in her booklet, *"123 Great Marketing Ideas to Grow Your Business."*

• **Place a small photo of yourself on your business card.** This connects your card with you.

• **Swap membership lists with colleagues in order to get fresh prospects.**

• **Keep a good supply of business cards with you wherever you go.** Even if all of your business is over the phone. Depending on what you sell, hand them out where appropriate ... to delivery people, stores you do business with, etc.

• **Submit feature articles to the trade publications that your prospects and customers read.** Make it full of useful content regarding how they can improve their business in some way, naturally tied into the use of your type of product or service. But don't try to promote your specific product or service (that wouldn't get printed anyway—as an article). But do insist that your name, company, and how you can be contacted appear at the end of the article. You might be pleasantly surprised about how this positions you as an expert, and prompts some calls. If you do get articles published, send them to customers and prospects.

• **Send notes to customers on the anniversary of your first sale to them.** Thank them for doing business with you and for their continuing support.

• **Use commemorative first-class stamps when mailing to a limited list.** This makes the envelope look less like "junk mail."

• **Use a P.S. at the end of your letters to reiterate an important point or call to action.** The P.S. generally is the most frequently read portion of the letter.

(SOURCE: "123 Great Marketing Ideas to Grow Your Business," a booklet by Barbara Leff. The Marketing Menu, 70 W. Burton, #1804T, Chicago, IL, 60610. 312-604-1620.)

Summarize Your Understanding

Before even considering talking about the results of what you can deliver, ensure you have a clear picture of what he wants. Paraphrase, or restate, what you understand his desires to be.

For example,

> **"So that I'm sure I understood what you said you're looking for, let me summarize ..."**

> **"To be certain I'm thinking along the same lines as you are ..."**

> **"So I know we're together on this, let's go over ... "**

Your Voice Mail Greeting

Use your own voice mail greetings as a mini advertisement. One of my printing sales reps leaves on his,

> **"Oh, and be sure to ask about the new ideas we have on promoting your business."**

Also, listen to the greeting you put on. Be sure your tone of voice conveys the enthusiasm you hope your prospects will also have when you call.

Correct Speech Habits, Ya' Know

In listening to calls I hear quite a few occurrences of certain words and phrases that detract from the professional images reps want to convey. Watch out for, and avoid these:

"Really?", at the end of prospect's statements. (As if the prospect should respond, "No, I was lying."

"Ya'know"

"Yeah"

Using *"Like,"* as in, *"It was, like, cool."*

Using, *"I mean"* constantly. You shouldn't use this too much, I mean, *like, not all the time, ya know?*

General to Specific

When early questions in a call immediately deal with specific, perhaps even sensitive information, the tone can be interpreted as pushy. For example, *"OK, bottom line, what are you paying for your widgets, and in what ways is the vendor screwing up?"* A better way is to ease naturally into the specifics by fist beginning with general questions on the topic:

> **"Let's talk about the widgets you're using now. What brand do you prefer?"**

Then you can conversationally move to the more need-related questions.

Tease Them a Little

During your questioning, you undoubtedly uncover need areas you can fill. Many sales reps prematurely jump in and begin a presentation too early after learning just one potential hot button. It's to your advantage to hold off on the presentation until you've fully developed the needs, and then make a much more on-target presentation. To transition between questioning topics and whet their appetite for what will follow, "tease" them. For example,

Prospect: "... and we really need a service that will handle the reporting from start to finish."

> **Sales Rep: "I think you'll like the way we handle that, and I'll tell you about it in a minute. Tell me about your maintenance requirements."**

Use Statements to Get Information

Tell people to give you information by using instructional statements. For example,

> **"Don, give me some idea of how you're handling this situation now."**
>
> **"Fill me in on ..."**
>
> **"Share with me ..."**
>
> **"Tell me about ..."**

Explain the Jargon

If you use technical or industry-specific terms, explain them to be sure the other person understands. If it goes over their head, they might just let it slide, and your point will be meaningless.

> **"Chuck, the Dooley Rating on this is 99.9%. That's the measurement of customer satisfaction, based on independent customer surveys."**

Ask What Influenced Them Before

During your questioning, ask how they made buying decisions in the past for your types of products/services. For example,

> **"Jan, the last time you selected a contractor, what criteria did you use?"**

Or, **"What were the most important things you looked at when you chose your present vendor?"**

Then you could follow those answers with,

> **"What other factors would you have considered if you were to do it all over again?"**

Give the Results First in the Opening

An approach that works is to mention the results of what you can do, before even giving your company name on prospecting calls. For example,

> **"Ms. Duncan, the reason I'm calling you is that my company provides a line of cutting tools that typically last twice as long under stress as conventional tools. If I caught you at a good time, I'd like to ask as few questions about your experiences with what you're using now to see if this would be something worth taking a look at. By the way, our company is Incision Industries."**

The rationale here is that unless they're familiar with your company, the name is meaningless. What they really care about is what you can do, and that grabs their attention at the very beginning.

What Image are You Projecting?

Isn't it such a breath of fresh air when you hear someone pleasant, willing, and eager to help you when you call an organization to inquire about, or buy something?

I called two glass companies last week to inquire about having a crack repaired on my windshield. Here's what happened:

Company 1- After 8 rings, a guy—who sounded like I just got him out of bed—answered with *"Yeah."* Taken aback, after getting confirmation it was indeed a glass company, I asked if he did chip repairs. *"Yep,"* he responded. It was a short call.

Company 2- The guy answered with a jovial tone, asked me about the chip, asked me when I wanted it done, told me it would take only 20 minutes, and offered to come to my office within the hour to fix it. Guess who got the business?

Call During the "Bad" Times

Sales managers often hear excuses from reps as to why they're not calling more frequently, or getting top results: "It's a slow season," "Friday afternoon is a bad time," "Everyone is in meetings on Monday morning," etc. However, the superstars recognize that the key to success is in consistent activity, especially during these times. Call when everyone else isn't and you'll have a greater chance at succeeding.

Isolate the Problem

It's senseless to deal with smokescreens or vague signs of resistance that aren't contributing to the real reason for the person's hesitancy. You must first isolate the problem to the one, core issue that's stopping them. For example,

> **"Can we narrow down your reason for not moving forward to just this price issue?"**
>
> **"If we completely took the minimum order size requirement out of the discussion, would you agree**

that this is the best offer you've seen?"

"Other than total number of years of experience, is there any other issue that is stopping you from selecting us?"

Open Accounts Just Like Your Best Ones

The 80/20 rule applies to many of us: 80% of our business comes from 20% of our customers. Therefore, when going after new customers, try to ensure that you're going after people who will be like the 20% of your customers who now give you most of your business. Do an analysis of that 20%. What characteristics do they have in common? Target your prospecting at groups possessing similar traits. Best yet, ask for referrals from your best customers. You might find they'll refer you to buyers similar to them.

Clarify the Time Frame

When discussing time frames with prospects and customers, ensure you both have an understanding of the terms used. For example, one person's summer might be another's early fall. Also, 1st quarter would be January-March if they're on a calendar year basis, but could be something else depending on their fiscal year.

How to Advise of a Price Increase

If you ever need to call customers and inform them of a price increase, ensure you soften the blow first. For example, you can contrast the actual increase with a larger one that might have been contemplated:

"We looked at what other suppliers in the industry have been doing, and some have raised their prices as much as 20% because of the rise in material costs. We decided that by maintaining our volumes and efficiencies we could manage with just a 10% increase."

Compliment the Competition

When discussing the competition, don't be afraid to pay them a compliment. The listener will appreciate you for it, plus he'll view you as possessing the same characteristics you're commending the competition for. For example,

Prospect: "So, what do you think about Geezer Services?"

Sales Rep: "Well, I know they also have a good maintenance department."

Don't Prejudge, or Be Intimidated

For many of us there are certain personality types, that for whatever reason, we tend to either be annoyed with, or intimidated by. It's imperative that you don't let this personal bias negatively affect your behavior on the phone upon reaching one of these individuals. For example, a person who usually falls to pieces when talking with a gruff-sounding, non-talkative, no-nonsense decision maker must deal with this problem the second the other person answers the phone. Otherwise, they'll allow themselves to be intimidated, and the call will be lost.

Get Caught Up in the Excitement!

Everyone needs motivation, and often a pick-me-up comes from the enthusiasm of others. One rep told me that when she hears another rep in her area getting excited about a sale he or she just made she'll tune into the conversation, getting pumped up by the other rep's excitement, and also picking up on the tactical details of the call.

Plant Now for a Future Harvest

Many people look at January 1st as the traditional starting point for the year ... a time to begin working on the New Year's resolution, to go after those goals. Consider this: If you wait until January to start work on your goals, you'll already be behind. Jim Rector with Motivational Technologies points out that what you do today determines how well you'll do in January. You're now planting seeds which you'll harvest later. If you plan on starting the year off with a flourish, keep that in mind every day, starting now, and make it happen!

Verify the Spelling

This next point seems painfully elementary, but can't be emphasized enough, since not following it can do irreparable damage: Be sure that when hearing your contact's name by phone for the first time to also get the spelling. I've learned this the hard way several times. Oh, sure, we always ask for the spelling of the difficult names—it's the "easy" ones that trip you up. I ended a call, talking to a Mr. "stoo-ert." After the call, I wondered if it was Stuart, or Stewart. After calling back to the company's switchboard, I learned it was Stuarte. When you have a "tray'-see" on the line, is it Tracey, Traci, Tracie, or Tracy? Just yesterday I talked to a "Tracye."

Prospect Their Former Companies

At a Telesales Rep College, Mena Natale, with Torpac, Inc., had a suggestion for getting referrals: If you run across a start-up company while prospecting, ask your contact for someone to talk to at their previous employer. Often, start-ups are spawned from larger companies ... companies that are in similar businesses, buying like-items.

The "Three Sentence" Rule

Mena also shared a useful tip on presentations and listening: Try not to make more than three statements without getting some type of feedback, or asking a question to elicit their response. This way, you ensure you're not talking too much about irrelevant points. Hearing their feedback keeps you on track.

Eliminate Telephone Tag

Telephone tag is a hair-pulling, wasteful exercise in futility. Judy Coco with Praxair leaves voice mail messages designed to cut down the message ping-pong:

> **"... and if you reach voice mail when you call me back, please let me know the best time to call you, a time when you'll be at your desk."**

She also suggests letting them know you'll call at a specific time.

Determine if Their Deal is For Real

John Ellis with Virtual Telecommunications gave a suggestion for responding to people who tell you the terms you'll need to beat in order to win the business. In cases where you're offering essentially the same product/service, and they've already told you price is the only factor, and there's no way you could match the price (indicating they might not be telling the total truth), respond with,

> **"That's a great deal you have there. I can't beat it, and you probably ought to take advantage of it. One thing though: if you find that you're not getting everything you expect for that price, please give me a call, because I can guarantee what you'll receive with us."**

This is a tactful way to allow them to admit that just maybe they are not comparing apples to apples.

Pause ... to Grab Their Attention

I've long promoted using the pause as a way to get more information when listening, and as a speaking tool to ensure you're not using filler words such as "uh" and "umm." Jim Crowley, with Kaskor added that using the pause while speaking brings back their attention to what you're saying. Sometimes listeners might tune out, and stay tuned out as long as the other person is speaking (remember that boring teacher in high school or college?) The pause has a subtle way of snapping their attention back to the conversation.

Place Relationship-Maintenance Calls

Many sales reps call customers to stay in touch with them, which is a fine way to keep a relationship healthy.

When making these calls have a specific relationship-maintenance objective in mind, not a selfish one like, *"We haven't heard from you in a while so I thought I'd check in with you. Is everything OK? Would you like to place an order while I have you on the line?"*

In George Walther's book, *"Upside Down Marketing: Training Your Ex-Customers into Your Best Customers,"* he gives his rule of thumb for relationship-maintenance calls: If the customer hangs up feeling glad you called, you're on target. Ask yourself before you dial, "What am I going to do in this call that will make the customer feel glad that I called?"

Walther suggests having a "tip of the day" in mind when you call. Think of yourself as an expert business consultant who is constantly in contact with many companies whose operations are similar. Without divulging any competitive secrets, pass along tips they can use. Often—but not always—these ideas will involve using your products or services. Your tips might be like,

> **"Steve, I picked up an idea from another one of my customers you might benefit from. They're a manufacturer like you, and are using an inventory control system that reduces their overhead costs. Let me tell you some of the basics, and you can see if it would be worth looking into ..."**

The more successful your customers are, the better able they'll be to buy more of what you're selling. And they'll also welcome every call from you with open arms, since they view you as a value-added partner.

("Upside-Down Marketing" by George Walther is a superb new book that shows you how to reach people whose buying has tapered off—or stopped completely—and convert them into your company's best customers. You're probably sitting on a goldmine of new business you could get from existing customers, and this book will show you how. It's only $19.95 + $2 shipping. Call 800-326-7721, or e-mail to arts@businessbyphone.com.)

Find Out What Has Changed

When calling customers or prospects you haven't contacted in some time, keep in mind that changes have taken place in their organization. Even though you might have hit a brick wall last time, circumstances might now be appropriate. Ask questions like,

> **"What has changed in your sales department since the last time we spoke in April?"**

> **"What are you doing differently since our discussion right after your major trade show?"**

Give Them a Home Number

I noticed this on a sales rep's card, and felt it was a nice touch: write your home telephone number on the back of your card if it's appropriate for your industry and customers. For example, there are some customers who might require questions answered or problems solved during off-hours. Making yourself accessible during those times has a positive perception that far exceeds any inconvenience it might cause you. By the way, *writing* the number adds to the exclusiveness of the gesture. The chances anyone will call are slim, but the impact is made on *everyone*.

Do You Understand Them?

Ensure that you completely understand your customers/prospects. Words can be interpreted many ways. For example, think of how the word "hit" would be interpreted by, a baseball player; a boxer; a Mafia member; and, by a movie producer. Likewise, analyze the language you use, and be certain it's clear.

Motivate Yourself to Squeeze More Productivity From Your Time

You'll only make more efficient use of your time if you want to. What would it mean to you if you could make five more calls per day? How about ten? Fifteen maybe?! Attach a dollar figure to it. Then ask yourself, "Why not?" You'll find the possibilities are easy when you look for them.

Who Asked You to Call?

Amy Bernstein with Executive Express gets lots of inquiries in response to magazine ads. She often hears from the inquirers, "I was given this ad and was asked to call you to get more information." Instead of just reactively complying and sending the material, she questions the caller. Amy particularly wants to find out who gave the ad to the caller, and what role they might have in the decision making process.

An Alternative to "Ask a Few Questions ..."

We need to ask questions in order to make the best sales recommendation, no doubt about it. And in looking back at virtually every opening statement tip I've made over the years, I've included a phrase similar to, " ... and I'd like to ask a few questions to determine ..."

It works, and I still suggest it, although I've recently heard another option that sounds like a fresh alternative. Kim Horna, with Midwest Computer Supply, proposes

> " ... **and I'd like to exchange some information with you** ..."

For example, on a prospecting call, after introducing herself, she might say,

> " ... **depending on your current method of computer**

back up, I have some ideas that have worked well for other MIS Directors that resulted in improved efficiency of their computer operations. If I've caught you at a convenient time, I'd like to exchange some information about the systems you support ..."

Kim feels it's a smooth, non-salesy way to flow into a dialogue.

They Might Not Buy Today, But When?

You've reached the point in the call where you've bumped into one dead end after another. You're at your wit's end searching for a fiber of potential to keep the call breathing, but you're coming up empty in the brilliant phrases department. What do you do? If all of your options are exhausted they probably aren't a prospect for you—today. No problem. But they might be in the future. Let them tell you when, and what will need to change with their situation for that to be true. Ask them,

"Under what circumstances would you consider upgrading?"

"What would have to happen with your organization in order for you to look at adding personnel?"

"At what point would you see yourself increasing your ad budget?"

"What changes would need to take place before you'd implement this type of program. What are the chances of that happening within the next year?"

"What do you see happening in your department over the next couple of months that might have an effect on what you'll do regarding this issue?"

These questions get them thinking of possibilities. And if they can visualize those changes and possibilities, that's the first step in at least considering them as an option.

Have The Boss Read It

Sending out material to prospects and customers is an obscene waste of time and money unless they **do** something with it. Marlene Watson with Access IBM suggests saying,

"When I send it, after you read it, will you have your boss read it too?"

This is appropriate when they've told you their boss is involved in the decision making or approving process.

Give Them Satisfaction On Your Voice Mail

Some of you have voice mail that intercepts your calls while you're busy talking to other customers or away from your desk. To minimize the chance of missing sales let your callers know that you will call them right back, and be precise with the time frames so they know you will. Everyone says, *"I'm talking to another customer right now ...",* and it's often viewed with skepticism (especially when you hear it after hours). Add to that greeting something more specific,

> **" ... and from 9:00 to 11:45 this morning I will check my messages every 15 minutes, so leave your name ..."**

Sure, you'll need to change your greeting a few times per day, but that will indicate to your callers that you really are there and will call them back. Otherwise, just think what might happen if an antsy prospect gets your recording, doesn't have a clue as to when you might call back (and doesn't want to wait), and therefore calls your competition. It happens. So give them satisfaction, now.

Sales Tips to Use Right Now

Here are a few profitable tips from Joe Verde's excellent sales newsletter, *"Selling Cars Today."* (I've adapted the ideas for generic products/ services.)

❑ **People like to own things, but with some items and services, they don't like buying them.** So quit using the words *"buy," "sell,"* and *"sold"* when talking with your customer. Instead of *"Is this the machine you'd like to buy?"*, try,

> **"Is this the machine you'd like to own?"**

It sounds better, and customers feel more comfortable.

❑ **Present a "similar situation."** People are interested in people— especially those they can relate to. When you have a customer who says they can't afford what you sell, try,

> **"You know Bob, I was talking to someone the other day who was in the same budget situation you are, and here's what he did ..."**

Be prepared for such instances.

❏ **Use the "Why not try ...?" closing question.** It's a nonthreatening way for them to make a decision.

"Pat, why not try the deluxe model?"

Psychologically they're trying, not buying.

(SOURCE: Joe Verde's "Selling Cars Today," P.O. Box 267, San Juan Capistrano, CA, 92693)

Soften the Impact of a Negative

When your prospect or customer makes a request you're unable— or unwilling—to fill, don't hem and haw, or give in. Let them know you won't be able to grant the wish, but soften it first in a positive way.

> **"I would love to be able to offer free shipping. The fact is, the price you're getting is the lowest around, and our margin is razor thin already, and we're just passing on the actual shipping cost in order to offer that low price."**

> **"I wish I could get it quicker for you. The manufacturing process dictates that the machine burns in for 24 hours before we can ship it. This way you get a unit that's already been tested, minimizing the chance it will go down later, causing an ever bigger headache.**

Using the Fax to Drive Inbound Calls

Robert Bolton with L.A. Cellular shared with me how his telesales department uses mass faxing in their marketing and telesales. He calls it "fishing with a net instead of a pole."

Instead of making cold calls to prospects, their objective is to contact both prospects and customers (whom they wish to upgrade) with an offer by fax in order to stimulate a phone call from them.

For example, a rep working from a directory would call a selected prospect company and say to the person answering,

> **"I'm with L.A. Cellular, and I'd like to fax over some information on a special cellular phone promotion that might be of some interest there. Whose atten-**

tion should I direct that to?"

They then get the contact name and the fax number, and the fax offer goes out. One promotion they've been running offers three cellular phones for $100. This generates responses from both existing customers interested in upgrading, and non-customers. One rep in particular noticed even a higher response because of an added twist: his fax messages were handwritten.

This system also provides leads—which are not icy cold—for the sales reps. On outbound calls to non-responders the reps reference the fax special. Even if the prospects don't buy in response to this offer, an added benefit is that L.A. Cellular has the fax numbers on file for future offers.

Motivation is Also Critical

Robert also shared a couple inspirational quotes.

"Attitude: Keep yours positive. Approach each call as if it's your first of the day."

"Enthusiasm: Energy and excitement will move the prospect. Your enthusiasm will affect your environment. Show it in your voice."

Learn the One Reason Behind Their Resistance

When you hear an objection, be certain you're isolating the real reason for the resistance. Otherwise, you're running on a treadmill—a lot of activity, but no forward progress. After hearing the objection, question it with,

"If I understand what you're saying, if it weren't for the price, this is the program you'd choose, is that right?"

"Let me be sure I understand. If we included the workbooks, we'd be the ones to win the bid, correct?"

"Let's confirm we're talking about the same issue here. You would get the system from us, it's just that the delivery time is holding you back, right?"

Listen for Changes

When your prospect or customer volunteers information on any changes at his company, find out what his feelings are about them. This can provide tremendous insight about his personal needs and ideas. For example,

Prospect: "Yeah, we've had a major restructuring here regarding how we need to report our inventory to corporate."

Sales Rep: "I see. How is that affecting you?"

Prospect: "It's created a lot more work for my people."

Sales Rep: "What are your feelings about the change?"

Prospect: "It stinks. I need to get twice the work done with the same staff."

If you just happen to sell something that helps to save time (in this case) you've uncovered a goldmine of information to help them sell themselves.

Put Yourself on Their Level

Gerry McKay, a manager with Thompson & Thompson suggests that asking *"Would it be OK to call you back in a couple of weeks?"* implies that you're not at the same level as the prospect/customer. In her business, her reps talk to busy paralegals at law firms and who often say they'll get around to reviewing the literature "in a couple of weeks." What she finds to work well is,

"Why don't I plan on calling you in two weeks? This way you won't have to worry about calling me back."

She made another good point on the price issue. Often prospects might say they can get a similar product for less money from a competitor. Gerry knows that the competition often quotes a low "bare bones" price, but then loads up the customer with additional charges for things they consider extra. She simply has her reps ask,

"What other charges would you incur in addition to the base price of the service?"

This helps them think about what they'll pay, bottom line, instead of the base price.

What Next?

The success of your follow-up call is always directly proportionate to the success of your previous call, and how well you positioned what's to happen between now and the next contact, and then set up the agenda of the next contact. At a training program I did for ERM Computer Services, Marilyn Watson suggested this question at the conclusion of a call:

> **"What do you suggest we should cover on our next call?"**

This gets them thinking about the next step.

Cheaper Now, But Ultimately More Expensive

Here is another question you might use in a situation where the price might seem low up front, but would ultimately be more in the long run:

> **"You're paying (or being quoted) a smaller price up front, but will it end up costing you more long-term?"**

This should evoke a "Huh?"-kind of response—which is exactly what you're looking for. It would lead naturally into a discussion about your long-term value vs. a one-time lower price. For example, if you know your product lasts longer than the el-cheapo competitor's, say,

> **"Well, how long do you plan on using the product?"**

Their answer might help point out that a replacement would ultimately cost more in the long run. If their product requires more service, more labor to operate, or anything of that nature, ask,

> **"What have you figured your costs to be for maintenance/labor/servicing with that product?"**

Again, this is designed to get them thinking about the hidden costs that aren't apparent with the cut-rate initial price tag, but nevertheless come back to bite them in the long run.

Purge Your Follow-Up Files

You will immediately increase production by cleaning up your follow-up files, therefore avoiding wasting time with people who will never buy. Pick one prospect per day who continually puts you off and ask,

> **"What's the probability we can move forward on a purchase within the next month?"**

They Can Hear Your Body Language

You wouldn't dream of plopping down in a chair, slouching so your head was barely visible in a face-to-face sales presentation. Don't do it on the phone either. They can hear how you are sitting.

They'll Never Hang Up on Themselves

Hans Dippel, a Senior Wine Broker with Windsor Vineyards sent me a few of his thoughts on objections. As I have long believed and taught, Hans says that when you get an objection, what the prospect is saying is not that you need to give more information to him, but you need to **get** more information from him. You need to ask more questions. He said, "No one will hang up on you when they're doing the talking." Therefore, it's up to you to get and keep them talking. Upon hearing resistance, don't attack their intelligence with a slick rebuttal; instead prompt them to open up with a well-thought-out question that is designed to get them thinking about why they feel the way they do.

How to End the Call Gracefully

To end a call after the constructive business portion has concluded, talk in the past tense to signal it's time to wrap up and move on. For example,

> **"Hey, it was great talking with you again ..."**
>
> **"I'm glad we had the opportunity to hammer out these details on ..."**
>
> **"It looks like you've given me everything we need to get this processed for you ..."**

By the way, small talk can help build relationships, but too much of it wastes time.

What to Ask Yourself Before Every Call

Here's a tip that I should repeat on every page of this book, because it's the foundation for all persuasion and sales. Before you place your call ask yourself, "What does this person want most, and want to avoid as it relates to my types of products/services?" Your answers provide ideas for opening statements, responses to screeners' questions, and it helps you develop your questioning plan.

Review Your Call

I've long advocated replaying every call in your mind immediately after you've finished, asking yourself the question,

"What did I like about this call?",

and for the trouble spots, posing the action-oriented query,

"What would I have done differently if I had the chance?"

Shari Wilkens, a sales trainer with Fred Pryor Seminars shared a fabulous variation of the second question that I believe I'll now suggest instead: **"What will I do <u>next time</u> if I run into the same situations?"**

"Objections" Might Be Symptoms of Bigger Problems

Here's a piece of wisdom to ruminate over: An objection really isn't an objection if there simply isn't a fit or a genuine need in the prospect's mind for what you sell. If you're encountering objection after objection on your calls, those might simply be the symptom of the real problem: A lack of incisive questioning before presenting.

Discuss It Over Coffee

Marilyn Mitchell with Sigma Diagnostics sets herself apart from the competition by mailing coffee mugs and packets of coffee to targeted accounts and prospects. She has little trouble getting through, since they remember her gesture when she calls.

They Don't Care About Your Products

No one cares about your products or services, other than maybe you and others in your company. Your prospects and customers are concerned most with the **results** they'll derive from owning and using the products/ services. And if you begin a call, a voice mail message, or an answer to the screener's question regarding the nature of the call by talking about products/ services, you'll likely create resistance. Their thought is, "We already have/ use/own that." Or, "I'm happy with my vendor." Which makes sense, because the focus is on the product/service, not on the result. Instead, brainstorm for the precise results people enjoy from using and owning what you sell. To generate interest, talk about the ideas, methods, concepts, processes, techniques, programs, and procedures that just might be able to help them to ... (fill in here with the results you're pretty sure they desire.)

Listen To Your Elected Officials; At Least You Might Learn Sales Ideas

Usable sales techniques surround us every day, in all areas of our lives. The morning after New Jersey Governor Christine Todd Whitman's Republican response to the President's State of the Union Address, one of the TV wake-up shows questioned her, attempting to blow holes in the content of her speech. The smug interviewer said, "Your critics have said that your own tax cuts favor the wealthy. How do you respond to that?" (This question is a sales tactic itself. It's the third-party technique; masking your feelings and what you want to say by attributing it to someone else, i.e. "Your critics say ...")

Her response was brilliant, since she not only refuted the premise of the question decisively by citing facts and figures, but what really struck me was the way she prefaced the response. She said,

"There are two things I love about that claim ..."

She then explained two pieces of faulty logic behind the assertion, then answered them. And she did it with a mischievous smile and a tone that implied, "I can't believe people say that!" Since then I've tried this idea, and found it to work well when someone repeats false claims they've heard elsewhere. Also, you're able to disprove a belief without fear of offending the speaker, since (ostensibly) it's likely not yet *their* belief; it's something they've heard elsewhere.

If They're Buying, Continue Selling

I heard a great comment from a sales rep at a seminar:

"Don't quit selling before they quit buying."

Which means when you have a customer in dire need of what you have (especially on incoming calls, or when they initiated the contact through a mail or phone inquiry), don't let your preconceived notion of how much (or how little) you think they're willing to spend stop your selling. For example, I've seen reps answer a question on just the one item a caller inquired about, and the customer bought it instantly. In retrospect, these reps could have continued questioning and recommending to help the customer even further fill his need or solve his problem. If you quit selling before they quit buying, you're missing sales.

Call the During the Second Shift

Karen Kubiak with Graphic Controls will occasionally call later in the evening and speak with workers on the second shift at hospital labs. This helps her collect valuable information—from people who actually use her products—that she might not otherwise learn.

Don't Leave Them On Hold

During a Telesales Rep College we debated the merits of placing someone on hold vs. leaving them on the line waiting while we look up information in the computer. For example, some reps are caught off guard when a prospect returns a call, causing them to say, *"May I please put you on hold for a moment?"*, while they scramble to pull up the person's record and attempt to remember why they called the person in the first place. Susan Mattson with United Stationers suggested *not* putting the person on hold. Using the time resourcefully by asking a few questions while you buy time is one option, small talk is another. Even if you're silent, Susan said, it's better than having them waiting on hold listening to music.

Understand Needs From Their Perspective

A key to successful selling is understanding, from your buyers' perspective, what they really want. Sarah Stewart with Medline Industries was formerly a buyer with her company, and now that she's in sales she can easily relate to that perspective. She knows, firsthand, that all buyers don't have the time to do cost analyses on multiple products and lines. Therefore, she offers to do this for selected prospects she feels she has a good chance of closing. She asks,

> **"If I did a comparison for you, would this make your job easier?"**

She asks this knowing full well it would. She then does a detailed comparison between what they're buying now, and what they could get from Medline. She can cross-reference inventory and compare prices on single units, boxes, cases, etc., providing a breakdown that the buyer might never do himself, but nevertheless could be very beneficial.

If You Promise It, DO It

Have you ever completely blown it and forgotten, or ignored plans to carry through on a promise you made? Most of us have. I'm in the process of dealing with several building and trade subcontractors right at this moment, and sadly, I'm genuinely shocked when someone actually does call me back or show up when they said they would. Be careful of how you communicate your reason for the blunder to the offended party. For example, you don't want to say, *"I've been just swamped lately. I'm so busy."* This admits that you didn't place a high priority on their request or your promise to them. And if you can't meet the deadline you both agree to when promising something, it's quite simple: don't commit to it in the first place. It's better that you have that understanding up front than let them down later, damaging your credibility in the process. If it doesn't look like you'll come through, let them know before the deadline. Either you can make contingency plans, or revise the deadline. If you simply forgot, apologize, take complete responsibility, and focus on what you're willing to do.

Let Them Put You On Hold

If the forward movement of your buying process is contingent on them doing something (gathering facts and figures, filling out and returning credit apps, etc.), avoid delaying it for another call if possible. Kathleen Ashbey with International Automated, suggests saying,

> **"OK, let's do it now while I have you on the line. I'll wait on hold while you get it."**

If they truly are sincere about doing something, this is a great way to qualify them and determine that. If they're resistant, and had no real intention anyway, now is a better time to learn that than later.

Think About "Decision Making Process," Not Just the Decision Maker

Oh sure, you might have done a fine job of identifying, getting to, and talking to the buyer, but do you know the buying process and who else is involved, or who else impacts it? Your contact might be sold, but is there a purchasing agent who wants to "shop it around" for a better deal? How about Larry in Operations? Maybe he has a personal favorite, and you don't even know he exists? Is there someone else at a peer level to your contact, who, perhaps is vying for the same money your contact is looking to spend with you? To ensure you can impact the entire process ask questions about it.

> **"What will need to happen on your end to finalize this purchase?"**

"What other people or departments might have impact on this decision?"

"Is there anyone who would rather see this not happen?"

"He's Out Goofing Around Today"

When you are out of the office, or even just away from your desk, ask
other people who answer your phone to say to your callers,

"He'll be in tomorrow," or,

"She'll be back in an hour."

It leaves a better impression, and is more service-oriented than *"He's
not in today,"* or, *"She's not here."* Better yet, have them say,

"Is there something I can help you with, or would
you like to leave a message?"

Overdeliver, and You'll Build Relationships

When I can hit a key on the computer I wrote these words with and
instantly send messages to thousands of people all over the world, why
does it take "3-4 weeks" for a company to fill my order for something like
wallpaper or to get a rebate check? If you want to stand out from the
crowd, it's not that difficult. Simply go the extra inch—a mile isn't necessary—for your prospects and customers. Surprise them. If you say you'll
have it there within the week, get it there in two days. If you tell them you'll
overnight the proposal, fax a copy now, with a note saying

"Thought you'd like to see this sooner."

You'll be remembered.

Watch Your Language

The words "love" and "hate" evoke emotion that can aid in your
sales effort. For example,

"Wouldn't you love to go a month without having
your copier fail?" And,

"Don't you hate it when your order is late?"

Another language tip is to use active verbs. For example, *"Our products are used by the Smith Company,"* is dull compared to,

"The Smith Company uses our products."

Reinforce Their Purchasing Decision

You might think the sale is cemented when they tell you "yes," but those of us who've had sales canceled by customers who later were bitten by buyer's remorse know that the sales process continues in the customer's mind long after delivery of the product/service. You might not be able to change the product itself, but you can enhance their perception and enjoyment of it after they've made the decision. For example, if they've negotiated with you, and you tossed in a few extras, you might congratulate them with,

"You've made a fantastic deal here. Most people don't get that."

Or, point out another benefit that they should be sure to look for, "The first time you use the service, notice how easy it is to install." Your words—and their decision—will be reinforced when it actually happens.

Some Brief Tips

❑ When speaking (and writing) avoid the use of "obvious" and "obviously." People can become defensive, and those to whom it's not obvious will be offended.

❑ If your phone system has an automated menu, save your customers time by suggesting specifically which numbers to select in order to bypass the instructions and quickly be routed to you or the departments they need.

❑ Chit-chatting with cohorts who stroll by consumes your valuable time. Learn to tell people you just can't talk now because you're working on a call or proposal that must be done.

❑ To encourage prospects to continue speaking, ask them to expand on what they just said.

(SOURCE: communication briefings, 700 Black Horse Pike, #110, Blackwood, NJ, 08012, 609-232-6380)

Help Them Understand What's Most Important

When your prospect compares you to his current vendor laundry-listing all of the competitor's benefits, particularly ones you don't offer, ask him,

"Which of those are most important to you? How many of the others do you really need and use?"

Chances are, only a few are truly meaningful ... probably ones you can also offer. Focus on the real value he wants, the value you can deliver.

Learn Exactly How to Win the Business

A technique that theoretically is solid, but often sounds cheesy and amateurish is, *"What's it going to take to get your business?"* Better attempts to learn their decision-making criteria are questions like,

> **"How, specifically, will you make your decision?"**
> Or,
> **"What decision-making criteria will you use, and which areas will be most important to you?"**

Personalized Letters Increase Sales

In response to an article I wrote about why you shouldn't send canned form letters after a phone conversation, Phoebe Morrow, a National Account Rep with Travelodge wrote a note (personalized, of course) to concur. One of the reasons she feels she was the top rep in their division last year is that she sends many personalized letters to clients along with her rates and proposals.

Discussing the Competition

Knocking the competition is not a good idea, particularly if they are already doing business with your prospect, and the prospect is satisfied. However, in some cases, there is such a glaring deficiency in your competitor's product or service that you want your prospect to be aware of the facts.

Blurting out that *"Johnson Publishing blatantly lies about their readership numbers so they can charge more for their advertising,"* may meet with a feeling of defensiveness. On the other hand, by stimulating their thinking about the issue, you can help them feel more open minded.

For example, consider a statement such as

> **"I'm not sure what other publications tell you about readership. What I do know is that ours is the only one which is audited by an outside firm. What this means to you is that with us, you know that when you make an advertising decision expecting your**

> **message to be delivered to 40,000 paying subscribers, those numbers are what you'll get."**

By planting an idea in the prospect's mind, it is they who may doubt the competitor's claims, instead of you making the statement.

When They Just Don't Get It

There are instances on the phone when your listener obviously hasn't comprehended your message. This becomes apparent when your prospect/customer makes erroneous statements based upon information you've shared. What you **don't** want to do is say something like *"You don't understand what I'm saying,"* or *"You're not following me."* These statements are harsh, and serve to put the listener on the defensive. Nobody likes being told they are wrong. Instead, place the blame on yourself. For example,

> **"Based upon what you said, I'm not sure if I clearly explained myself..."**

Take Control

Ever been caught unprepared when someone returns your call after you've left a message? Here's a way to quickly refamiliarize yourself with your reason for calling that person: If you use files or some other type of paper system for tracking your calls, put a post-it note on each file you've left a message for. Jot down your objectives/reasons for the call, and keep the files in an easily-accessible place. When the call comes in, immediately review the note, so you're reminded of why you called.

If You're Disconnected ...

Everyone has probably had a call terminate for some reason or another in the middle of a conversation due to technological reasons. Regardless of who placed the call, it's YOUR responsibility to call the prospect/customer back. Don't wait for them. Be proactive. Another point: Whenever you get an incoming call such as an inquiry, be sure you get their name and phone number right away just in case you are disconnected. You'll have a way of recontacting them.

When You're Not Familiar With the Competitor

What should you do when a prospect compares you to a competitor you're not familiar with? Ask them for more information.

"I'm really not familiar with that company Mr. Mason. Please tell me about them?"

Some prospects will even send you price lists, brochures, and proposals from the competitor. Or, get the phone number from them and call for the information yourself.

Some Terrific Tips

Here are ideas from *"TELEPHONE TERRIFIC!,"* a fun book of telephone ideas from Dartnell (1-800-621-5463).

✆ **The next time you've got a bear** of a prospect or customer on the phone, stand up and speak. Researchers at the University of California found that we can process information 5% to 20% faster when we're standing than sitting.

✆ **If someone is getting angry,** maybe even loud, with you, do the opposite. Lower your tone, perhaps down to a whisper. It will calm them.

✆ **Ever had a steamed customer** who called you with a problem on an order? Don't hesitate diffusing the tension. State your "make right" phrase immediately.

"Pat, I'm going to make this right for you."

✆ **It's frustrating to have that brilliant idea** strike you over the weekend, or perhaps somewhere else away from the office where pen and paper aren't available, and then ... a couple of days later you can't remember what it was. Remedy that by calling in to your own voice mail and recording the idea or reminder to yourself.

✆ **When you do decide to leave a voice mail message** for someone else, give your name and number first, just in case they don't hear the entire message. Also repeat it at the end.

✆ **Imagine your prospects and customers at a fork in the road,** and they must make a decision regarding which way to turn. Help them by asking questions like,

"Why don't you try it?"

"Does this fit the bill?"

"When would you like to get started?"

"Have a Nice Day"

I've seen people threaten to take a fireman's ax to their phone if they ever again hear, "Have a nice day." *TELEMANAGING* reported that another fine newsletter, *communication briefings* (1-800-888-2084) asked its readers for alternatives to the ubiquitous and trite "Have a nice day." Here are a few suggestions:

- **Take care.**
- **Enjoy your day.**
- **Thanks for calling.**
- **Make it a good one.**
- **Talk to you soon.**
- **I'll be in touch.**
- **I'm glad you called.**
- **Have a productive day.**
- **Keep smiling.**
- **Good luck on your ...**
- **Thanks for doing business with us.**

Do You "Connect" or "Transfer"?

Angela Vasquez-Anderson with Amerus Bank says that her people say,

"I'll connect you,"

instead of *"I'll transfer you"* when sending a call to another person. Her reasoning is that "connect" is more personal than "transfer."

Don't Confuse Them

Every company has quirky internal acronyms and terms used to define departments, procedures, even products. Often these might make perfect sense to insiders, but cause total confusion when used with prospects and customers. Jim Stenger with Central States Industrial Supply shared the story of how customers would call his company to place an order, and the person answering the call would say, *"Is that for EPD or General Line?"* Normally the caller would say, "Huh?" Now, the standard first question is,

"Are you calling for pipes, valves and fittings, or for air compressors?"

This prompts the exact reason for the call, and it's routed appropriately.

Stay Sharp at All Times

With the repetition of phone work naturally comes the temptation to become lax with some of the basics, especially when you're quite busy. Here are two areas to especially be cautious with.

☐ **Leaving rushed voice mail messages.** Particularly your phone number. If your goal to have them return your call, a rushed phone number that's unintelligible negates that possibility. And most of us are unaware we're doing it. Here's a good strategy: According to Nancy Tuckerman and Nancy Dunman, authors of the *"Amy Vanderbilt Complete Book of Etiquette,"* before you leave your phone number, say, **"Here's my number,"** and then pause for one or two seconds. It gives them a chance to retrieve a pen. Then pause every few digits, and repeat the number at the end so the person can check what he has written. *(Source: "Bottom Line Personal" , 1-800-274-5611.)*

☐ **Blurting out your name, and your company name.** I've heard introductions that sounded like the speaker's mouth was taped shut. Articulate your introduction, and speak at a rate so you're understood. Be proud of your name and affiliation.

And remember, even though you might be repeating something 30 or more times daily, they're hearing you for the first time.

For Talkative Prospects ...

To tactfully direct a long-winded prospect or customer back to the topic at hand,

- Say his name first. It grabs attention.
- Agree with him.

  "That's interesting." Or,

  "That's a good point."

- Redirect.

  "Getting back to what you mentioned earlier." Or,

"You had mentioned something earlier ..."

Your Purpose Is NOT to Talk

When planning your next call, remind yourself that you're not calling to talk. Your objective is to listen. And you can only listen by first getting them interested with a great opening, and then asking well-prepared questions.

Deliver Value on Every Call

Placing calls to your regular accounts, and consistently having something of value to say or offer, is perhaps one of the most challenging you face. Doubly so if detailed notes aren't taken from previous calls.

You want to avoid, *"Just touching base," "Wanted to see how it's going," "Checking in to see if you needed anything."*

Instead, personalize the greeting for greatest impact.

"Last time we spoke you mentioned."

Or, **"I noticed in my notes that you are ..., and we have ..."**

Go to Purchasing Last

When prospecting, go to the purchasing department, and specifically purchasing agents, last. Why? Their main mission in life is to secure goods and services at the lowest possible price with little regard for the value you deliver. And it makes sense, doesn't it. For most of them, it's not their job to understand how what you have will help the company. Therefore, you need to make sure that your user, the one who will reap the greatest value, is the person you start with, and try to make an advocate for you.

Your Call is Important

Keep this in mind: if you and your company didn't deliver value to customers, you wouldn't be in business. Especially remember this as you're planning and placing calls. Too often reps will have the feeling that they're calling busy people and they don't want to interrupt the prospect ... or what they're calling about is insignificant. Nonsense! Get that out of your head. As long as you're able to clearly and concisely articulate your potential value to a valid recipient, you're not wasting their time. Their job relies on evaluating and implementing new ideas, products, and services.

Another Taping Benefit

I've always advocated taping your calls as one of the best tools for self-improvement. It allows you to evaluate and make changes to your method of speaking as well as your content. Another benefit: taping enables you to review your calls and take notes on material you might have missed. Therefore it helps you prepare for the next call. *NOTE:* Some states have a goofy statute that says you need to let the other person know you're taping the call (that really sets the mood, eh?), even if it's solely for your own personal training purposes. If you're concerned about turning into a hardened criminal, check this out in your state. Otherwise, to tape your calls, get our Recorder Link, a simple device that connects to your phone and tape recorder to tape both sides of your conversation. Call us at 1-800-326-7721 for current pricing.

Don't Be Against Their Idea;
Be FOR a Different Solution

A way to politely disagree is to stand *for* a different alternative as opposed to being against one the prospect or customer might propose. For example, consider the negative connotations of this transaction,

Customer: "Let's implement it over four weeks."

Salesperson: *"Nah, that wouldn't work."*

Instead, consider,

> **Salesperson: "How about three weeks? This way we can maximize the return over a shorter period."**

Question the Implications Of Their Problem

After getting a prospect on the topic of a problem, Ramon Williamson, President of Williamson Sales & Leadership Inc., suggests asking the question,

> **"How do you see that hurting/holding you back/disrupting you in achieving your goals?"**

What to Ask When They Say "Send Me Something"

Here's a technique that sales coach Dave Mather suggests to address the stall, "Send me something in the mail." Respond with,

"Within a few minutes, we'll both know whether we want to pursue this further. Does that sound fair?"

Mather says this positions you as a partner, where you're collaborating on making a decision on meeting or speaking further, not just them deciding. The key at this point is focusing more on the reasons for getting together, not on features/benefits of your product or service, like *"Oh, but we could save you a lot of money."*

Be Prepared to Defend a Lower Price

If you're the lowest priced in your market that can be as challenging as being the price leader. Low price can denote low value. As with any resistance, be prepared to explain why you're lower priced than the competition, while value is still high ... such as small overhead, lower distribution costs, cheaper labor, and so on.

What Do You Earn Per Call?

Calculate how much you earn per call. Take your average weekly earnings and divide by your average number of calls per week. Motivate yourself by hanging that amount of money on your wall (a $5 bill) for example, and then trying to increase that average per call every month.

Compare Your Advantages Directly

When selling against the competition, be sure you're specific in presenting your advantages compared directly to the alternatives. For example, instead of just stating your warranty terms, say,

"And naturally you'll get our standard three-year full warranty, compared to the two-year, parts-only plan you said is offered in the other proposal."

Regarding Big Ticket Items, High Dollar Sales

Don't prejudge someone early in a call, thinking they wouldn't be a prospect, wouldn't have the money, that when they hear the price they'll shy away, etc. And for really big potential sales, don't act as if it's out of the ordinary for you. Some reps become awestruck when they work on a huge quote, and present the price in an almost-apologetic manner. What you might think is a mammoth-sized order is mundane, everyday business for them.

They Don't Always Need a Problem to Switch

When prospects tell us, "I'm not having any problems with my current supplier," our first thought typically is to ask questions to get them to admit, or realize problems they might have. R. Scott Winters, with The Vendo Company, suggests an alternative method. Respond with,

> **"I'm glad to hear you're not having problems ... but are problems the only criteria you use when making the decision to change suppliers?"**

Generally, the answer will be no. Then you have the perfect opportunity to question further along that path, learning more about the other criteria, and then following up with your appropriate product/service recommendations.

(SOURCE: THE COMPETITIVE ADVANTAGE, P.O. Box 10828, Portland, OR, 97210.)

Help Them See a Problem

Even though the previous point presents an alternative, asking about problems is still an effective way to open up their mind. However, don't simply say, *"Are you having any problems now?"* That forces them to think too much for you, and they're likely not going to do that, or at least come up with anything worthwhile. Instead, in response to "I'm happy with my present supplier," ask something like,

> **"I see. When you've had difficulty in the past with _____, what were the specific problems?"**

You fill in the blank with something you're pretty sure they have challenges with. For example,

> **"When you've had difficulty in the past with compatibility, what were the specific problems?"**

Humor Can Sell

Levity can sometimes make a point, and a sale. Rich Goldman, a sales pro with Lou Bachrodt Chevrolet in Pompano Beach, Florida, says that when a customer claims, "Another dealer is selling this Cavalier for $500 less," he asks, **"Well, why didn't you buy it?"**

If they respond, "They didn't have one in stock," he quips,

> **"When I don't have one in stock, I'll beat his price by $1000."**

Lock in the Sale Today, Even When
It Won't Happen for a While

If they like what you have, and say they'll buy the next time they have the need, do everything you can today to ensure that sale. Open the credit-approved account, get a blanket purchase order from them ... whatever, to make the purchase easier.

Send it Only When There's Potential

Don't mail information just to get it out the door, especially with people who have no short-term potential. Instead, let them qualify themselves.

> **"Would it be worth it to send you information for your files, just in case things change with you?"**

Don't Let the Guarantee Be The
Main Reason for Buying

Guarantees are necessary for credibility, but don't sell your guarantee harder than you sell your value. Some reps use the negative sell just to get a "yes," and then later get exactly what they sold: people asking for their money back.

When You're the Higher-Priced Alternative ...

Question to ask when they are comparing you to a discounter:

> **"What other expenses have you considered in the long-term if you went with the lower-price alternative?"**

Write the Numerals as You Say Them

Even if your prospect or client has a fancy voice mail system that lets them rewind and replay the message, it's much easier for them if they can jot it down the first time they play it. Therefore, when leaving a number on voice mail, slow down! Here's a test: jot down each digit on paper after saying it. Then say the next one. The right pacing becomes habit after a while.

Give the Entire Price

Doesn't it just annoy you to no end when you're shopping for something and are quoted a bare-bones price, but then you watch the cash register tape get longer as all the "extras" are added on to give you what you really want? It's like when you see the latest speed-of-light computer advertised in the paper for what seems to be an unbelievable price, and then you realize *it is* unbelievable when you get out the magnifying glass and see in minuscule print: "monitor not included." The point here is, always state the total price.

"Look" at Their Office Walls

In Harvey MacKay's best seller, *"Swim With the Sharks Without Being Eaten Alive,"* he's a strong advocate of learning as much about your customer as possible, citing the fact that all things being equal, people buy from people. One suggestion he has for outside sales reps is to make mental notes of status symbols decision makers have adorning their offices, and then asking about them or dropping those topics into the conversation. We can do the same thing by phone. The unconventionality of this idea is what makes it so effective. When you're speaking with the executive assistant, or anyone in close proximity to the decision maker, ask about him/her personally. Learn their interests, hobbies, and status symbols hanging in his/her office. By bringing up these topics appropriately during a call you have a great chance at making a personal connection.

Brief Tips

Here are a couple of tips pulled from the *"PHC Profit Report"* (800-837-8337) a plumbing and heating contractor's newsletter that I read every month solely for the great marketing tips adaptable to anyone.

❏ **Don't just say,** *"I'm going to transfer you to so-and-so,"* or, *"You'll have to talk to so-and-so about that."* Instead, put a little sizzle into it:

"Pat Davis is our expert on that, and I'm sure she

will be happy to answer all of your questions. I'll transfer you."

(Original Source: Customer Service Newsletter, 212-228-0246)

❑ **When you hear,** "How much would this cost me?", a possible reply is,

"Do you mean if you do, or don't take advantage of my product/service?"

Then you can begin talking about the value they'll receive. *(Source: The Guerrilla Selling Newsletter, 800-247-9145)*

The following tips appeared in *"The Executive Edge"*:

❑ **By acting more outgoing** than you think you are, you might boost your self-image, according to psychologists. Experiments found that test volunteers who were instructed to act very friendly and exhibit exceptionally high self-esteem remained more amiable and confident afterward.

❑ **According to** *"The Professional Consultant"* newsletter, a hand-written message on the envelope gets seven out of 10 obvious direct mail pieces opened.

From *"Bottom Line Personal"* (800-234-3834), Mary Kay Ash presented this time control technique:

❑ **Do two things** in the time it takes to do one. If you're doing something mundane like stuffing brochures or standing at the copy machine, listen to motivational or sales tapes, or an audio book. Many people set aside blocks of time for a singular activity, and only work on that task during that time. Sure it helps you focus, but it doesn't maximize your efficiency.

❑ **Regardless of how many** calls you placed or received today, your next one is the first one to that person. Treat it like the only one for the day.

❑ **When you greet** someone on an incoming call, view it as escorting a friend into your home. You wouldn't frown or act indifferently. Greet them warmly, with enthusiasm.

❑ **Practice tongue twisters** to articulate clearly. Recite this one now, several times while picking up speed each time: "Frank phoned four pharmaceutical factories feeling fresh and fulfilled."

For Seasoned Sales Reps:

If you've been selling the same things for the same company for a few years, you're very intimate with the understanding of your products/services. But other people are not. Keep that in mind. As monotonous as it might seem for you, they need a clear explanation of what you might think should be obvious.

Tips from Seminar Attendees

Here are a few fine tips heard from the participants at a training session I did for The Knoll Group, an office furniture manufacturer.

❏ Joy Graves wisely likes to have plenty of information about the company before speaking with a decision maker. She surfs the Internet to access companies' home pages, or locate news articles that give useful information. Another tactic she uses is to contact personnel departments and gather information. These departments are often quite helpful in providing company info, since they're mission is to "sell" the organization to potential applicants.

❏ Kathy Kelly mentioned that on her calls she doesn't just set one objective for the call; she'll typically set five or more. For example, on a prospecting call she'll have her primary, ultimate objective, which might be, after the prospect is qualified, to set an appointment to further discuss specific expansion or addition plans. A secondary objective (in case the primary isn't reached) would be to get the buyer's agreement that he would review the literature and check the current status of projects throughout the organization before their next scheduled follow-up call, in order to determine specific needs if any. Another objective would be to ask for names of other buyers within the organization. Having multiple objectives helps Kathy to also have another direction to turn during a call in case she hits a brick wall.

When Your Time is What You Sell ...

Bev Cavanaugh gave a tip for those of you selling your time ... consultants, accountants, anyone selling a personal service. Occasionally you have prospects and customers asking you to either throw in additional time free, or to cut your price. Bev suggests putting their request into a context that helps them realize what they're requesting. For example, she has said,

> **"Pat, that would be like me asking you to drop off a truckload of your products at my office, free. Would you be agreeable if someone asked you to do that? You see, my time is what I sell. It's my inventory, and they're not making any more of it."**

Obviously you want to do this in a courteous way, and then shift back to the discussion of the value you provide them.

Questioning About Their Present Vendor

Bev also contributed some very good points on questioning. First, many sales reps routinely ask prospects "how it's going" with their present vendor. If there's a big problem, some might tell the truth. Others, however, might say everything is OK. Why? Because they were the one who made the vendor choice initially, and divulging a problem could be an admission of failure regarding their decision. *Instead:* consider talking to other people within the organization who are affected by the vendor, users of the product or service ... those without a vested interest in the selection of the vendor, but with a personal stake in the results of what the vendor provides.

Hand-Write Your Fax Message

Use handwritten faxes to break the ice with prospects you plan on cold-calling, says Dave Mather. This is how he has gotten in the door with some of his largest clients.

Business Cards Can Bring Huge Returns

Randel Thompson with MicroTech provided a tip that has helped him generate several extra thousand dollars worth of sales. Simply include **two** business cards with everything you mail to prospects and customers. Granted, most people might toss them, but you're banking on the potential returns from the few who don't. It's the same premise as direct mail: you only need a small response to get a profitable return. If you're reluctant, has this ever happened to you: Someone calls you out of the blue and says, "I'm not sure how I got your business card, but here's what I'm interested in ..."

It's a Pain in the Neck If You Don't Use One

If you don't yet use a headset, for whatever reason, consider the experience of Jean Linendoll. For years Jean pooh-poohed the merits of headsets, preferring instead the old handset, most often nestled between her head—tipped at an awkward angle—and her shoulder. Today Jean uses a headset, and swears by it. She also swears *at* her back and neck problems, and accompanying pain. Her advice: use a headset. Get used to it. You'll be thankful in the long run.

Listeners Focus on the Fillers

During our discussion of eliminating filler words and sounds from your presentation ("ahh," "umm," "ya know") Vilma Lawrence, with TV Data, shared the story of how one prospect had such a bad habit of using the word "naturally" throughout their conversation, she started focusing on the use of the word instead of the content of what he was trying to say. For example, she'd say to herself, "It was appropriate there. Not there. THAT was a comical use of the word ...", and so on throughout the call. This point is not intended to be a model for good listening; it's to illustrate how annoying habits can distract listeners from the message. And as sales-people, we all know it's difficult enough to get people to listen, therefore we don't want them to focus on habits at the expense of our message.

Don't Assume

Vilma made another interesting point that highlighted our discussion on false assumptions. When we make assumptions about what we think the prospect or customer could afford, what they will or won't buy, and even if they'll be a good prospect or not, we're operating in sort of a virtual dreamland. We make decisions and statements that are based on incomplete and inaccurate information. Vilma followed-up with a prospect to close a sale. Much to her surprise he said he wanted a price on "Everything." Since her company has quite an extensive menu of offerings (they provide TV listings to newspapers), she felt this guy would be blown away by her price quote for everything, since he appeared to be a smaller paper. She said, "Are you sure you want everything?" He said, "Yes, everything." Vilma worked up the quote, shaking her head, just knowing he'd be floored. She held her breath, then gave the quote. Wisely, instead of presenting it in a "See, I told you that you wouldn't want 'everything' tone of voice," she stated the price confidently ... she bit her lip, then paused.

There was silence. The prospect finally said, "That's not a bad price." He bought. Everything.

Don't assume. Unless, of course, you'll assume you're going to get the sale.

A Sticky Business Card Situation

We've talked about the merits of sending business cards along with your written materials (do it; most get tossed, but the few that don't more than pay for the effort), and here's a similar idea used by Jeffrey Jones with Ryan Herco products. Ryan Herco has business cards printed on peel-off stickers, which the reps then attach directly to the mailed information. This way if the prospect files away the information—or tosses it on a pile like most of us—the rep's name and number stays attached instead of disappearing as paper clipped-on cards tend to do.

A Quote From a Seminar Attendee

Gary Bonner wrote this note to me: "*After attending the College last March in Orange County, I wanted to share with readers the difference in the reception I'm getting from people on the phone. The key has been to treat people as individuals, not just as numbers to burn. Anyone in tele-sales should remember that people they speak with by phone face the same difficulties and uncertainties they themselves face. Keeping this in mind makes the phone conversation go a lot more smoothly.*

"*I had an administrative assistant actually compliment me this morning on my professional attitude, candor, and straightforward approach to what I wanted to accomplish by speaking with her boss. I was able to win her over, and in doing so, will get the attention of a CEO of a very well-known company. You see their ads every time you watch TV. The administrative assistant said she speaks to many people on the phone each day and she was impressed by my approach. It boils down to good manners and allowing class to come through on the phone. We're not trying to push or sell anyone; we just want to help them.*"

Don't Think Out Loud

When you're searching for what to say, don't think aloud. Be sure your comments add to the conversation. Otherwise you might utter some random thoughts you could regret later.

Delay When Hit With a Negotiation

Picture this: Out of the blue like a lightning bolt arrives a phone call from a prospect or customer who wants to negotiate (lower) price or terms, or wants you to throw in something on an order. Oh, by the way, he's also going to put you on the speakerphone since there are several others in the office. This customer was the furthest thing from your mind before the call. What do you do?

It could be dangerous to dive into the conversation at this point. He and his team are obviously well-prepared for this session; you are not. The advisable route would be to delay until you can prepare—even if just for a few minutes.

> **"Mr. Prospect, I want to make sure I have all my facts and figures right before I proceed with you. Let me call you back in 10 minutes."**

They're Looking for Something to Object To

If you barge blindly into a call with a prepared presentation and no up-front questioning, keep in mind that they are likely looking for the first piece of data they can object to.

Get Agreement

Here are more examples of "temperature-checking" questions, or trial closes, to ensure you're presenting something they're interested in.

> **"Does this make sense so far?"**
>
> **"Is this helpful?"**
>
> **"Is my reasoning sound?"**
>
> **"Would this fit?"**
>
> **"Am I on target?"**
>
> **"How am I doing?"**

How to Keep the Door Open After Losing a Sale

Let's say you've been informed you lost a sale to a competitor. You could become indignant, rip the competition, and tell the prospect to go pound sand. Of course you wouldn't even consider that (although it might *feel* good). A better alternative is to keep the door open, and set the stage for the future, maybe even plant some doubts. Tell them you'd love to talk with them gain at some point, and let them know you're available if anything happens. Then ask them,

"Were there any reservations at all about the selection?"

This could point out the one or two weaknesses in the competitor—valuable info for your next contact. Also ask,

"What could you see happening that might cause you to need another vendor, perhaps as a backup?"

Action Steps

Now the Work Begins ...

Congratulations on reaching the end of this book. (Or, maybe you're like me and skim through books, often reading the end first.) Regardless, to have anything from this book work for you, **you** must work first. Do that, and I'm confident you will show the sales results you are truly capable of.

And don't let this be the last we hear from each other. I want to e-mail you every week: I'll send you my *"TelE-Sales Hot Tips of the Week"* free e-mail newsletter. Zap a message to me right now at arts@businessbyphone.com with "join" in the subject. Better yet, also include how you've shown results from using the ideas in this book.

For even more telesales tips you can use, you should also receive my **TELEPHONE SELLING REPORT** monthly sales tips newsletter. This contains my newest, freshest material, plus columns by other sales experts, as well as proven ideas from your peers out in the trenches. Call, fax, write, or e-mail us.

And finally, I take on a limited number of customized telesales training workshops and in-company training programs. If you liked what you read here, I'll bring these ideas to life in an entertaining, results-getting program for your company, group, or association. From one-hour to a couple of days, I will research your situation, listen to your calls, listen for your wants and needs, and design and deliver a session that will leave you and your people motivated to hop on the phone, and get measureable results. I am regularly booked around 3-5 months in advance, so if this sounds interesting to you, call me right now at 800-326-7721, or (402)895-9399, or send over an e-mail.

I look forward to continue contributing to your success.

Go out and have your best week ever!

Art

Art Sobczak
President, Business By Phone Inc.
13254 Stevens St.
Omaha, NE 68137
(402)895-9399
e-mail: arts@businessbyphone.com
www.businessbyphone.com

Here Are Other Resources You Can Get Right Now to Help You Close More Sales Using the Phone!

Go to Our Website for Lots of FREE Telesales Tips, Special Offers, and Other Resources to Help You

www.businessbyphone.com

Have Information In Seconds With Business By Phone's Fax-Back Service

You can have detailed descriptions of plenty of sales-building products in your hands as soon as you want. Go the handset of your fax machine, call (402)896-9877, listen for the prompts, press "1," and follow the instructions. When asked, press "101" as the document you'd like. This is our Fax Information Directory listing all of the brochures and samples available to you by return fax. Receive this document, pick the additional information you'd like, then call again to receive your choices. Or, simply use the document numbers below to make your selections.

FREE! "The TelE-Sales Hot Tips of the Week" Newsletter

Each week you will have sales tips and words of motivation from Art Sobczak e-mailed to your desk, free! Sign up by e-mailing to **teletips @businessbyphone.com** with "join" in the subject line, or go to **www.businessbyphone.com** and sign up yourself. Plus, you will get a free special report for simply sigining up.

Get a FREE Subscription to the Business By Phone Catalog of Tapes, Books, Telesales Rep College Seminars, Other Training Materials

Call our offices at 1-800-326-7721.

The Telesales Rep College Two-Day Training Workshops

Throughout the year Art personally delivers 8-10 public training programs across the U.S., covering every step of the professional telesales call. Valuable for rookies and veterarns alike, you'll leave energized, armed with new ideas to deploy right away to grab more business on your very next call. Only 20 participants accepted per session.Call 1-800-326-7721 for the current schedule, or select Fax Information Document 108.

Sales-Building Materials By Art Sobczak You Can Order Right Now

The Monthly *"Telephone Selling Report"* Sales Tips Newsletter

If you enjoyed this book, get more of this same type of sales-building material delivered to your desk every month in the eight-page *"Telephone Selling Report."* Fax Information Document #110 for all eight pages. **$109** for a one-year, 12-issue, subscription.

"Getting Through to Buyers . . . While the Others are Screened Out" Video

If you ever get tired of playing phone tag, getting tangled in the web of voice mail, or being screened with questions like, "What's this in reference to?", you'll get through to more buyers, more quickly with this 50-minute video developed and presented by Art Sobczak. (Just think, the next person you can't get through to could have been the big one you were looking for! Get this program today.) Includes an Action Guide workbook. Fax Information Document 102. **$98** (plus $4 shipping)

"Ringing Up Sales" Audio Tape Training Program

Six-tape, twelve-module program taking you step-by-step through the ideal telesales call. Includes over 100 call examples. Interactive Action Guide included. Fax Information Document 103. **$98** (plus $4 shipping)

"Hello Success" Training Program, Everything You Need to Run Your Next 12 Months Worth of Training Meetings

Run a complete sales training session every other week for the next year using the step-by-step, word-for-word instructions, audio tapes, and newsletter/worksheets in Hello Success. Twelve separate, independent training topics. Manager's Kit Includes Leaders Guide, 12 audio tapes, full set of newsletter materials. Each Rep Kit includes newsletter/worksheet materials and three-ring-binder. Fax Information Document 113. **$149** for Manager's Kit, **$30** per set of Rep Materials.

To Order Any of These Items

1. Mail your check, U.S. funds only, to Business By Phone, 13254 Stevens St., Omaha, NE, 68137.

2. Call us at 1-800-326-7721.

3. Fax your order with credit card number to (402)896-3353. *(Overseas shipping billed at cost. Candian shipping 2x listed rate.)*

Get More Copies of This Book, and Volume 1

To get additional copies of this book, and/or Volume 1, photocopy or remove this form, or call, fax, or e-mail us with the necessary information. *(Inquire about quantity discounts for your entire sales staff. Also, bookstore and dealer inquiries welcome.)*

☐ ___copies of "How to Sell More in Less Time ... **VOLUME 1**" @ $29.50 (+$3.50 shipping U.S., $7 foreign, US funds)

☐ ___copies of **VOLUME 2**" @ $39.95 (+$3.50 shipping U.S., $7 foreign, US funds)

Special Set Pricing Discount!

☐ Save! Get both books for only $59. (+$6 shipping U.S., $10 foreign, US funds) Send ___ sets.

Name_____

Company_____

Address_____

City_____**State**_____**Zip Code**_____

Phone_____

Fax_____

Method of Payment

☐ Visa/MC/AMEX/Discover

　　#_____

　　sig._____exp._____

☐ Check /Money Order Enclosed *(U.S. Funds Only)*

Ways to Order

Phone your order to 1-800-326-7721, or (402)895-9399.

Fax your order to (402)896-3353.

**Mail your order to Business By Phone,
13254-B1 Stevens St., Omaha, NE, 68137.**

E-Mail your order to teletips@businessbyphone.com.